MARCO  POLO

BUDAPEST

D1334005

WW

05056212

Sightseeing Highlights

Buda, Chain Bridge and Parliament – the most famous sights in the city panorama can hardly be missed. For the rest of your tour we've collected all of the places that you should definitely not miss.

Do You Feel Like...

...visiting Budapest's marvellous coffee houses, enjoying cultural pleasures, relaxing in the famous spas and bath houses, having impressive views or wandering along the traces of Art Nouveau? Discover Budapest as you please.

COFFEE HOUSES

- **BookCafé**
  An elegant and classy coffee house in a former casino.
  page 99, 132
- **Central**
  The late literature café was founded in 1887.
  page 97
- **Gerbeaud**   ▶
  The most famous of the Budapest coffee houses, a must see.
  page 96, 247

FESTIVALS

- **Budapest Spring Festival**
  A renowned festival with Hungarian and international stars.
  page 80
- **Sziget Festival**
  Party and dance at the largest open-air of central Europe.
  page 80
- ◄ **Summer Concerts**
  Atmospheric concerts in varying locations such as Vajdahunyad Palace and in front of the palm house in the zoo
  page 81

Lively Liszt Square

PRACTICAL INFORMATION

PRICE CATEGORIES
Restaurants
(main dish without a drink)
££££ = over 5000 HUF
£££ = 3500 – 5000 HUF
££ = 2000 – 3500 HUF
£ = up to 2000 HUF
Hotels (for a double room)
££££ = over 45 000 HUF
£££ = 30 000 – 45 000 HUF
££ = 20 000 – 30 000 HUF
£ = up to 20 000 HUF

BACKGROUND

Things to know about the city on the Danube, the country and the people, economy and politics, society and everyday life...

Facts

Population · Politics · Economy

Budapest is aglow, emanating a new self-confidence and optimism. It knows how to live too. Rarely does it rest, for a generation of dedicated young Europeans work the world markets during the day, so they can meet in the bars in the V district until late into the night.

POPULATION

The independent towns of Óbuda, Buda and Pest had a combined population of 12,200 in 1720. By the time they were incorporated into Budapest in 1873, the total number of inhabitants had already passed the 300,000 mark. As the capital of Hungary at a time when it was associated to Austria, the city experienced a boom without precedent, which also took the form of a dramatic increase in population. By the early 20th century, a million people lived in Budapest. Incorporation of surrounding districts during the 1970s resulted in the two million mark being passed, but in the 1990s many Budapest residents turned their backs on an increasingly expensive city. Today Budapest has around 1.6 million inhabitants at a density of approx. 3200 per sq km/9300 per sq mi.

Development

The development of the Hungarian capital was influenced by immigrants from former German and Austrian territories, as well as by Czechs, Slovaks, Serbs, Croats and Bulgarians, particularly during the 18th and 19th centuries. After the Second World War many Greeks came to the city. In recent times, numerous immigrants, officially »tourists«, from the Ukraine, Russia and countries from the Near, Middle and Far East have settled in greater Budapest. Hungarian Jews, whose deportation and murder during 1944/1945 comprised the last major crime of the Holocaust, have survived mainly in Budapest (►MARCO POLO Insight, p. 180). Before World War II over 200,000 Jews lived in Budapest. Their present 80,000-strong community is the largest in all of eastern Europe. The main synagogues are situated in the VII district (Elizabeth Town). The largest ethnic minority in terms of numbers is the Sinti and Roma. Instability in Hungary's neighbouring countries since the 1990s has caused an additional influx from these groups to the wider Budapest area. The second-largest minority in the country consists of approximately 87,000 Hungarian citizens who describe themselves as culturally German Hungarian.

Immigrants

Váci utca: a chat in the popular shopping street in Pest

Location:
47° 29' north latitude
19° 08' east longitude
Highest elevation:
János-hegy:
527m/1729ft

Area:
525sq km/202 sq mi
(173sq km/66sq mi on
the right bank of the
Danube and **352sq km/**
135sq mi on the left)

©BAEDEKER

Population: **1.74 mil.**
In comparison:
Paris 2.24 mil.
Berlin 3.4 Mio.
London 8.41 mil.

Population density:
3200 people per sq km/
1235 per sq mi

▶ Coat of arms

The coat of arms was
introduced in 1873 when
Buda, Pest and Óbuda
were united.

▶ Religion
(census 2011, in %)

No answer 34.1

Roman catholic 29

No religion 22.9

Calvinist 8.5

Orthodox 3.7

Lutheran 1.7

Jews 0.4

▶ Governance

The 23 city districts of Budapest are
marked with Roman numerals. Not all
districts have an official name. Head of
adminstration is the mayor.

I	Vár	**XII**	Zugliget
IV	Újpest	**XIII**	Angyalföld
V	Belváros	**XIV**	Zugló
VI	Terézváros	**XVII**	Rákoskersztúr
VII	Erzsébetváros	**XIX**	Kispest
VIII	Józsefváros	**XX**	Pestszenterzsébe
IX	Ferencváros	**XXI**	Csepel
X	Kőbánya	**XXIII**	Soroksár

▶ Airport

Ferenc Liszt airport is Hugary's busiest
airport with about 8.5 mil passengers
annually.

▶ Public transport

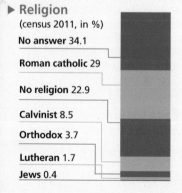

200 bus lines

40 tram lines

5 suburban commuter lines

3 metro lines

▶ Economy

As Hungary's financial and economical capital Budapest accounts for 39% of the national income (2013).

Employment structure:

74 %
service

26
others

Unemployment rate (2014):
8.9 % (Hungary: 7.3 %)

▶ Tourism

4.3 mil visitors (2013)

▶ Education

Budapest is Hungary's centre of education with 19 universities and academies

▶ Climate

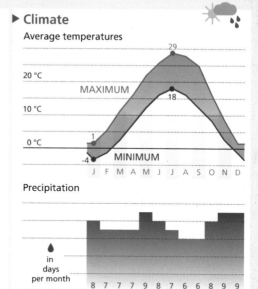

Average temperatures

29
20 °C
MAXIMUM
18
10 °C
1
0 °C
-4
MINIMUM
J F M A M J J A S O N D

Precipitation

in days per month
8 7 7 7 9 8 7 6 6 8 9 9

in hours per day
2 3 5 6 8 9 10 9 7 5 2 2
J F M A M J J A S O N D

▶ Little Balkan

Approx. 10 % of Budapest's population come from foreign countries. The city is a real melting pot.

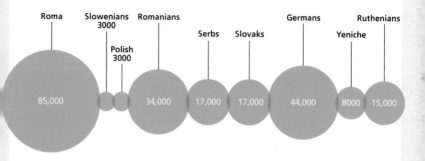

Roma 85,000
Slowenians 3000
Polish 3000
Romanians 34,000
Serbs 17,000
Slovaks 17,000
Germans 44,000
Yeniche 8000
Ruthenians 15,000

Religion   The majority of Budapest residents who acknowledge a religious affiliation, presently 65%, are traditionally Roman Catholics. A quarter are Protestants, the overwhelming majority followers of the Reformed (Calvinist) Church. The rest consists of other religious groups, in particular Orthodox Christians, Baptists and Jews

ADMINISTRATION

Districts   The city of Budapest is divided into 23 municipal districts or boroughs. The central shopping district of the Hungarian capital is almost identical in extent with the V district Beváros (at Pest city centre and Leopold Town): not only numerous department stores, shops, boutiques and top-class hotels can be found here on little more than 2.5 sq km/1 sq mi, but also government offices, financial and trading institutions, and significant cultural and scientific establishments. Far in excess of 100,000 workers commute daily to the V district.

City administration   The city is ruled by the Senate (Közgülés). The city's leader, the mayor, is nominated by the party or coalition that has a majority in the Senate. The administration of the municipal districts is managed by a magistrate controlled by the Senate.

The Hungarian capital is twinned with the German financial metropolis of Frankfurt am Main, the Finnish capital Helsinki, the Lithuanian capital Vilnius and the Texan city of Fort Worth in the United States. Others include Berlin, Germany; Lisbon, Portugal; Zagreb, Croatia; the most recent addition is Dublin, Ireland in 2006.

HEART OF THE HUNGARIAN ECONOMY

Important economic metropolis   Budapest is one of the leading economic centres of eastern central Europe. At present almost a quarter of Hungary's gainfully employed work in the economic area of Budapest. The vast majority work in the service sector, administration and trade. Furthermore, the city is characterized by a high number of export-orientated industrial sectors. To these belong in particular the car and machine production industries, the chemical and pharmaceutical industries, as well as the electrical and electronic industries.

Industrial development   The particularly good transport links and coal deposits in the near vicinity were and remain the ideal basis for Budapest's economic development. After the cities were united 1873 and Budpest became the capital it soon became the main seat of significant industrial companies. After the Second World War, raw material imports from the

There is a wide variety of goods at the central market hall

Soviet Union enabled the establishment of new oil-processing and chemical industries. The Ikarus plant not only delivered buses to countries in COMECON (Council for Mutual Economic Assistance, the eastern European counterpart to the European Union), but also to clients in the West. After the collapse of Communism at the end of the 1980s, the free market was quickly re-established and businesses were privatized. The fundamental political changes in eastern Europe attracted a huge stream of investment capital to Budapest, especially from Germany and companies – now not only multinationals – have created platforms by buying existing companies or establishing new ones.

Budapest has a long tradition as a centre of trade due to its good geographic and transport location. This applies in particular to the district of Pest, where all strands of Hungarian business management come together today. The large shopping centres and commercial

Trade

Welcome to Everyday Life

Really enjoying Budapest means getting off the tourist path and meeting ordinary people – therefore some tips from a qualified expert of the city.

STUDY AND INTERNSHIPS

A study term or at least a semester abroad at one of Budapest's universities is the best way to get to know the city intensively. There are often special seminars in English so the language barrier is not that high. Also internships give an understanding of the local everyday life. Legal formalities for a stay abroad are manageable within the EU. Further information can be found on the British embassy's website: *ukinhungary.fco.gov.uk*

GUIDED CITY TOURS

Even some guided city tours allow a view of the everyday life of the local people. Beyond Budapest, with its detailed guided tours through the Jewish quarter plus its tours through the VIII district convey far more than just tourist sights. Even social and cultural issues are broached during these tours (►Tours and Guides)

LEARN HUNGARIAN

The Hungarian language is classified as an isolated language in Europe because in its proximity there is no other member of this language family. Learning Hungarian is fun though and gives a more intense access to the people and the country. The prestigious Debrecen summer school offers regular language courses for beginners and advanced learners.
Debreceni Nyári Egyetem,
www.nyariegyetem.hu

markets that have now arisen in the outer districts or on the periphery of the city can match those of any other European metropolis. Even after Hungary became a member of the European Union, Germany remains the most important trading partner. Budapest's Liszt Ferenc Airport has succeeded in becoming one of the most significant air-freight handling centres within the space of a few years, and the free port of Csepel has become the most important transhipment centre on the Danube.

Thanks to its economic strength, Budapest is now one of the principal financial centres of eastern central Europe. Numerous foreign banks have branches in Budapest and, as becomes a European capital, there is also a stock exchange in the city. Hungary's largest insurance companies are at home in Budapest.

Banking and insurance

As one of the leading trade fair centres of eastern central Europe, Budapest fully participates in the national and international calendar of exhibitions and congress activities. The internationally most important trade fairs that take place regularly include the Utazás Tourism Fair; the agricultural machine fair Agro-Masch in March; the Budapesti Nemzetközi Vásár (BNV), with its concentration on technical and consumer goods, in September; the Budapest car fair Autosalon in October; and Snowshow, the fair for winter sports in November.

Trade fairs

Budapest has been among the top destinations for European city breaks for years. The majority of the around 34 million annual visitors to Hungary visit Budapest. Austria, Germany, Italy, Great Britain, the Netherlands, Switzerland and Israel, as well as the USA and Canada, are the main contributors to tourist earnings.

Tourism

Foreign Rule

First came the Romans, then the Magyars; for a long time the Turks ruled. Only after that does the history of this city, which never really existed before, begin. It became the eastern seat of the Austro-Hungarian Dual Monarchy, experienced a golden age after 1867, was then a pawn in fatal world events, and now follows a European democratic path.

ROMANS, HUNS AND ÁRPÁDS

895/896	Invasion of the seven Magyar tribes
1000	Stephen (Istvan) I becomes King of Hungary
1241/1242	The Mongols destroy Buda and Pest
1308–1386	Rule of the House Anjou
1458	Matthias Corvinus becomes king

The earliest known traces of settlement are on the Buda side of the Danube and go back 50,000 years. By about the second millennium BC both banks of the Danube had been settled. Several fields of urns, which date from the Bronze Age, have been discovered over the entire area of the present-day Hungarian capital. Nomadic Scythians from the Black Sea region settled in the Budapest area in the 6th century BC, and in the 4th and 3rd centuries BC Celtic tribes appeared. **Pre- and early history**

The Romans conquered the region west of the Danube around 10 BC. The **Aquincum** in the present-day quarter of Óbuda became the capital of the province of Pannonia Inferior. The residential and garrison town experienced its heyday at the 2nd/3rd century AD. **Roman rule**

The power vacuum caused by the fall of the Roman Empire allowed the Huns to penetrate into Europe. In the year 409 Aquincum fell to the nomadic people from the east by treaty – a rarity in the history of the Huns. Bloody campaigns of conquest were the foundation for the Hun empire under **King Attila**. With the death of Attila the Hun in 453, the empire, already weakened by its defeat in Gaul in 451, collapsed. Ostrogoths, Lombards and Avars from the steppes settled along the Danube in the aftermath. **Invasion of the Huns**

Seven Hungarian tribes belonging to the Finno-Ugrian linguistic group moved into the Carpathian basin and continued their migra- **Invasion and rule of the Árpáds**

At first, the people cheered during the Hungarian uprising of 1956

The royal regalia of the Hungarian Kingdom

tion up the Danube, settling in present-day Óbuda around 895–896. These tribes, the Nyék, Megyer, Kürtgyarmat, Tarján, Jenö, Kér and Keszi, were led by the chieftains Árpád, Elöd, Ond, Kond, Tass, Huba and Töhötöm, who are all portrayed as a bronze equestrian group on ▶ Hösök tere (Heroes' Square). This phase, from 895 to 972, characterized by the Magyar invasion of the Carpathian basin as well as their raids into western and southern Europe, is known as the Age of Migrations. Árpád ruled the unified Magyar tribes as chieftain after the blood-brother union of Szeged, and his descendants ruled until 1301.

Feudal state and Christianity	Stephen I (István I) became King of Hungary in the year 1000. He organized a feudal state on the central European model and introduced Christianity. His residences were in Esztergom and Székesfehérvár. With the settlement of merchants from central and western Europe in Buda and Pest in the 12th century, these towns on the trade route to eastern Europe increasingly gained economic significance.
Invasion of the Mongols	In the middle of a period of economic boom, the up-and-coming Danube towns of Buda and Pest were stormed and destroyed in the years 1241–1242 by Mongols. After the terrible experiences of the Mongol invasions, King Béla IV had a castle built on the Buda hill and the Castle District was built to his plans. The new city was soon given the right to hold markets.
Houses of Anjou and Luxemburgs	With the death of Andrew III in 1301, the male line of the Árpád dynasty died out. The house of Anjou took over the throne. The rule of Charles Robert (1301–1342) and Louis I (1342–1382) gave Hungary an era of domestic political stability and economic recovery. Under the rule of Louis, Hungarian power stretched all the way to Bosnia, Serbia, and Bulgaria, and on to Walachia and Dalmatia – with access to the sea. From 1387 to 1437 **Sigismund** of Luxemburg, later Holy Roman Emperor, ruled Hungary and had a palace built on Castle Hill.
Matthias Corvinus	Matthias Corvinus (Mátyás Hunyadi), son of the conqueror of Turks János Hunyadi, was crowned King of Hungary by the nobility in 1458.

Buda developed into a **centre of Renaissance culture** during his rule, which lasted until 1490. The Buda royal palace was extended and the Corvina Library became one of the largest libraries in Europe.

In 1514, Captain György Dózsa gathered an army before Pest by order of the church, intended to fight the advancing Turks. However, this army, predominantly made up of farmers and serfs, turned against the despotism of the Hungarian nobility. The peasant revolt was brutally crushed by the feudal lords.

Peasant Revolt

THE COMING OF THE TURKS

1541–1686	Turkish rule
1686	Charles V, Duke of Lorraine, expels the Turks

After their victory over Hungarian troops at Mohács (1526), when the Hungarian King Louis (Lajos) II was killed, the Turks temporarily occupied Buda Castle.

Time of the Turks

The dispute over the succession after Louis II's death led to the division of Hungary: to protect the crown from Habsburg aspirations one faction of the Hungarian nobility elected King John I (János Szapol-

Division of Hungary

Historical illustration of Buda and Pest from 1617

yai), while another elected the Habsburg Archduke Ferdinand I of Austria, who was forced to restrict his rule to the western regions of Hungary. Through Ferdinand's rule over parts of the Hungarian territory, the country became the setting for warfare between the Habsburgs and the Ottoman Turks.

Second era of Turkish occupation

Buda and Pest were occupied by the Turks under Sultan Suleiman I from 1541 onwards. Many churches were turned into mosques during this time, fortifications were renewed, and magnificent bathhouses were built. Buda became the seat of a vizier. The Ottoman Empire's rule over central Hungary meant the country was divided into three. Óbuda, Buda and Pest were retaken for the Habsburgs by Charles V, Duke of Lorraine, only in the year 1686.

THE DANUBE MONARCHY

1740–1780	Rule of Maria Theresa
After 1789	Early attempts at civil reform
1848	Bourgeois revolution
1867	Hungary gains an independent government
1873	Óbuda, Buda and Pest became the capital of Hungary.

Rule of the Habsburgs

During the Hungarian Diet called in 1687, the Habsburgs were granted the right of accession to the Hungarian throne in return for freeing Hungary from the Turks, and Hungary was incorporated into the Habsburg Empire at the Peace of Karlowitz in 1699. However, opposition to rule by the Habsburg emperors, with their court in Vienna, developed as early as 1697. **Ferenc Rákóczi II** (1676–1735), Prince of Transylvania, who initially refused to lead the fight against the Habsburgs, took over as leader of the freedom movement from 1701, allying himself with the French king, Louis XIV. But, apart from feudal privileges guaranteed to the Hungarian nobility by the Peace of Szatmár in 1711, his military campaigns were mostly unsuccessful.

Enlightened absolutism

Maria Theresa's rule of **enlightened absolutism** as Habsburg regent (1740– 1780) was characterized by a modernization of the Habsburg Empire and a simultaneous strengthening of the absolutist feudal system. Technical, social and economic reforms did strengthen civil society, however, and led to tentative economic growth. Numerous immigrants from German-speaking regions, especially from Upper Austria and southern Germany, settled in Buda and Pest during this phase. The university founded in Nagyszombat by Peter Pázmány in 1635 was initially moved to Buda in 1777, and then to Pest.

The Hungarian nobility restricted the reform policies of enlightened absolutism. By clinging to its political and social privileges, however, it made the population receptive to the messages of the French Revolution. The emerging liberation movement was destroyed by repression: numerous Hungarian supporters of republican ideas were executed on the Bloody Field (Vérmezö) below Castle Hill in 1825.

Spread of revolutionary ideas

In 1825 the failed reform ideas of the late 18th century once more became the object of political discussion, during the course of which – among other things – the nobility's tax privileges were reduced. One of the key figures of the reform era was **Count István Széchenyi** (1791–1860), who aimed to counteract Hungary's economic, technical and social backwardness by the foundation of the Hungarian Academy of Sciences. He brought this project to fruition with a generous donation. The urban development of the two neighbouring cities of Buda and Pest during the first half of the 19th century followed the example of western and central European cities. Bourgeois society set the tone. Many areas of life received further reforms, and trade blossomed. The Hungarian language was also renewed: Latin was dropped in favour of Hungarian, and national consciousness awakened.

Renewed attempts at reform

Revolution broke out in the year 1848, led by liberal nobles fighting the Austrian hegemony in Hungary. Count Lajos Batthyány (1806–1849) formed a government responsible to the Hungarian parliament and Lajos Kossuth (1802–1894; ▶Famous People) rose to become a significant political leader; the poet Sándor Petöfi (1823–1849; ▶Famous People) died in battle. The Habsburg monarchy crushed the freedom movement with the help of tsarist troops from Russia. Kossuth fled into exile, and Batthyány was executed.

Bourgeois revolution

The Hungarian Compromise with the Austrian rulers was not achieved until 1867, with the help of **Ferenc Deák** (1803–1876). Hungary was granted a considerable amount of independence and its own government, although the Austrian emperor continued to be King of Hungary. Emperor Franz Joseph I and Empress Elisabeth (Sisi) were crowned in the Matthias Church in 1867, the final act in the establishment of the

MARCO POLO INSIGHT ?

Revolution song

The revolution of 1848 broke out when Sándor Petöfi recited his »National Song« in front of the Hungarian National Museum.
»Useless villain of a man
Who now, if need be, doesn't dare to die
Who values his pathetic life greater
Than the honour of his homeland
By the God of the Hungarians
We vow,
We vow that we will be slaves
No longer!«

The mural of the coronation of Emperor Franz Joseph and Elisabeth inside the Matthias Church

Austro-Hungarian Monarchy. In 1873, Óbuda, Buda and Pest were united to form the Hungarian capital. On the occasion of the **1000th anniversary** of the arrival of the Magyars in the Carpathian basin, an impressive jubilee exhibition was mounted. During the course of the millennium celebrations in 1896, the decision was made to honour the heroes of Hungarian history with a major memorial (►Heroes' Square). The first underground railway on the European continent was initiated. The Parliament building was completed in 1902.

HUNGARY UP TO 1945

1918	End of Habsburg rule and establishment of a republic
1920–1944	Miklós Horthy, Regent of Hungary
1941	War on the German side
1944	Invasion of German troops, murder of approx. 500,000 Jews
1945	Soviet troops liberate Budapest

First World War and inter-war years

Budapest suffered severe setbacks in its economic development during the First World War. With the defeat of Austria-Hungary, which fought on the side of the Germans, Habsburg rule was at an end in Hungary too. In 1918 a democratic republic was announced. Its first president was **Count Mihály Károlyi** (1875–1955). The Republic of Councils installed by Social Democrats and Communists in March 1919 only held for a few months. In November **Miklós Horthy** (1868–1957) took power and re-established the monarchy in Hungary. As a return of the Habsburgs was unthinkable, he ruled as their regent. Thousands of supporters of the council republic fell victim to his White Terror.

Peace Treaty of Trianon

The Treaty of Trianon resulted in Hungary losing two thirds of its territory and 60% of its population to neighbouring states. This decision by the victorious Allies shocked the Hungarian population, and parts of the population still haven't gotten over it. Trianon became a national trauma. Regent Horthy tried to retract this loss of territory. All means were acceptable to achieve the end of a revision of the treaty and any strong partner was a welcome ally. The closer association of Hungary with Hitler's Germany after 1933 should be seen in the context of these efforts for revision: Germany became the ideal alliance partner, an aggressive and effective support in the question of a cancelation of the Treaty of Trianon. By 1940, the lost territories had successively been handed back to Hungary through the two Arbitrations of Vienna in 1938 and 1940, as well as through the occupation of the Carpathian Ukraine by Hungarian troops in 1939. With Germany as its ally, however, Hungary had to pay a high price for its persistent policy of revision: joining the Second World War on the side of the German Reich in 1941.

Hungarian troops were not spared their Stalingrad: in January 1943, the second Hungarian Army was destroyed at Voronezh; almost 300,000 soldiers died. When the defeat of Nazi Germany became obvious the Hungarian leadership began to think about a timely exit from the war. Hitler's reaction was swift: German troops occupied Hungary on 19 March 1944. There were arrests in Budapest, which also affected renegade representatives of the Horthy regime who had wanted to cancel the pact with Hitler. The bombing of the city began in the summer. After Rumania's exit from the war coalition, Soviet troops easily moved in the direction of Hungary. Nevertheless the **deportation of hundreds and thousands Jews** to Auschwitz was initiated outside Budapest. The persecuted were gathered in so-called Jews' houses in the Hungarian capital. Later ghettos were established. The Swede **Raoul Wallenberg** (▶Famous People), the Swiss Carl Lutz, the papal nunciate, as well as other significant personalities and institutions tried to help the Jews (▶MARCO POLO Insight, p.180). Miklós Horthy tried to leave the alliance with Adolf Hitler on 15 October 1944. The German occupation removed the regent and handed power to the **Arrow Cross Party** led by Ferenc Szálasi. Shortly afterwards Soviet troops surrounded the Hungarian capital and there was heavy street fighting. Wehrmacht and Waffen-SS troops barricaded themselves in Buda Castle. Arrow Cross party members murdered many thousands of Jews in the ghettos and on the banks of the Danube. In January 1945, Soviet troops advanced towards the Danube from the Pest side. Hitler's troops destroyed all Danube bridges. The German soldiers barricaded in the castle failed to escape and the battles ended on 13 February 1945, when Budapest was liberated.

Second World War ◢

THE COMMUNIST ERA

1946	The Hungarian Republic is declared
1949	Hungary becomes a people's republic
1956	Popular revolt

Hungarian Republic

The first post-war elections during the national assembly of November 1945 lead to a defeat for the Communist Party, which had to make do with 17% of the votes. The winner, with 57% of the votes, was the Party of Small Farmers, and the first government leader of the post-war era was **Zoltán Tildy**. The **Hungarian Republic** was declared in Budapest on 1 February 1946. During the period that followed, the Communist Party tried to regain a share of power – trying to erode the power of the democratic government bit by bit. The goal was a socialist society on the Soviet model. There were ever fiercer disagreements within the coalition government.

Dictatorship of the proletariat

Arbitrary methods were used in an attempt to establish a dictatorship of the proletariat. There were show trials and other repressive measures, and even the smallest businesses were nationalized. Finally, the new constitution of the **People's Republic** came into force on 20 August 1949.

Development of infrastructure

The city of Budapest was substantially enlarged by incorporating surrounding districts in 1950. The new Ferihegy Airport was opened the same year, and good progress was made with rebuilding the destroyed neighbourhoods and the Danube bridges. The expansion of heavy industry around Budapest was promoted with great enthusiasm in the early 1950s. By comparison, housing development was seriously neglected.

Relaxation of the political climate

Changes within the Soviet leadership caused by the death of Stalin made for an improved political atmosphere, in Hungary as elsewhere, from 1953 onwards. **Imre Nagy** (1896–1958; ▶Famous People), Rákosi's challenger, who was considered a liberal Communist, became Hungarian prime minister in July 1953. Tentative changes were made under pressure from reformers within and without the Hungarian Communist Party. Nevertheless, Prime Minister Nagy was beaten by arch-conservative Stalinist Rákosi and pushed from office in 1955. Battles over the political direction brought economic development to a standstill. The disaffection of the population increased.

The 1956 uprising

After the 20th Congress of the Communist Party of the Soviet Union, groups pressing for a democratization and modernization of socialism formed. Rákosi gave his last speech in the Budapest Sports Palace, before he got exiled to the Soviet Union. But his successor Ernö Gerö had not the slightest interest in political reforms. On the occasion of a student demonstration on 23 October 1956, his resignation was demanded, along with a call for political renewal. A **popular uprising**, and finally an armed battle against the soviet Military ensued. Imre Nagy was reinstated as premier to calm down the situation. After hesitating in the beginning he negotiated a ceasefire on 28

October and started the democratisation of the country. The prohibition of parties was abolished, a multi-party government was formed, uncensored newspapers were published, and finally Nagy declared the withdrawal of the country from the Warsaw Pact. Nevertheless bloody retribution followed: On 4 November Soviet troops moved into Budapest, led by **János Kádár** (1912–1989; ▶Famous People), the resistance inspired by national and social ideas was crushed. Kádár was the first secretary of the newly founded Hungarian Socialist Workers Party. Once he was a companion of Nagy, but Kádár switched sides just before the Red Army invaded again. Budapest's city centre was devastated. 25,000 Hungarians were killed and thousands of people were arrested, including Imre Nagy and his companions. Over 200,000 left their homeland.

The first years after the national uprising were characterized by a settling of scores with the fighters of 1956. The execution of Imre Nagy and two of his closest associates for high treason in 1958 caused profound shock. At the same time the new Kádár regime tried to appease the population by raising the living standard and to consolidate the regime by political means. In the 1960s Kádár permitted a cautious, but nevertheless dynamic, development of the Hungarian economy

Socialism Hungarian-style

Soviet troops put an end to the revolution of 1956

and society. The education and healthcare systems were reformed and the development of science and technology was especially promoted. From 1960 onwards, large urban building programmes and the expansion of the transport system were realized.

Goulash Communism A new economic system – so-called Goulash Communism – was introduced at the end of the 1960s. It contained elements of a market economy, allowed personal freedoms and participation in decision-making by the collectives. The realization of this plan was continued even after the invasion of Czechoslovakia by Warsaw Pact troops.

Contact with the West With the exemplary restoration of the historic quarters of Buda, especially the castle and the Castle District and, after 1975, of Pest, tourism blossomed and several large hotels were opened. Hungarian foreign and economic policy sought contact with Western countries.

DEMOCRACY AND INTEGRATION WITH THE WEST

1987	The peaceful change of system begins
1989	The third Hungarian Republic is declared
1989	Hungary joins NATO
1991	The Soviet Army leaves the country
1999	Hungary becomes a member of NATO
2004	Hungary joins the European Union
2010	New controversial constitution

Turning away from socialism Small businesses were already permitted at the beginning of the 1980s. In 1985, several candidates stood in one local election, which was a novelty in the history of the Communist bloc. The General Secretary of the Hungarian Socialist Workers Party, János Kádár, was deposed in 1988. His post was taken by **Károly Grósz**, who had, in the meantime, been elected prime minister. That same year workers' organizations and political groups independent of the Party constituted themselves in a first step towards a multi-party system. In 1989, the Hungarian Socialist Workers Party was dissolved. Leadership of the Council of Ministers was taken over by **Miklós Németh**, who remained in office until the elections of 1990. A re-evaluation of the events of 1956 took place. On 16 June 1989, hundreds of thousands paid their respects once more to the former prime minister Imre Nagy, who was the most prominent victim of the 1956 uprising. An increasing number of features of a free market economy began to emerge in the system of the previously socialist planned economy.

The Iron Curtain along the Austro-Hungarian border was dismantled. The liberal attitude of the Hungarian authorities enabled tens of thousands of East German citizens to leave for Austria and the Federal Republic of Germany.

In the year 1990 Hungary had finally said good-bye to socialism and become a republic on the Western model. The conservative Hungarian Democratic Forum and the liberal Association of Free Democrats emerged as the strongest groupings after the first free elections in 45 years. The parties of the Left suffered defeat. **The writer Árpád Göncz** became state president. The constitution was changed in several points: instead of a Hungarian People's Republic, there was now a **Hungarian Republic**; the old state coat of arms with the Crown of St Stephen was reintroduced; the Hungarian Constitutional Court began work and the entire state apparatus was remodelled. The administration, military and police were given new structures. Hungarian economic and foreign policy turned to the West even more than before.

Free elections

The economic restructuring of post-Communist Hungary caused severe disturbances in 1992. Increasing unemployment and inflation were the result. In April 1994, the Hungarian government applied for membership of the European Union. An association agreement that envisaged the step-by-step reduction of customs duties within nine years had already come into force in February 1994. In the parliamentary elections of May 1994, the opposition Hungarian Socialist Party (MSZP) achieved an absolute majority with 209 out of 386 seats. **Gyula Horn**, who had signed up to a continuation of the path towards a free market economy, became the new prime minister of a coalition government with the liberals.

Integration with the West and free market economy

The opening up of the Hungarian market encouraged recession: the rate of inflation stood at almost 19% and unemployment at 10%, and there were few wage increases. The government took measures to reduce domestic debt by, among others things, reducing the value of the forint and limiting state expenditures by, for example, reducing wages in the public sector and shortening the period of income support after illness. In 1998 Viktor Orbán, member of the national conservative party Fidesz, became prime minister for the first time (until 2002).

Recession

The Kosovo crisis of 1999 affected life in the Hungarian metropolis. Hungary, which had been a NATO member since March 1999, and especially Budapest, not only became the destination for many refugees from the areas of former Yugoslavia hit by NATO bombs, but also became a logistical base for NATO troops.

Kosovo crisis and membership of NATO

2011: demonstration against the new constitution

Coronation jubilee of Stephen I

The year 2000 began with the thousandth anniversary of the coronation of Stephen I. During the course of celebrations, the Crown of St Stephen was carried from the National Museum to Parliament on the first day of the new millennium.

EU membership

The most recent highlight of the country's journey towards joining the community of democratic market economies was Hungary's membership of the European Union on 1 May 2004. In the summer socialist Ferenc Gyurcsány overturned prime minister Medgyessy with an intraparty coup and became leader of the second social-liberal coalition.

Disturbances in 2006

In September 2006, Hungary was gripped by protest. During a party meeting Prime Minister Ferenc Gyurcsány – only re-elected in April 2006 – discussed false promises made by his government in the recent elections. When a recording of his comments was played to the media, Budapest experienced its worst disturbances since the beginning of the post-Communist era. The increased cost of living since joining the European Union contributed towards a latent dissatisfaction in the population. 2009 Prime Minister Gyurcsány resigned and was replaced by Gordon Bajnai, who lead a minority government after the liberals had left. Due to the international financial crisis, Hungary turned from prototype to the worst country compared with the rest of Europe. Decreasing economic growth, high unemployment and huge public dept are indicators of a poor economic development. Viktor Orbán won the parliamentary election again in 2010 with 51% of the votes and scored a majority of two-thirds in the parliament. So Orbán and the Fidesz adopted a new and controversial constitution which includes the restrictive and internationally criticised media law. A Fidesz-politician, István Tarlós, became mayor of Budapest for the first time. The rightward shift in Hungary became obvious. Orbán lost his vast majority in a by-election in February 2014.

Hungary held the EU Council Presidency for the first six months of 2011 and most of the meetings were held in Gödöllő Palace. In 2012 Hungary stood under increasing pressure by the EU because of its national deficit.

Art and Culture

Architecture

Historicism was the formative era of urban construction in Budapest in the second half of the 19th century, which went back to great historical architectural styles. Due to the Millenium Celebration in 1896 architecture received an additional push. At the turn of the 20th century an own national style was developed – the Hungarian version of Art Nouveau – which was not influenced by other European styles but rather by oriental styles.

Far into the 19th century, the Buda side still had a mostly Baroque appearance. However, many houses of the Castle District that were rebuilt in the 18th century in the Baroque style after the reconquest of Buda from the Turks have medieval foundations from earlier buildings. Traces of this can often be found, most obviously in the seating niches with pointed arches or blind tracery in some entrance gates, for example at Országház utca 2. The appearance of Buda showpieces today, such as the royal palace and the Matthias Church, is characterized mainly by the designs given to them during the millennium years (1896) after a turbulent history.

Medieval remains in Buda

During the time of the Austro-Hungarian Dual Monarchy (1867–1918), **historicism**, with its multi-faceted use of the great historical architectural styles, was the characteristic building style in Budapest. It was during this time that all the public and commercial buildings, churches, private mansions and industrial headquarters with neo-Romanesque, neo-Gothic or neo-Baroque façades were created. The 1870s and 1880s are considered the true foundation years of the city. Many significant public building works were only undertaken after 1873, when the formerly independent towns of Buda, Pest and Óbuda were officially united. The buildings from this period include the **Nyugati (West) Railway Station** (1877); the **Keleti (East) Railway Station** (1884); the **Margaret Bridge** (1884); **Andrássy út** (completed in 1885), part of the **Great Ring Road**; the **Basilica of St Stephen in Lipótváros**; the **Opera House** (opened in 1884); most of the **university buildings**; the **Customs House** on the Pest bank of the Danube, as well as the massive **Parliament Building** (1885–1904). This rapid pace of development occurred on the busy Pest side, in particular, where an official commission for beautifying the city had been responsible for systematic urban planning since 1808. The grid

Historicism

Collector and patron: Count Ferenc Scéchenyi donated his art as the basis for the National Museum

of streets was planned and the first apartment blocks were built. Several surviving buildings in Lipótváros (Leopold Town), for example on József Nádor tér, or in Terézváros (Theresa Town), especially on Király utca, give an impression of the architecture of the first half of the 19th century. The cultural and political perspectives of the independence movement of the mid-19th century are evidenced by pioneering works such as the building of the **Chain Bridge** (1839–1849), the first Danube bridge, which was built from plans by the English engineer W. T. Clark; construction was supervised by Adam Clark. Other buildings that date from this era are the **National Museum** (1836–1846), the **synagogue** on Dohány utca (1854–1859), the concert hall known as **Vigadó** (1859–1864), and the **Hungarian Academy of Sciences**, whose main buildings on Széchenyi István tér were built between 1862 and 1864. **At the turn of the 20th century**, architects with a historicist perspective continued to win the most prestigious building contracts. For example, Alajos Hauszmann, who was responsible for the extension of the Buda **palace buildings** from 1891 to 1905, also supplied the plans for the former Palace of Justice, today's **Ethnographic Museum**. He adorned this building with architectural decorations and gilded adornments as sumptuous as those of the former headquarters of the **New York Insurance Company**, with its well-known café on the ground floor. The same generation also produced architects whose Hungarian variations on art nouveau still attract attention today. Ödön Lechner (1845-1914), the main representative of the Hungarian Secession style, sought his inspiration for an original and inde-

The oriental looking Arts and Crafts Museum

pendent architecture not in the academic European styles, but in the Orientalism. However, he later wrote of the ornamental decoration of the **Museum of Applied Arts** (1891–1896) that it had »turned out a little too Indian« after all. Apart from considerations of style, in his extensive use of washable ceramic elements he also already took into account problems caused by pollution in the city. From the beginning, Hungarian Secession had a second focus that worked to a different agenda: for architects such as Károly Kós (1883–1977) the roots of an architecture appropriate to a Hungarian style lay in folk art and medieval art. Kós was given commissions that gave him an ideal opportunity for experimentation in the use of traditional building methods from different Hungarian regions, even in the city, with buildings such as the **Budapest Zoo** (1910) and the **Wekerle telep** (from 1912) housing project in Kispest.

BUILDINGS FOR THE 1896 MILLENNIUM CELEBRATION

The urban architectural development which blossomed at the time of the millennium celebrations gave Budapest the characteristics that mark it as a 19th-century metropolis to this day. The architectural heritage of this epoch, which was decisive for the city, can be encountered by visitors on every step, especially in the city-centre districts on the Pest side. The 1896 millennium festivities were staged to recall the arrival of the Hungarian tribes in the Carpathian basin and to record the »glorious thousand-year past« as national history.

1896 – 1000 years of Hungary

The buildings that were constructed on the occasion of the millennium stand predominantly along the north-eastern end of Andrássy út. Even then, the massive Heroes' Square (Hösök tere), which is totally dominated by the millennium memorial, can be reached directly via the freshly inaugurated »Little Metro«, the first underground railway in continental Europe, which runs underneath the showpiece street. Work on the bronze equestrian statue of the seven Hungarian tribal chieftains by György Zala (1858–1937) was not completed until the late 1920s. The design for the columned architecture of the memorial was provided by Albert Schickedanz (1846–1915), who also designed the two museum buildings that flank the square: the Museum of Fine Arts and the Palace of Art.

Andrássy út, Hösök tere (Heroes' Square)

Few traces remain of the temporary millennium buildings that spread over the area stretching from present-day Heroes' Square to the distant wooded area of Városliget, far beyond. Of all those, the only survivors are the »group of historic main buildings«, called Castle Vajdahunyad (Vajdahunyad vára).

Temporary exhibition buildings

An Own Style of Art

In the end of the 19th century, the Hungarian intelligentsia was concerned with searching for national origin and identity and the question of the own tradiotion. A balance against the Austrian ascendancy was supposed to be established by creating a typical Hungarian style. Architecture and art became an instrument of national emancipation.

In 1886, the Budapest Museum of Applied Art bought the complete furniture of an Arabian room in Antwerpen. This purchase was important for the Hungarian national self-conception. Orientalism was in vogue. In their inscrutability the rich exotic ornaments on the furnishings gave cause to speculate about self identity and heritage.

Art and Identity

Art often provides evidence of daring theses in the form of deducing a national heritage and constructing a mythical origin. The Hungarians were interested in this Arabian interior because at this time it was acceptable to prove cultural origins even of regions far away, based on similarity of the decoration of implements. The Orient proved to be a sumptuous source for the Hungarian love of decoration while they simultaneously distanced themselves from European cultural traditions. They were looking for something of their own and original in opposition to Austrian domination in the field of visual arts.

Ödön Lechner

Some artistic circles adopted this synthesis of Orient and Occident enthusiastically. Among the architects, it was mainly Ödön Lechner who was inspired to his inexhaustible Ornamentalism by the mythical past, where by he interwove all kinds of suggestions. He combined old Hungarian subjects with exotic ornaments and elements from the Far Eastern colonial architecture.

For him all the qualities of his artistic demands were united in ceramics: the possibilities of rich color and ornamental design combined with popular traditions and modern use of material. He came from a family of brick manufacturers and maintained a friendship with Vilmos Zsolay, a famous terracotta and porcelain producer, so Lechner had a first-hand knowledge of the working techniques with clay. However, there were many coincidences and speculations in play during his search for subjects. As he revealed the design of the Museum of Applied Art, for example, was mostly inspired by Persian and Indian Art. To date the Museum of Applied Art, built together with Gyula Pártos, as well as the building of the Geological Institute, which was built at the beginning of the 20th century, and the national savings bank still count as classic examples of uniquely Hungarian architecture.

The building of the National Savings Bank is a master piece of Hungarian art nouveau

by different examples and directions – the common goal was just to get rid of the cultural background of the prevailing academic styles.

Ornament and Function

Some representatives even pursued an idiosyncratic form canon. These included, for example, Henrik Böhm and Armin Hegedüs, who opened a joint office in 1896. Ten years later they managed a sensational highlight: the Turkish Banking House (Török bánkház) at Szervita tér, executed according to their plans, was presented to the public. With its elaborate glass façade outwards and its largely freely allocated layout inside, the building became a symbol of modernity. In turn, the monumental Murano glass mosaic gable by Miksa Róth with the subject »Homage to Hungaria«, which functioned as a figurehead for the bank building, was totally devoted to the national zeitgeist.

Later on, Armin Hegedüs was still involved in well-esteemed and representative constructions of Budapest's economy and business world, for example, the construction of high-class hotel Gellért with its thermal baths.

Exemption From Academic Style

However, Lechner's way was not without controversy among his contemporaries. Outspoken opponents like historically working Alajos Hauszmann, a professor at the Technical University, called for a clear distinction between popular and national styles. But also Lechner's like-minded associates from the Secessionist camp were guided

MODERN TRENDS

New building A transitional position is held by Lajos Kozma (1884–1948), who took art nouveau as his starting point and attached himself to the avant-garde tendencies of Modernism. In contrast to many of his colleagues, who had planned in Modernist style elsewhere as emigrants since the 1920s, he was able to complete typical examples of Modernist architecture in Budapest. These include, among others, the **Atrium House** (1936) and the **cinema** at Margit körút 55, with its generous and elegant interior. A **showcase housing development** in 1931, in which most of the modern architects working in Budapest at the time participated, lies in the II district, on Napraforgó utca.

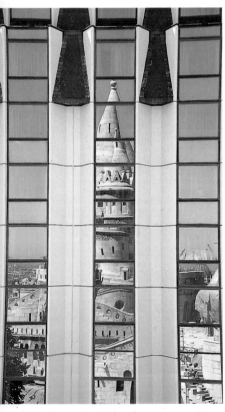

However, the ideas of classic Modernism could only be revisited and developed into functional solutions, especially for industrial, transport, leisure and housing buildings, after the Second World War and after the »iron« Fifties. Buildings, such as the **Hotel Budapest** (Szilágyi Erzsébet fasor 47), built by György Szrogh in 1969, emerged, as well as **terraced houses and apartment blocks** such as the complex on Körösi utca, built by György Vadász between 1967 and 1969. The **Elizabeth Bridge** was built between 1961 and 1964, and the **Metro 2** line was opened in 1973.

In the 1970s and 1980s, elements of Secession architecture came back in fashion. During Expo 1992 in Seville, Hungary presented itself with a pavilion by Imre Makovecz (1935 – 2011), who said of his return to pre-industrial building designs: »I call my work, which is influenced by the turn of the 20th century, **organic architecture**... «. In Budapest, it is possible to get an idea of this organic architecture in the wealthy neighbourhoods of the II district, from several private villas such as the

Reflections of architecture:
Hilton hotel and Fishermen's Bastion

house Pete at Kondorkert utca 9, or the house Gubcsi at Törökvész lejtö 25. Today, in contrast to these buildings, there are architectural concepts that work with ideas of urbanity and try to underline what is typical in the city. An example of this trend thatcomes under the heading of Deconstructionist is the interior of the **Nane Gallery** (IX district, Lónyay utca41), by Gábor Bachman.

Much has changed in the Budapest cityscape since the end of the 1980s. Street names were changed, sculptures and memorials were removed, and the red stars disappeared from public buildings and squares. Post-modern department stores appeared with impressive rapidity, their glass façades contributing to the appearance of the inner city today.

Change

Fine Arts

Since 1867 a fruitful Hungarian national artistic work began in consequence of the political compromise with Austria. The interwar period (1919 – 1939) in Hungary was characterised by political repressions, which restricted the development of artistic freedom. Also Communism only allowed some politically opportune works. Not until the establishment of democracy in the late 1980s did artists have freedom for artistic development.

Mihály Munkácsy (1844 – 1900), born as Michael Lieb, belonged to the highl-valued painters of the 19th century due to his rich clientele. His repertoire contained conventional salon paintings, masterful landscapes and virtuosic still lifes with flowers. He spent his life mostly abroad but due to his national pride he adopted the name of his birthplace Munkacsy as pseudonym in 1864. In 1878 he received the Hungarian title of nobility. He combined scenic dramatic art with rich colours in a pastose brushstroke in huge representational compositions, its contents are partly religious and often patriotic symbolism. His painting style became shallower over time also because of overproduction. A whole hall in the National Gallery is dedicated to him.

Mihály Munkácsy

Guests entering one of the coffee houses in the district of the capital's art and exhibition centres during the time of the Dual Monarchy (1867–1918) would, in all probability, have met a social gathering in lively debate about the cultural and political questions of the day. For the artists of that time, the circle of regulars at the local café was the most important forum for discussing their concerns. The composi-

Golden Age

tion of the individual circles more or less mirrored the main artistic trends and their adherents at the time.

The older generation, representatives of the academic style, met in a side room at Virágbokors (flower bouquet). To these belonged **Bertalan Székely** (1835–1910), a friend of the Munich historical painting movement, who liked commissions for monumental wall paintings best; **Károly Lotz** (1833–1904), the most successful fresco artist of his day, who from the 1870s onwards worked on the majority of new buildings for official representation, such as the great hall in the Palace of Justice, the staircase of Parliament, the ceiling in the auditorium of the opera house, and the main hall in the Academy of Sciences; **Gyula Benczúr** (1844–1920) dazzled visitors to the millennium exhibition with his 3.5m x 7 m (11ft x 23ft) oil painting on the Reconquest of Buda Castle, which today hangs in the country's National Gallery. The different circles of the popular Salon and genre painters gathered in the Abbázia Café or the Royal Café. Several groups of youthful Secessionists met at the Mücsarnok kávéház, the café in the Palace of Art.

At the end of the 19th century and the beginning of the 20th century, the Café Japán was the most important artists' meeting place. It was the favourite café of innovators, such as **Pál Szinyei Merse** (1845–1920) who, independent of Parisian influences, had already experimented with painting outdoors around 1870. His main work, *Breakfast Outdoors*, of 1873, is in the Hungarian National Gallery. **Károly Ferenczy** (1862–1917) also dropped in here when he had business in the city, and was not at the artists' colony of Nagybánya. He was one of the most influential exponents of non-academic methods and directions, from Pleinair to Impressionism, and from art nouveau to Symbolism, that were represented and developed by the »Nagybánya School« from 1896 onwards. Examples of his work can also be admired in the National Gallery, such as *The Painter* (1903) or *Sunny Morning* (1905). The »greats« that patronized the Japanese café also included **József Rippl-Rónai** (1861–1927) who, after his intensive and frequent visits to France, reported on the latest artistic events there. He became a painter of Hungarian small town scenes. A not very sociable and, in his day, not seriously respected member of the circle was **Tivadar Csontváry Kosztka** (1853–1919), who was convinced that his pictures would one day »shine as lone stars in the sky«. This attitude, which he expressed in monumental landscape paintings in expressive colours with motifs from the Near East or southern Italy – such as, for example the picture *The Ruins of the Greek Theatre at Taormina* from 1904/1905, in the National Gallery – still gives him a special position. At the beginning of the 20th century the art scene began to split more and more. Béla Czóbel (1883 – 1976) was a primary promoter for new impulses. In Paris he was acquainted with Matisse, among others. He was one of the cofounders of the painters group »The Eight« (Nyolcak) along with Róbert Berény. Both spent a long time abroad during the interwar years. Aladár Körösföi-Kriesch (1863 – 1920), who had founded an artist colony, dealt very much with art nouveau in Hungary.

Most of the artistic avant-garde that began to develop in the revolutionary climate of the 1910s had to continue its activities abroad after the collapse of the People's Republic in 1919. Vienna and Berlin, where the relationship with German Expressionists and Dadaists, Italian Futurists or Russian and Dutch Constructivists could be intensified especially, became the centres of Hungarian emigration. Today the career of **Lajos Kassáks** (1887–1967), the main organizer of the Hungarian Activist circle, and his activities as an artist, writer and publisher of a number of avant-garde publications, can be viewed in the Budapest Kassák Museum in Zichy Palace in Óbuda, as the artist returned to his homeland after years of exile.

The inter-war years

Quite a few artists connected with Hungarian Activism taught at the Bauhaus in Weimar and later on in Dessau, where they received international recognition. The most famous among them are **László Moholy-Nagy** (1895–1946), **Marcel Breuer** (1902–1981) and **Farkas Molnár** (1898–1944).

Lajos Kassák remained a defender and supporter of the avant-garde right up to his death, even of the newest trends of New Abstraction, Happenings, Flux and Pop Art. In the 1960s and 1970s, however, several exhibitions oriented towards the international scene were closed down early, despite support from famous personalities. Newspaper projects were foiled, and several theatre productions banned. Protagonists of that underground era were, for example, **Sándor Altorjai** (1941–1979), **Ilona Keserü** (born 1933), **Béla Kondor** (1931–1972) and **Dóra Maurer** (born 1937). The heroic sculptures that were created for Budapest's streets and squares on official commissions from the 1950s to 1980s will probably not leave their present location any time soon: they are all gathered in silent pathos in the ▶sculpture park /Memento Park on the city's edge, designed as if it were a final resting place.

Art after 1945

Imre Varga (born 1923), the most important Hungarian contemporary sculptor, created a very wide range of artistic work, which ranges from communist-leaning sculptures to clerical work and also representations of Konrad Adenauer and Charles de Gaulle. Parts of his collection are exhibited in Óbuda.

Another museum in Óbuda is dedicated to the painter and graphic artist **Victor Vasarely** (1908 – 1997), who came from Pécs in southern Hungary and then emigrated to Paris, where he became the founder of Op art. His work makes use of optical ilusions due to his use of geometrical elements.

Contemporary art scene — A unique aspect of the Hungarian art scene is that it is less characterized by private galleries and more by the associations, free groups and independent initiatives of the artists themselves. This is still the case today, as the Hungarian avant-garde's desire for independence from official tastes in art has a strong tradition.

Already in the years of the Hungarian People's Republic, the art scene laid claim to several unconventional places in which to offer its newest work for public discussion. For example, such exhibitions and art events took place in the Budapest zoo, in the Research Institute for Physics, at the airport and, very often, in private apartments or studios. Beyond the traditional art institutions, many forms of expression which challenged social conventions were tried out. The confrontational and scandalous performances and actions in the 1970s and 1980s by **Miklós Erdély** and **Tibor Hajas** still resonate today. The painters J. Barcsay, A. Bernáth and I. Szöny had given new impulses to the Hungarian painting scene during the last two decades. Today, too, the liveliest sector of the art scene is sustained by initiatives of the artists themselves, which occur at changing venues without fanfares or publicity. These events are almost always exclusively advertised by word of mouth.

City of Culture

Budapest is Hungary's most important cultural centre. It is not only the home of the Hungarian Academy of Sciences, but also the city in which most of the country's universities and colleges are concentrated. The Music School, the Opera, as well as the Operetta, make the city on the Danube a centre of music. Furthermore, over two dozen theatres, superbly equipped museums and galleries underscore Budapest's reputation as a city of culture. Several poets and writers have succeeded in helping a rich Hungarian literature to achieve international fame, despite its linguistic isolation.

Music — »In relation to songs and other forms of entertainment, Pest is ahead of Vienna«, thus wrote the Vasárnapi Ujság (Sunday News) in 1873. In fact, Budapest was so successful that connoisseurs such as Johannes Brahms travelled there especially to hear a good performance of Mozart's *Don Giovanni*. That was around 1890, when Gustav Mahler was the director of the Royal Hungarian Opera. External influences were many and various during the development of the city's culture. Conversely, however, Hungarian traditions were also received in the cultural centres of Europe, a phenomenon particularly evident in music. Musicians such as Brahms and Franz Schubert liked to use themes that originated in the Verbunkos instrumental dance music of the 18th century. Originally, Verbunkos melodies and dances were used in recruiting of soldiers.

First-class music can be experienced at the Budapest Opera, which has been under the artistic direction of such eminent persons as Gustav Mahler, Sergio Failoni, Aladár Tóth, Kálmán Nádasdy, János Ferencsik and András Mihály. Furthermore, there are concerts at the Academy of Music, the Pest Redoute, in the new Congress Centre and in the Matthew Church and the Dohány Street Synagogue. During the summer months, there is a programme of operatic and ballet performances on the open-air stage on Margaret Island. Significant musical occasions are the annual cultural events: the »Budapest Spring Festival« and the »Budapest Autumn Festival«.

Music performances

Budapest is also known for excellent klezmer music, headed by Budapest Klezmer Band. The band's founder Ferenc »Fegya« Jávori helped to provide a revival of the very emotional klezmer music in Hungary. Even the klezmer musical *Bridal dance* (Menyasszonytánc) is performed in the Budapest Operetta Theatre – of course with the Budapest Klezmer Band.
Jazz is also played in a lot of pubs and clubs. Benkó Dixiland Band has a significant postion in the jazz scene and has performed energetic concerts for decades.

Klezmer music

THEATRE

Theatrical venues in the Hungarian capital reflect cultural changes and influences. In the second half of the 19th century, the Viennese architectural practice of **Ferdinand Fellner and Hermann Helmer** built countless theatres. In Budapest, their first commission was a theatre that no longer exists; their last was the Vígszínház Theatre on Szent István körút, which was built in 1895–96. Their most interesting project was the Somossy Orfeum, today the home of the Operetta (Fövárosi Operett Színház), which they had to fit into a narrow plot at Nagymezö utca17, in 1893–94. The stages and auditoriums of the two Viennese architects always followed Baroque models. In contrast, the Erkel Theatre in VIII district, Köztársaság tér, was built in art nouveau style in 1911 by pupils of Lechner, Marcel Komor, Dezsö Jakab and Géza Márkus, though many renovations had to be made. Today around fifty ensembles covering a wide spectrum perform theatre in Budapest. Popular opera, Hungarianized musicals, well-known operettas and light music dominate the programmes of the major Budapest stages. However, the Opera House (Magyar Állami

Venues and ensembles

Operaház) increasingly offers out-of-the-ordinary productions. Built to designs by Miklós Ybl between 1875 and 1884, the Opera House remains the city's most significant venue, even if, in recent years, artistic innovations and experiments in content and organization have generally been developed for small stages, such as the József Katona Theatre on Petöfi Sándor utca 6. The inauguration of the structurally and politically controversial Hungarian National Theatre (2002), a building on the banks of the Danube in the IX district, designed by Mária Siklós, has added yet another inportant stage to Budapest's rich collection.

The Palace of Arts (Művészetek Palotája) opened in 2005 next to it. Apart from the Museum Ludwig the biggest concert hall of the country is also placed inside this cultural building. The Hungarian Philharmonic Orchestra and the National Dance Theatre enter its stage consistently. The parent house of this prestigious dance theatre is former Castle Theatre near Buda Castle.

UNIVERSITIES

The first permanent Hungarian university was founded in Nagyszombat (present-day Trnava in Slovakia) in 1635 and initially moved to Buda in 1777, and finally to Pest in 1784. From this emerged today's Eötvös Loránd Tudományegyetem, the city's and the entire country's foremost university. It is named after the physicist and researcher of gravity Loránd Eötvös (1848–1919), who invented the torsion balance that carries his name.

The Franz Liszt Academy of Music has a good reputation among experts

Of the almost 60 institutes of higher learning in the country, a quarter are found in Budapest alone. Many subjects can be studied only there. The most important seats of learning and research, which also played a significant role in the development of the city, are the Technical University (Budapest Müszaki Egyetem), the School of Veterinary Medicine (Allatorvostudományi Egyetem), the Music School (Liszt Ferenc Zenea Akadémia), and the Art School (Magyar Képzömüvészeti Föiskola).

Other important universities are the Corvinus University of Budapest on the Pest bank of the Danube, which developed from the University of Economics, and the University of Technology on the opposite side of the river.

The German-language Andrássy Gyula University was founded in 2002 and housed in the palace of the Festetics noble family, behind the National Museum. The name is taken from Count Gyula Andrássy, the most significant Hungarian reform politician of the 19th century. The university has a European focus and offers subjects such as International Relations, Comparative Schools of State and Law, and Central European Studies.

Andrássy University

ÁRPÁD (PROBABLY 850 TO 907)

Árpád was the founder of the first Hungarian royal dynasty, the Árpáds, who ruled the country from the 9th century until the year 1301. The nomadic Hungarian tribes of the ninth century had two types of leaders, the kende (religious leader) and the gyula (chieftain and judge). Árpád was a chieftain when he penetrated the Carpathian basin via the Verecke Pass in present-day Ukraine, and conquered the regions east of the Danube during the first phase of the Great Migrations. After the death of the kende in 904, Árpád took over this role too and became sole leader as chieftain.

First king of the Hungarians

BÉLA BARTÓK (1881–1945)

Béla Bartók became famous as a composer far beyond the borders of Hungary. He studied at the Budapest Music School and took on a

Composer

professorship for piano there in 1907. His interest in folk music, which he researched himself in Hungary and in formerly Hungarian regions, was inspired by his friendship with Zoltán Kodály. As a composer, Bartók succeeded in joining the European avant-garde; his works combine modern musical language with Hungarian folk music. With his *Mikrokosmos*, comprising 153 piano pieces, Bartók created a progressive textbook between 1926 and 1937. On the occasion of the 50th anniversary of the unification of Buda and Pest in 1923, he composed the *Dance Suite*, which had its premiere together with Kodály's *Psalmus Hungaricus*. Developments in Hungary caused him to emigrate to the USA in the autumn of 1940, where he died in impoverished circumstances in 1945. His remains were transferred to Budapest in 1988.

DÉNES (DENNIS) GÁBOR (1900–79)

The Budapest-born physicist Dénes Gábor went down in the history of science in 1947 when he invented holography. After his studies in Budapest and Berlin he emigrated to England in 1934, where he became a lecturer at London's Imperial College from 1949, and Professor of Electrophysics from 1958 to 1967. After the invention of laser light in 1960, his technology gained great practical significance. Dénes Gábor was honoured with the Nobel Prize in Physics in 1971.

Physicist

Lajos Kossuth fought for independence from Austria.

THEODOR HERZL (1860–1904)

Zionist   Budapest is the birthplace of Theodor Herzl, the founder of political Zionism. Herzl studied law in Vienna and after the completion of his final examinations in 1884 worked as a foreign correspondent for an Austrian newspaper in Paris. He came to Zionism there, where large sections of society were increasingly anti-semitic. In *The Jewish State*, published in 1896, he demanded the foundation of a sovereign Jewish state with the argument that Jews were not only a religious group, but also a nation. He called the first Zionist Congress in Basel, in 1897, which elected him as President of the World Zionist Organization. The foundation of a Jewish state, for which he campaigned energetically, was not to become a reality until more than forty years after his death.

IMRE KERTÉSZ (BORN 1929)

Writer   In 2002 the **Nobel Prize for Literature** went to Imre Kertész, for »a literary work that upholds the fragile experience of the individual against the barbaric arbitrariness of

history«. The author was initially deported to Auschwitz, and later to Buchenwald, at the age of 15, due to his Jewish roots. After his rescue, he became a journalist and then lived as an independent author in Budapest, and wrote musicals and drama; he earned his living through his work as a translator. He began to write his autobiographical *Fatelessness* as early as 1960. Today it is one of the most important works of contemporary European literature and helped Kertész gain an international breakthrough in 1995.

Nobel prize winner Imre Kertész

MIHÁLY KERTÉSZ (MICHAEL CURTIS) (1888–1962)

Film director   The movie *Casablanca*, filmed in 1943, with Ingrid Bergman and Humphrey Bogart, made the Hungarian-born Mihály Kertész, pseudonym Michael Curtis famous and gave him the highest American film honour, an Oscar. Curtis already made his first film in 1912, at the age of 24. After periods in Vienna and Berlin he arrived in Hollywood in 1927, where he was already working in colour in 1930. His most famous films are *Robin Hood* (1938), *Virginia City* (1940), *Yan-*

kee Doodle (1942), *Mission to Moscow* (1943) and *The Life of Francis of Assisi* (1961).

ZOLTÁN KODÁLY (1882–1967)

The composer and musician, who was born in Kecskemét, became   Composer
famous above all for his systematic research of Hungarian folk music,
whose special characteristics he worked out by a comparison with the
folk music of other Finno-Ugrian peoples. After completion of his
studies at the Budapest School of Music, he taught theory of music
and composition there from 1907 and, from 1937, folk music as well.
His compositions, which reflect his detailed work with Hungarian
folk music, were popularized abroad as well, by Toscanini and Furt-
wängler. Beginning in the 1920s, but especially after the Second
World War, his focus was on the reform of music teaching in schools.
The system of music teaching developed by him is still well-known
throughout the world.

GYÖRGY KONRÁD (BORN 1933)

György Konrád is among the leading representatives of the intellec-   Writer
tual opposition in Hungary which from the 1970s fought for the democratization process in the country. Until the political changes at
the end of the 1980s, the writer could only publish his work abroad
or in the underground press. His first novel *Látogató* (The Case
Worker, 1969) evolved from the experiences of this former philosophy student when working at the youth protection unit of a Budapest
government organization. In this and his later novels, among them
The City Builder from 1975, or *A Feast in the Garden* (1986), the social and political problems in a socialist society are portrayed. He
received the International Charlemagne Prize of Aachen and the
Peace Prize of the German Book Trade and was, among other things,
president of the Berlin Academy of Arts. His recent works (*Departure
and Return* 2001 and *Pendulum* 2008) deal intensely with survival
during the Holocaust, his experience in the opposition and the condition of modern Hungary.

LAJOS KOSSUTH (1802–94)

Kossuth was one of the leading figures in the battle for Hungarian   Freedom
independence and civil rights in the 19th century. He campaigned for   fighter
secession from Austria, social reforms, the abolition of feudal privileges, taxation for all, and the establishment of representative bodies.

In April 1849, the Hungarian Parliament under his leadership voted for independence, as well as the deposition of the House of Habsburg, electing him as regent. After the revolution Kossuth fled to Turkey and then through Europe, where he continued the fight for Hungarian independence. Even though he was granted amnesty in 1867, he never returned to Hungary. His work of several volumes entitled *My Writings in Exile* was published in 1880–1882. Already a national hero in Hungary during his lifetime, the revolutionary died in his elective home of Turin, in 1894.

FERENC (FRANZ) LISZT (1811–86)

Composer   Franz Liszt, who is now considered one of the country's greatest sons, was born in present-day Raiding, in the Austrian Burgenland, which

at that time was Hungarian. The piano virtuoso lived in Paris from 1823 to 1835, where he was influenced by Berlioz, Paganini and Chopin. In Weimar, where Liszt was engaged as director of music at the court of the grand duke, he composed, among other things, various piano pieces, with which he founded the so-called New German School. Between 1861 and 1869 he lived, at various times, in Rome, Weimar and Budapest. In Budapest he took over the leadership of the Academy of Music whose foundation was inspired by him. His close relationship with Hungary is particularly evident in his *Hungarian Rhapsodies*. The composer was ennobled by the Duke of Sachsen-Weimar in 1859 and died in Bayreuth in 1886.

Virtuoso pianist Franz Liszt

GYÖRGY LUKÁCS (1885–1971)

Philosopher and historian of literature   György Lukács, a philosopher and historian of literature was born in Budapest, and became a member of the Communist Party in 1918. After the collapse of the People's Republic, he emigrated via Vienna to Moscow. His writings, in which he outlined the core themes of Marxist aesthetics and artistic philosophy, had a permanent influence on left-wing European intellectuals. In the 1930s Lukács concentrated on working with European literature of the 19th century, especially the realistic novel. After the end of the war he returned to Hungary and taught aesthetics and philosophy of culture in Budapest from 1945 to 1958. As one of the main movers of the Hungarian uprising in 1956, he suffered great discrimination after it was crushed and was relieved of all his posts. Lukács withdrew into internal exile for some years and his books were published abroad. He re-emerged into Hungarian intellectual life in the mid-1960s, but did not live to complete his planned final work on ethics.

LÁSZLÓ MOHOLY-NAGY (1895–1946)

The multi-talented artist, painter, sculptor, graphic artist and photo-   **Artist** grapher, born in the north-eastern town of Bácsborsod, is widely known as an influential teacher at the Bauhaus in Weimar, where he taught from 1923 to 1928. After Hitler took power, he initially emigrated to England, and then to the USA in 1937. He founded the »New Bauhaus« in Chicago. Moholy-Nagy embodies the modern artist of the early 20th century, who liberated himself from traditional forms and single tracks of expression and experimented with new materials, media and techniques, touching on and influencing various contemporary trends, such as Dadaism, Constructivism and de Stijl. His extensive repertoire included abstract compositions, collage, stage sets and photo montage.

IMRE NAGY (1896–1958)

Nagy, a locksmith from Kaposvár joined the Russian Bolsheviks to-   **Politician** wards the end of the First World War. He became a member of the newly founded Hungarian Socialist Workers Party in the 1920s. He qualified as an agrarian specialist in Moscow in the 1930s. He returned to Hungary with the Russian troops in 1944 and, as Minister for Agriculture, oversaw the dispossession of the large landowners without compensation. Nagy, who held important party posts, was forced to work with Stalinist trends. He was elected as Hungarian prime minister in 1953, as representative of the »new course«, but was already forced to resign under pressure from the Stalinists by 1955. Imre Nagy became prime minister once more at the beginning of the Hungarian uprising in 1956. He took the lead in the uprising and proclaimed Hungary's neutrality in the Cold War. After the suppression of the uprising by Soviet troops Nagy was carried off to neighbouring Communist Rumania. He was returned to Hungary in 1958, and sentenced to death in a secret court, along with several fellow activists. In 1989, Nagy and his comrades were officially rehabilitated by a formal act of state. His mortal remains were buried at the new city cemetery (Új köztemetö).

SÁNDOR PETÖFI (1823–49)

Poet Sándor Petöfi is honoured as Hungary's greatest poet. The characteristics of his poetry are unpretentious language and a confession of
personal feelings, which is particularly evident in his love poems, but
also in other genres. In his heroic epics, fairy tales and songs – his
Hero János (1845) was particularly famous – he portrayed the traditions and landscapes of the great Hungarian plain in the daily lives of
the farmers and cowherds. His revolutionary tendencies made him a
leading figure of the freedom movement, and on 15 March 1848,
Petöfi led Pest's youth and recited his revolutionary *National Song* on
the steps of the National Museum. Convinced of the need for armed
resistance, he took part in the Hungarian War of Independence as a
captain in the revolutionary army, and is believed to have fallen at the
Battle of Segesvár (today Sighisoara in Rumania).

FERENC PUSKAS (1927–2006)

Football The career of the great Hungarian footballer Ferenc Puskas began in
legend 1943 in his birthplace of Kispest, a suburb of Budapest. The short and
stocky Puskas gave his debut performance in the Hungarian national team aged 18, against Austria. In 1953, he was captain during the
legendary match of Wembley, when Hungary won 6-3 against the
English national team, which was regarded as invincible. After four
Hungarian championship titles with Kispest Honved, Puskas moved
abroad in reaction to the political events in Hungary in 1956. He
signed for Real Madrid in 1958 and along with Alfredo di Stefano he
became part of the most feared international pair of strikers of his
time. While at Real Madrid he won the Spanish championship six
times, was European Footballer of the Year and World Footballer of
the Year twice. As captain of the Hungarian national team between
1950 and 1956 he only suffered one defeat, against Germany at the
World Championships in Bern. In 84 games for the Hungarian team
Puskas scored 83 goals. Ferenc Puskas was elected as Hungary's Footballer of the Century in 1998. He died of Alzheimer's in Budapest,
aged 79, in 2006.

IGNÁC SEMMELWEIS (1818–65)

Doctor The doctor from Buda went down in medical history as »the saviour
of mothers«. During his work as a birthing assistant he discovered
that dirty hands, instruments and bandages could cause an infection
at childbirth that was usually fatal. He therefore advised doctors to
disinfect these with chlorine water before beginning treatment. He

returned to Budapest from Vienna in 1850, and became consultant gynaecologist at the Rókus Hospital. From 1855 onwards, he taught at the Medical University that today carries his name. Even though his method, which paved the way for the antiseptic treatment of wounds, had great success he was denied international recognition beyond Hungary during his lifetime.

ISTVÁN SZABÓ (BORN 1938)

István Szabó began his film studies in Budapest, in 1956, the year of the Hungarian uprising, and already achieved international recognition in 1963, with his short film *Concert*. His first full-length movie, *The Age of Dreams*, followed in 1964. Since then he has numbered among the most creative and artistically influential filmmakers in Europe. His early films reflect the political trauma of the suppression of the Hungarian uprising in allegorical, deeply poetic and melancholy visual language. Szabó began his European career in the 1980s, with his film *Mephisto* (1981). To this day he continues to work on his theme of the relationship of artists to political power, and the damage done to the individual by social circumstances. István Szabó was born in Budapest in 1938. Between 1956 and 1961 he studied film direction under Félix Máriássy at the Theatre and Film School. In 1959, he was a founding member of the Béla Balázs Studio; his first short films were created there in 1961–62 (*Variations on a Theme*, 1961; *You*, 1962). During his years of study he was hired by the Hungarian State Security. The consequential internal conflict is obviously reflected in his movies.

Director

ENJOY
BUDAPEST

Where to eat Hungarian specialities? Which celebration should you not miss? Where to buy nice souvenirs? Read about it – best before you start your journey!

Accommodation

Hotels for Every Taste

In general, it is not difficult to find a room in Budapest, since the offer has grown considerably in the last years. From private rooms or pensions and middle class hotels to luxury hotels, the choice is very large. There are also apartments, flats and campsites.

Most hotels are concentrated around the Pest city center or in Buda near the Danube or the roads leading towards Vienna. Some guesthouses and hotels are located in the Buda hills. This means long travel time to the center, but beautiful residential areas with fresh air. | **Location**

There is a wide range of four- and five-star hotels in the upscale sector. Some of the top hotels offer a wonderful view over the Danube, others have their own spas and still others have thouroughly modern design look. In the mid-range, there are comfortable three-star hotels. It is often more convenient, however, to choose a guesthouse because these can also have very high standards. | **Categories**

Especially in the high-class hotels prices can vary considerably depending on the occupancy rate, day of week and time of year; the difference to three-star hotels may disappear. You should compare the prices exactly before you book a hotel. The effort can be worthwhile. Also the low season from November to March provides significant discounts. | **Prices**

Private guesthouses are booming. During the summer months there is additional accommodation in student halls of residence. Here you can quickly get in contact with other travelers. | **Private guesthouses**

The accommodation service in Budapest can help you find a room, especially if you are looking for an apartment in the city or arrive without a reservation. On the internet you often find the best deals for booking a hotel. Usually a credit card is required as a guarantee for booking. | **Accommodation service**

In the summer months, Easter and New Year's Eve a reservation is always recommended, also during the Formula One weekend in July/August at the Hungaroring. | **Reservation**

The Gellért Hotel still reflects the splendor of the old baths architecture

Recommended accommodation

ACCOMMODATION SERVICE

Best Hotel Service
V., Sütő utca 2
Tel. 1 3 18 48 48
www.besthotelservice.hu
Booking service for hotels, guest-houses, private rooms and apartments.

IBUSZ
V., József Attila utca 20
Tel. 1 5 01 49 10
www.ibusz.hu
Booking service for private rooms and flats.

Hotels via internet
www.travelport.hu
www.budapestinfo.hu
www.budapesthotelreservation.hu
www.flatrentbudapest.com

Price categories
Price for a double room
££££ from 45 000 HUF
£££ 30 000 – 45 000 HUF
££ 20 000 – 30 000 HUF
£ up to 20 000 HUF

❶ etc. ►map p.94/95

❶ Budapest Marriott Hotel ££££
Apáczai Csere János ucta 4
Tel. 1 4 86 50 00
www.marriott.com
Thanks to its location on the Pest Danube Corso, this hotel ranks among the most desirable choices in Hungary's capital. Many of the 364 luxury rooms enjoy a superb view of the Castle District opposite.

❷ Corinthia (Grand Hotel Royal) ££££
VII., Erzsébet körút 43 – 49
Tel. 1 4 79 40 00
www.corinthia.hu
Looking for a gorgeous and luxurious accomodation directly on vibrant Great Ring? The Royal was built in 1896 for the Millennium exhibition to give an international flair to the city. After extensive renovation a few years ago the renowned Hotel has regained its old status. In the vast complex of buildings there are excellent restaurants, cafes and even an original spa from the end of the 19th Century.

❸ Four Seasons Hotel Gresham Palace ££££
V., Széchenyi István tér 5 – 7
Tel. 1 2 68 60 00
www.fourseasons.com
Adjacent to the Chain Bridge, with a view of Castle Hill, lies the Gresham Palace Hotel, re-opened in 2003 after restoration work. Even if you cannot afford a room at the hotel where Sophia Loren stays, at least take a look at the entrance hall: wonderful art nouveau windows, intricate mosaics of Murano glass, and silk wallpaper from Belgium. The palace is a breath-taking spectacle, especially at night.

❹ Hilton Budapest ££££
Hess András tér 1 – 3
tel. 1 8 89 66 00
www.budapest.hilton.com

Hotel Gresham Palace

This modern luxury hotel in the heart of the Castle District, close to the Fishermen's Bastion, was built during the era of »goulash communism«. The architects incorporated architectural remains of the Gothic Dominican monastery. The Hilton has 322 comfortable rooms and suites, and the restaurant is one of the city's best.

❺ Inter-Continental Budapest ££££
Apáczai Csere János ucta 12–14
tel. 1 3 27 63 33
www.interconti.com
Built in 1981, the Budapest Inter-Conti stands on the Danube Corso on the Pest side. This hotel with its 398 rooms and suites is mainly frequented by business travellers.

❻ Kempinski Hotel Corvinus ££££
Erzsébet tér 7–8
H-1051 Budapest
tel. 1 429–3777
www.kempinski.com
The Budapest Kempinski in the Pest city centre opened in 1992 and is considered a post-modern architectural highlight to this day. The luxury hotel has 369 extremely comfortable rooms and suites.

❼ Le Méridien ££££
V., Erzsébet tér 9–10
Tel. 1 4 29 55 00
www.lemeridienbudapest.com
Right next to the Kempinski the Le Méridien also offers luxurious accommodation in a building that was originally built for an insurance company, but later housed the headquarters of the Budapest Police. The central and convenient location is a plus for the hotel.

❽ Sofitel Budapest Chain Bridge ££££
V., Széchenyi István tér 2
Tel. 1 2 35 12 34
www.sofitel.com
This luxury hotel stands on the Pest side of the Danube, near the Chain Bridge. The 355 rooms and suites are arranged around an inner courtyard with piano bar. Of course the hotel also has a swimming pool, as well as a gym with sauna and solarium.

❾ Art'otel £££
I., Bem rakpart 16 – 19
Tel. 1 4 87 94 87
www.artotel.com
Located directly below the Castle Hill, overlooking the Danube. From the front rooms you have a magnificent view on Parliament. The interior and the paintings date back to the American artist Donald Sultan, who gave a special flair to the house.

❿ Best Western Hungária £££
VII., Rákóczi út 90
Tel. 1 8 89 44 00
www.bestwestern.com
This reasonably comfortable 1000-bed hotel is very centrally located by a major road junction and opposite the East Railway Station.

⓫ Danubius Grand Hotel Margitsziget £££
XIII., Margitsziget

Tel. 1 8 89 42 79
www.danubiushotels.com
Guests taking a cure feel most at
home here, in the 164 rooms on
Margaret Island. The spa facilities
of the neighbouring Danubius
Thermal Hotel Margitsziget can
be reached by underground
tunnel.

**⑫ Danubius Hotel Astoria
City Center £££**
Kossuth Lajos ucta 19–21
Tel. 1 8 89 60 00
www.danubiushotels.com
Things are friendly and familiar in
this hotel in the centre of Pest. It
has over 129 nicely decorated
rooms. Connoisseurs of art history
will enjoy the unadulterated Empire style here.
The in-house café-restaurant has
all the charm of the old
world and is a relic of
the past coffeehouse
time. **Insider Tip**

**⑬ Danubius Health
Spa Resort
Margitsziget £££**
XIII., Margitsziget
Tel. 1 4 52 62 00
www.danubiushotels.com
Those who want to relax in an at-
tractive environment away from city
noise are well served by this spa ho-
tel with 248 comfortable rooms.

⑭ Gerlóczy £££ **Insider Tip**
V., Gerlóczy utca 1
Tel. 1 5 01 40 00
www.gerloczy.hu
Above the atmospheric epony-
mous café, the Gerlóczy offers
comfortable rooms in a quiet and
very central location. Breakfast

can be enjoyed in the morning in
the café – a little bit of Paris on
the Danube!

⑮ k + k Hotel Opera £££
VI., Révay utca 24
Tel. 1 2 69 02 220
www.kkhotels.com
This modern and well-run hotel
lies in a quiet side street behind
the opera and has more than 200
tastefully decorated rooms. The
service is first rate.

⑯ Mercure Korona £££
V., Kecskeméti utca14
Tel. 1 4 86 88 00
www.mercure-korona.hu
This hotel, one of the Hungarian
capital's large establishments
with its 424 rooms, has a very
central location on the Little
Ring. The rooms are relatively
small, but nevertheless quite
comfortable

**⑰ Radisson
Blu Béke £££**
VI., Teréz körút 43
Tel. 1 8 89 39 00
www.radissonblue.com
This hotel, which has a long tradition and 239 somewhat small
rooms, is located quite centrally
on the Great Ring near the West
Railway Station and the opera. It
is also the home of »Zsolnay«,
one of the city's best café-restau-
rants.

⑱ Carlton ££
I., Apor Péter utca 3
Tel. 1 2 24 09 99
www.carltonhotel.hu
Guests at the Carlton can stay in
95 attractively decorated rooms,

at the foot of Castle Hill and near the Chain Bridge.

⑲ City Hotel Mátyás ££
V., Március 15. tér 8
Tel. 1 3 38 47 11
www.cityhotel.hu
A central middle class hotel between the Danube and the Váci utca. Unfortunately only very few rooms offer a view on the Danube, but the major attractions in the city center are just a few minutes walking distance, and the Elizabeth bridge quickly leads to the other side of the Danube.

**⑳ Erzsébet
City Center ££**
Károlyi Mihály utca 11 – 15
Tel. 1 8 89 37 46
www.danubiushotels.com
The modern city hotel is located in the pedestrianized part of downtown Pest. It is especially favoured by price-conscious business travellers, who can eat well for a good price in the hotel restaurant. The hotel bar is always lively.

**㉑ IBIS Budapest
Centrum ££**
IX., Ráday utca 6
Tel. 1 4 56 41 00
www.ibishotel.com,
Modern city hotel at the beginning of the trendiest street Ráday Street at the Little Ring. The rooms offer a good middle class standard. Breakfast and parking in the garage must be booked extra.

㉒ Peregrinus Elte Hotel ££
V., Szerb utca 3
Tel. 1 2 66 49 11
www.peregrinushotel.hu

Directly in front of the Serbian Orthodox Church in the heart of downtown Pest the university hotel is located in a quiet side street of Váci utca. The rooms are modern and tastefully decorated. The price is okay for the location. The hotel does not offer parking, but has a perfect ambience.

㉓ Soho Boutique Hotel ££
VII., Dohány utca 64
Tel. 1 8 72 82 92
www.sohoboutiquehotel.com
Behind the narrow façade of the chic, modern design hotel a relatively large number of attractive rooms are hidden. With a little luck you can catch one of the special offers, so you can save about a third of the regular price.

㉔ Bara £
XI., Hegyalja út 34-36
Tel. 1 3 85 34 45
www.hotelbara.hu
This small and fairly basic hotel with 36 rooms lies at the foot of Gellért Hill and near the road to Vienna. The Gellért Bath is also just a few minutes' walk away.

㉕ Benczúr £
VI., Benczúr utca 35
Tel. 1 4 79 56 50
www.hotelbenczur.hu
This hotel is situated in a more or less peaceful location near Heroes' Square and Városliget Woods. The exterior is not very appealing, but the 93 rooms are OK.

㉖ Connection Guesthouse
VII., Király utca 41
Tel. 1 2 67 71 04
www.connectionguesthouse.com

Gay and lesbian guests feel very comfortable in the Connection. However, not all rooms have a private bathroom / WC. Around the Király utca the nightlife of Budapest takes place, but the house itself is very quiet – of course, the guests will also find tips for Budapest scene life.

㉗ Medosz £
VI., Jókai tér 9
Tel. 1 37 4 30 01
www.medoszhotel.hu
Andrássy út and night life venue Liszt Ferenc tér is just a few meters from this Hotel. You should not expect too much comfort, but some rooms are modernized so that the standard has increased significantly. The cheap price is hard to beat for the good location.

HOSTELS
In Budapest there are numerous private hostels and several dormitories, which are converted to cheap hostels. A comprehensive overview of the offer can be obtained on the internet: http://de.hostelbookers.com.

Bánki
VI., Podmaniczky utca 8
Tel. 06 30 7 76 22 62
www. hostels.hu
Hostel with 80 beds located in the middle of a shopping centre, near the western railway station; also double rooms

Red Bus Hostel
V., Semmelweis utca. 14
Tel. 1 2 66 01 36
www.redbusbudapest.hu
In the heart of downtown Pest, the hostel is located in a typical residential block, offering authentic accommodation for backpackers; also double rooms.

YOUTH HOSTELS
Information
Hungarian Youth Hostel Association
Tel. 3 43 51 67
www.youthhostels.hu

Diáksport
Dózsa György út 152
Tel. 1 3 40 85 85
www.youthhostels.hu
One of Budapest's most popular hostels; the 138 beds are in demand all year round so making a reservation in good time is recommended.

Landler Universum Hostels
Bartók Béla út 17
Tel. 1 4 63 36 21
www.universumyouthhostels.hu
250-bed hostel on the Buda side near to Gellért-Bath.

Children in Budapest

No Boredom

Children can spend very exciting days in Budapest as soon as they are a bit more independent. Those who visit children´s attractions, such as the zoo or children´s railway in the Buda hills, can see some of the most beautiful corners of Budapest at the same time.

Visiting Budapest with toddlers in strollers can be exhausting: steps onto buses and trams are often very high and there are not yet many elevators at metro stations. Escalators are long and the main trams and buses are constantly overcrowded. If children are a bit more mobile, however, it is not difficult to arrange a visit to the city in such a way that both offspring and parents have a good time.

Exploring Budapest

Kids under the age of six ride free on public transport; after that they pay full price. There are, however, reduced weekend tickets for families, or you can choose to buy a »Budapest Card« from the outset (▶Prices and Discounts). Almost all museums and sights offer significant child discounts, and hotels very often even offer free additional children's beds in parents' rooms. A friendly request for a child's portion is normally acceptable should restaurants not offer a specific children's menu.

Discounts

A good starting point is a boat trip on the Danube, past the biggest attractions of the city. Especially in the forest park, on Margaret Island and the Buda hills numerous child-friendly attractions can be found.

Danube tour

The ▶Vàrosliget woods is one of the most favoured destinations for families with children, as there are a host of »child-friendly« attractions very close together: you can go boating on the small lake in the summer, the zoo is a great destination for a family afternoon, and right next door is the large metropolitan circus with guest performances by famous circuses from all over the world. The theme park nearby is an alternative, full of attractions like a Ferris wheel, roller coaster and shooting galleries. In bad weather, you can make for the Transport Museum, and in winter the ice-skating rink is fun. A ride on the cable car to the ▶Royal Palace is a must, and a trip to the ▶Buda hills to take a ride on the children's railway should not be missed on any account. Rides on the funicular railway and on chair-

Excursions with kids

**Ship ahoy! A boat trip is always a fun experience –
for young and old**

A ride on the funny Bringómobil on Margaret Island is fun guaranteed

lifts will also be a popular alternative if the younger generation is not keen on going for walks. On ▶Margaret Island children can really run around: there is almost no traffic, but playgrounds and broad meadows. At the Palatinus Bath, with slides and a wave pool, it is easy to spend an entire summer day. A ride on the bicycle carriages (for 2–6 people) can also be fun. They can be rented at the northern end of the island, at the »Bringó-vár«, opposite the hotels along the Danube quay. Outside the open-air swimming pool season, a visit to the ▶Gellért Bath is highly recommended. The large pool has artificial waves and small children are happy in the warm water of the paddling pool. And when your legs won't carry you any further after a long day in the city, a relaxing boat cruise on the Danube (▶Transport, ▶City tours, Sightseeing) or a tour of the ▶Castle District in a horse-drawn carriage are good options. This is also the site of the underground labyrinth, which is fascinating and just a little scary to explore by oil lamp. In bad weather, a puppet theatre performance can while away the time, though language problems might be unavoidable. The Palace of Wonders (▶p.67) can enthuse the whole family or you can sink into seats at the Planetarium.

Attractions for children

THEATRE
Puppet Theatre Budapest, Bábszínház
Andrássy út 69, tel. 321–5200
www.budapest-babszinhaz.hu
Show: 10am
The performance is comprehendable, even without knowledge of the language.

Planetarium
Népliget, tel. 263–1811
www.planetarium.hu
Looking at the stars is always a special experience for children and also for adults.

MUSEUMS
Museum of Science
VIII., Ludovika tér 2
www.nhmus.hu

April – Sept. Mon, Wed – Sun
10am – 6pm
Oct. – March
Mon, Wed – Sun
10am – 15pm
This museum gives a fascinating insight into the natural history of the Carpathian basin with many fossils, minerals, plants, animal and human remains and artifacts.

Palace of Wonders
(Csodák palotája)
II., Feny utca 20 – 22
Tue – Fri 9am – 5pm
Sat, Sun 10am – 6pm
Housed in a former factory building technical and scientific correlations are conveyed in an interactive and playful way.

City vacation does not have to be boring: in Memento Park

Entertainment

»Paris of the East«

As far as nightlife is concerned, Budapest deserves its reputation as the »Paris of the East«. Theatres and concert halls of the city offer high cultural pleasures and you can enjoy a relaxed atmosphere in the nightlife area around Liszt Ferenc tér and Ráday ucta where locals and tourists get together. In downtown Pest around Váci ucta, the Danube promenade and around St. Stephen´s Basilica are mostly taken up tourists, which also applies to the Castle District. A more student-oriented atmosphereIn can be experienced at the University District, between Egyetem tér and the little Mikszáth Kálmán tér in the »Palace District« behind the National Museum.

Hungarian music enjoys world renown and its heritage is especially well tended in Budapest. In addition to Franz Liszt (▶Famous People), its fame is especially based on the compositions by Ferenc Erkel, Béla Bartók (▶Famous People) and Zoltán Kodály. Budapest's musical life offers something for every taste, from symphony concerts, opera and operetta to bold productions of modern musical theatre. Those who enjoy folk music can find programmes in many places. And Budapest also caters for fans of rock and pop, as famous bands regularly perform here. Real highlights are performances at the Opera house and the Operetta Theatre, which is considered to be the flagship of »Pest's Broadway«. The world of theatres is localised around the intersection of Andrássy út and Nagymezö ucta, which has led to this nickname.

Music

Over forty theatres vie for an audience in Budapest. Most performances are in Hungarian and only a small number of international productions can be understood by non-native speakers. The following selection of theatre venues concentrates on those that include foreign-language productions in their programme.

Theatre

Budapest is also known for fine jazz music. A special highlight are concerts on the restaurant boat Columbus below Vigadó tér. The Benkó Dixieland Band is full of rhythm and brings a touch of New Orleans to the banks of the Danube. Bandleader Sándor Benkó has been in the business for over 50 years, but still puts on a youthful and agile stage performance.

Jazz

Typical for Budapest is also the Jewish klezmer music, which experienced a small revival in the last 20 years. Concerts of the Budapest

Klezmer

You can spend the evenings in Pest pleasantly outside

Klezmer Band, led by Ferenc Jávori are a musical pleasure. Jávori has managed to inspire the younger generation of traditional Jewish music and has made klezmer an integral part of the music scene with his commitment and imagination.

Roma music Places where classic »gypsy« bands appear are less common than in the past. The Roma music is in a crisis because state funding was eliminated and modern style bars prefer to have a different image. Due to a lack of demand, entire musicians dynasties are struggling for survival. Today the performances of Roma musicians are mostly limited to tourist spots. The dance performances of the National Folklore Ensemble are also geared towards tourists, but are the most professional. Tickets are not only available in the hotels but also at info booths in the city centre. Also the group ExperiDance takes up folklore themes, but performs it in modern arrangements with an incredible pace. The performances of the National Dance Theatres are also on a high artistic level.

Cinema Of course there are many cinemas in a city such as Budapest, some of them also offer movies in the English original.

Gay Budapest is the only city in Hungary with a significant gay scene. There are a number of gay-friendly cafes and nightclubs.

Programme tips In the Hungarian capital you can obtain programme tips in many ways: the free weekly appearing magazines »Exit« and »Pesti est« (in Hungarian) provide current cinema programme as well as live performances of music bands in pubs and clubs. In hotels and tourist information officess the monthly published magazine »Where« is available in English. Also the weekly-published Budapest's newspaper obtains some programme tips.

Tickets Theatre, opera, and concert tickets should be bought in advance at the ticket desks of the relevant theatres or from advance booking offices. Tickets are also available at the evening ticket booths and at the tourist office.

TICKET SALE
Publika Jegyiroda
VII., Károly körút 9
Tel. 01 3 22 20 10
Rózsavölgyi és Társa Zeneműbolt
V., Szervita tér 5

Ticket Express
VI., Andassy út 18

Internet
www.eventien.hu
www.kulturinfo.hu
www.jegymester.hu

THEATRE
National Theatre
IX., Bajor Gizi park 1
Tel. 4 76 68 68

www.nemzetiszinhaz.hu
The programme includes plays
from Shakespeare to Botho
Strauß.

International Buda Stage
II., Tárogató út 2 – 4
Tel. 1 3 91 25 25
Theatre performances in English;
also concerts and film premieres.

József Katona Theater
V., Petőfi Sándor utca 6
Tel. 1 3 18 37 25
www.katonajozsefszinhaz.hu
The world-famous theatre is almost always sold out; its repertoire includes drama by Shakespeare and Kleist.

Merlin Theater
V., Gerlóczy utca 4
Tel. 1 3 17 93 38
www.merlinszinhaz.hu
Comedies and tragedies in
English.

Thália Theater
VI., Nagymező utca 22 – 24
Tel. 1 3 12 42 36
www.thalia.hu
One of the theatre scene flagships
with a sophisticated programme,
opposite the Operetta theatre,
sometimes also concerts

Trafó
IX., Liliom utca 41
Tel. 1 2 15 16 00
www.trafo.hu
Contemporary avant-garde pro-
ductions of foreign ensembles.

Víg Theater
XIII., Szent István körút 14
Tel. 1 329–23 40

Classics, including modern inter-
pretations, in a building that is
well worth seeing.

CONCERT HALLS
Budapest Congress Centre
XII., Jagelló út 1 – 3
Tel. 1 3 72 57 00
Classical concerts, opera and ballet galas, but also performances
by international jazz and soul legends

Danube Palace
V., Zrínyi utca 5
Tel. 1 2 35 55 00
Concerts by the Danube Sym-
phonic Orchestra and the venue
of the annual opera gala. The
Danube Folklore Ensemble, which
is characterised by folklore dances
and music at a high level, performs here as well.

Palace of Art
IX., Komor Marcell utca 1
Tel. 1 5 55 33 00
www.mupa.hu
Hungary's biggest concert hall offers plenty of scope for high-quality concerts and is the domicile of
the Hungarian philharmonic orchestra. The biggest organ of
Hungary is integrated into the
concert hall. The National Dance
Theatre, among others, performs
in the smaller festival theatre.

CHURCH CONCERTS
Matthias Church
I., Szentháromság tér
Organ concert pieces are performed on Fridays, and oratorios
on Saturdays.

An experience: a performance in the magnificent Opera House

St Michael's Church
V., Váci utca 47
Works by Bach, Bartók and
Kodály, among others, are per-
formed on Budapest's oldest or-
gan.

St Stephen´s Church
V., Szent István tér

Organ concerts underneath the
basilica's beautiful dome.

OPERA/BALLET
Hungarian State Opera
VI., Andrássy út 22
Tel. 1 35 30 1 70
www.opera.hu

Superb productions of ballet and
opera performances; book early!

National Dance Theatre
Szinház utca 1 – 3
Tel. 1 4 57 08 48
www.nemzetitancszinhaz.hu
The stage provides the entire
spectrum of Hungarian dance:
from folklore to ballet.

OPERETTA/FOLKLORE/
MUSICAL
Budapest Operetta
VI., Nagymező utca 17
Tel. 1 3 53 21 72
www.operettszinhaz.hu

Well-known operettas by Hungarian composers such as Lehár and Kálmán; also musicals.

Buda Redoute
I., Corvin tér 8
Tel. 1 3 17 27 54
The Hungarian State Folk Ensemble, with its famous gypsy orchestra, performs gypsy music, folk dances and folk music.

Madách Theatre
VII., Erzsébet körút 29–33
Tel. 1 4 78 20 41
www.mardachszinhaz.hu
Internationally famous commercial musicals are performed here.

OPEN-AIR STAGES
Szabad Tér Színhaz
Tel. 1 3 75 59 22
www.szabad ter.hu
The theatre has three open-air stages: on Margaret Island, the park stage (XI., Kosztolány tér) and the Városmajor stage in the park with the same name. They present operettas, cabaret, pop concerts and folk programmes.

DISCOS/CLUBS
❶ etc. ▶map p.74/75

❶ A 38
IX., Petöfi híd
Bank of the Danube, 150 m south of Petöfi Bridge on the Buda side.
Tel. 1 4 64 39 40
www.a38.hu
An unusual location: underground music, bar, artists' lounge, art and exhibitions on a decommissioned Ukrainian stone freighter. It is especially pleasant on the deck in the summer.

❷ Alcatraz
VII., Nyár utca 1
Tel. 1 4 78 60 10, www.alcatraz.hu
Thematically styled disco, where jazz and salsa concerts take place, afterwards disco until dawn.

❸ Bahnhof Budapest Music Club
VI, Nyugati pu (West Railway Station) by the car park
Funk, rock, alternative club with two dance floors; occasional live gigs.

❹ Bamboo Music Club
VI, Dessewffy u.44
Tel. 428 22 25
Gay club: disco, Latin nights, 1980s music and also techno and house.

❺ Capella
V, Belgrád rkp.23
Tel. 17 05 97 77 55
www.capellacafe.hu
Legendary café on three levels with predominantly gay audience. Midnight shows

❻ Fat Mo's
V, Nyáry Pál u.11
Tel. 12 66 80 27
www.fatmo.hu
Well-frequented music club with daily live concerts from jazz to rock & roll music, disco every Friday and Saturday from 11pm.

Insider Tip

❼ Gödör Klub
V., Erzsébet tér
Tel. 1 2 01 38 68
www.godorklub.hu
Central party location under the former bus station, providing live performances and disco.

Budapest Going Out

Going Out
1. A 38
2. Alcatraz
3. Bahnhof Budapest
4. Bamboo Club
5. Capella
6. Fat Mo's
7. Gödör Klub
8. Holdudvar
9. Morrison's Music Pub
10. Moulin Rouge
11. Old Man's
12. Budapest Jazz Club
13. Columbus
14. Hades
15. If Kávézo
16. Paris, Texas
17. Vian
18. Spinoza
19. Szatyor/Hadik
20. Szimpla Kert
21. Wine Bar

A-38 is an airy location

⑧ Holdudvar
XIII., Margitsziget
Tel. 1 5 44 23 64
www.holdudvar.net
Located on Margaret Island. The inviting café beer garden provides bistro cuisine in the daytime and open-air cinema and DJ music on warm summer evenings.

⑨ Morrison's Music Pub 2
V., Szent István körút 11
Tel. 1 3 74 33 29
www.morrisons.hu
Popular destination for long disco nights; several dance floors. The Morrison´s has two branches: at the opera in Révay ucta live shows are available, a nightclub is in Morrison´s Liget in Népliget út 2, near the international bus station.

⑩ Moulin Rouge
VI., Nagymező utca 17
Tel. 1 4 34 99 95
www.moulinrouge.hu
The traditional club with plushy and sumptuous interior features a restaurant and a coffee shop.

⑪ Old Man's
Insider Tip
VII, Akácfa u.13
Tel. 1 3 22 76 45
www.oldmans.hu
Legendary music bar with live music every night from Jazz to Rock music, followed by DJ sounds.

JAZZ
⑫ Budapest Jazz Club
VIII., Múzeum utca 7
Tel. 1 2 67 26 10
www.bjc.hu
Fine salon Jazz in a venerable palace next to the National Museum.

⑬ Columbus
V., Vigadó tér (Pier 4)
Tel. 1 266 90 13
www.columbuspub.hu
Excellent Jazz concerts on the restaurant ship below the Pest Danube Boulevard.

⑭ Hades Jazztaurant
VI, Vörösmarty u.31
Tel. 13 52 15 03
Pub/Restaurant with piano Jazz from Tuesday until Thu. and live jazz on Mondays and Fridays.

⑮ If Kávézó
IX., Ráday utca 19
Tel. 1 2 99 06 94
www.ifkavezo.hu
Free jazz concerts with soft tones take place in the little, friendly coffee shop in the evening.

BARS/PUBS
⑯ Paris, Texas
IX., Ráday utca 22
Tel. 1 2 18 05 70
www.paristexaskavehaz.hu
On the trendy nightlife mile Ráday ucta the sympathetic café is al-

most an institution. Casual atmosphere and tables outside.

⑰ Vian
VI., Liszt Ferenc tér 9
Tel. 1 2 68 11 54
www.cafevian.com
The cozy Liszt Ferenc tér has been one of the most important meeting places for a relaxing evening. The Vian is also a good starting point for a coffee or a cocktail in the daytime.

⑱ Spinoza
VII., Dob utca 15
Tel. 1 4 13 74 88
www.spinozahaz.hu
This charming bistro-café is a silver lining in Elizabeth City. The atmosphere is nice and the kitchen good. In the evening there is occasional piano music. An insiders´ tip are the klezmer concerts. Above the café are apartments for rent.

Insider Tip

⑲ Szatyor/Hadik
Insider Tip
XI., Bartók Béla út 36 – 38
Tel. 1 2 79 02 90
www.szatyorbar.com
www.hadikkavehaz.com
This newly reopened in reduced form, rather dignified coffee house Hadik and the youthful, colourfully decorated bar stimulate the nightlife in Újbuda. There is a beautiful terrace.

⑳ Szimpla Kert
VI., Kazinczy utca 14
Tel. 1 2 61 86 69
www.szimpla.hu

The oldie of the so-called ruin pubs has set the standard for the alternative scene. Trendy pubs open in the summer in empty courtyards in the city. The Szimpla has proven stamina and provides subculture and atmosphere at its best.

㉑ WineBar
V., Hercegprímás utca 4
Tel. 1 2 66 29 29
www.winebar.hu
Stylish ambience near the St. Stephen´s Basilica characterize this cozy wine bar, where you can also buy the Hungarian wine directly. It presents a good blend of wines from top winemakers and aspiring colleagues.

CASINO
Las Vegas
V, Roosevelt tér2
Tel. 1 2 66 12 34
www.lasvegascasino.hu
In the large casino with the highly original name of »Las Vegas«, within Hyatt Hotel Atrium, American roulette is played, as well as blackjack and poker. Also slot machines are available. Relaxed atmosphere, no black tie required.

CINEMA
Corvin
Corvin köz 1
Tel. 1 4 59 50 50
www.corvin.hu
The historic theatre – it was part of the 1956 uprising – is very popular. Some films are shown in English.

Festivals · Holidays · Events

Busy Festival Calendar

Budapest has a very busy festival calendar throughout the year, which offers something for every taste. From classic opera and theatre festivals to casual wine and funky open-air events a wide range is offered.

The festival season starts in March with the internationally prestigious Budapest Spring Festival. Hungarian and international stars perform for two weeks, while first-class exhibitions and other cultural events are held at the same time.

Budapest Spring Festival

In particular, in the summer between June and mid-September the programme is more condensed. In this time the cultural life shifts out onto the outdoor stages. The jazz and klezmer concert in the courtyard of the Vajdahunyad castle and the zoo are very atmospheric – ideal venues in the summer. A cultural highlight is the Jewish Summer Festival, as well as the wine festival in the Buda Castle. It offers a good view into the scope of Hungarian wine culture.

Summer

A magnet for young visitors is the Sziget Festival on a Danube island in the nothern district of Óbuda. In Central Europe´s largetst open-air festival the music is turned up for one week and tens of thousands celebrate extensively.

Sziget Festival

The second mega-event of the summer is the Formula One stop at the Hungaroring east of Budapest. When Louis Hamilton and his competition drive their rounds there, the hotels of the city are mostly completely booked.

Formula One

Highlight of the summer season are the fireworks on National Day on August 20, dedicated to the founder of the state King Stephen I. When the rockets are fired from Gellért Hill thousands crowd on the Pest Danube Promenade to enjoy the spectacle. Soon afterwards, the Jewish Summer Festival marks the ending of the summer season.

National Day

Before several years, the tradition of Christmas markets arrived in Budapest. The central market is located on the Vörösmarty tér at the nothern end of Váci ucta.

Christmas markets

The city information booths (►Information) often have quite extensive monthly events programmes available, such as »Budapest Pano-

Events programme

On National Day the Chain Bridge is flagged

rama« (▶Media). Dates for events can also be found in the daily press and in publicity from the Hungarian Tourist Office. An up-to-date events calendar can also be found on the internet at www.budapestinfo.hu

Spectator sports **Football** is still the most popular game among Hungarian sports fans, even if the days of great international success, such as reaching the finals of the 1954 World Cup, are long gone. Hungarians continue to be a nation of horse lovers and the **horse-racing season** runs from April to October.

HOLIDAYS
1 January: New Year
15 March: National holiday in remembrance of the Liberation War oTel. 1848
Easter Monday
1 May: Labour Day
Whit Monday
20 August: St Stephen's Day, state holiday with big fireworks display on the banks of the Danube
23 October: Day of the Republic (day of the 1956 uprising and establishment of the republic in 1989)
1 November: All Hallows
25/26 December: Christmas

Carnival
Budapest »Carnival« is comprised of dance events, concerts and various other performances (end of Feb/early March).

Budapest Spring Festival
Extensive series of cultural events over a period of several weeks, with opera and operetta performances, concerts and folklore (mid-March to early/mid-April; www.festivalcity.hu).
The most prestigious festival of Hungary brings international stars to the Danube. The main events take place in the Palace of Arts, but there are also venues which are usually unused, open for a varied programme. At the same time high-profile exhibitions are held, so that art lovers get their money's worth during the Spring Festival.

IN JUNE/JULY
International Danube Carnival
Folklore ensembles present Hungarian musical and dance tradition, for example on Vörösmarty tér and Margaret Island.

Sziget-Festival
On the Óbuda Danube island Hajógyári-sziget the biggest outdoor event of the region takes place in the summer. Tens of thousands of young people flock to the island festival and celebrate to the booming beats. In addition, an extensive cultural program is offered, including crash courses in Hungarian. The Sziget Festival presents Budapest from its youthful side. End of July/ beginning of August; www.sziget.hu.

BudaFest
The Dominican Court behind the Hilton Hotel, the square in front of St. Stephen's Basilica and Mar-

garet Island become an outdoor theatre for opera, ballet, jazz and klezmer music in the summer. July/August; www.viparts.hu

Hungarian Grand Prix
Formula One Grand Prix on the Hungaroring (end of July/mid-Aug; information and tickets: www. hungaroinfo.hu/formula1)

Summer Music Festival
Atmospheric open-air concerts in varying locations such as Vajdahunyad Palace and in front of the palm house in the zoo: klezmer, jazz, classic (July/Aug) www.vajdahunyad.hu

National Day
Concerts, markets and a fireworks finale celebrate the foundation of the state (20 Aug).
St Stephen's Procession is held on the same day, when the saint's right hand – the famous relic in St Stephen's Basilica – is carried through the streets of Budapest (20 Aug).

Jewish Summer Festival
Concerts, film and book days, and exhibitions on Herzl Square, in the synagogue on Dohány utca, and at various other places (end of Aug/beginning of Sept)

St Stephen's shrine is the focus of the National Holiday

IN SEPTEMBER
International Wine Festival
Hungarian wine regions present themselves in the Castle District (early/mid-Sept).

OCTOBER/NOVEMBER
Budapest Autumn Festival
Dance events, film and theatre productions, photography exhibits and much more in various venues; contemporary art festivals; early/mid Oct. to late Oct./early Nov. www.festivalcity.hu

DECEMBER
Christmas Markets
Christmas markets are held at several places around the city in December.

Food and Drink

Not Only Gulyás

The days when the people of Budapest preferred to eat only traditional hearty fare are gone. The restaurant scene of the Danube metropolis has opened up tremendously and has become more international. Nowadays it is even hard to find a simple and good traditional restaurant in downtown that is not recognisably designed for tour groups.

Traditionally Hungarians love native meat dishes. These are often flavoured with paprika and served with plenty of potatoes. Small dumplings and rice are also popular. On the other hand the salad and vegetable side dishes usually turn out meager, which is suprising, since the climatic conditions make for plenty of vegetables. Accordingly, they often serve salad only as side dish not as a main dish.

Gulyás is not the same as goulash! Disappointment results when the culinary novice visits Hungary for the first time, hoping to eat the world famous goulash – braised meat chunks in a spicy sauce – only to be served with a well-spiced stew of beef and potato cubes, with paprika, onions, tomatoes, garlic and caraway. In Hungary goulash has a different name. The Hungarian »gulyás« is the strong beef stew, while »goulash« is called »pörkölt« in Hungary. Then there is Gulyásleves, a beef soup with potatoes and diced peppers and onions (▶MARCO POLO Insight, p. 90).

Gulyás and pörkölt

Also very popular are fish dishes, even though the great rivers Danube and Tisza are not as rich in fish as before. Carp, perch, catfish and trout are on many menus, some restaurants are specialized in fish.

Fish dishes

The variety in vegetarian dishes is slowly increasing. In Budapest however some possibilities present themselves. In this way the rising demand for lighter food is met. Now, there is even a demand for organic meals.

Vegetarian dishes

The pancakes (palacsinta) are famous, and are offered both sweet and salty and even with meat-containing variants.
Very popular is also lángos. This deep fried flat bread is offered at diners and spread with garlic and sour cream. But for a snack the people of Budapest eat, of course, everything from burgers to kebabs.

Pancakes

Budapest's cafés invite for a refreshment

International dishes

As cosmopolitan as the city is so international is also the restaurant scene: there is no national cuisine that is not represented. The spectrum ranges from simple kebab stalls to French gourmet restaurants. Also Japanese and Indian restaurants are very trendy. The young Budapest people are very open-minded and want to eat diversifiedly.

Sweet dishes

The sweetest temptations of Hungarian cuisine are undoubtedly the various strudels, and pancakes filled with quark and dusted in icing sugar; or Gundel pancake with nut filling and chocolate sauce, as well as Schomlau dumplings. Budapest's coffee houses and pastry shops complement the repertoire of sweet dishes with their own artful cake creations.

Restaurants

The next good restaurant in Budapest is never far away. Many very good addresses are located on the Pest side of the Danube within the Great Ring and in Buda in sight of the Danube. Very touristy and correspondingly expensive are the restaurants around the Váci ucta and the Danube promenade. But in return the Danube promenade offers an incredible view. In the Castle District there are good and not

Hungarian cooking is down-to-earth, hearty and spicy

so good restaurants. Some restaurants and cafes there however are top. In general, a table for the evening should be reserved in advance if you do not want to wait or would like a special table. People in Budapest traditionally have dinner quite early, in restaurants the typical time to dine is between 7 and 9pm

Incidentally, many restaurants offer discounted lunch specials at lunch time between noon and 2.30pm. Particularly those venues where local employees and students have lunch offer budget-priced dishes.

Many restaurants and cafes have menus in English available. Also many waiters speak English.

The tip should be 10% of the bill. Often the service is listed on the bill as an extra item up to 20% of the amount, then no tip is necessary. In many venues gypsy bands play on their own account; an amount of 500 forints is appropriate.

> ! MARCO POLO
>
> *Hot and Healthy*
>
> Paprika, which is almost as a synonym for the Hungarian cuisine today, was used until the mid 19th century only as a remedy for fever.

For Budapest tourists a visit to a coffee house is almost compulsory! And the Hungarian capital offers countless stylish old cake shops and cafés. Some of the best and most famous are described in more detail in ►MARCO POLO Insight, p. 96. A selection of pleasant coffee houses is listed on page 99.

Coffee houses and cake shops

DRINKS

Wine-growing enjoys a long tradition in Hungary, going right back to Roman times, and the selection of good wines has increased rapidly in recent years. Dry wines are also increasingly being cultivated these days, and many local wines can be tasted in many Budapest wine cellars.

Wine (bor)

The region around Tokaj produces the **Tokaj dessert wine** from Furmint and Hárslevelü grapes. The grapes are prone to the »noble rot« or botrytis fungus, which has a positive effect on sugar content and taste. Tokaj comes in three quality levels: furmint (light and dry), szamorodni (mild and sweet), and aszu (from selected grapes with three, four or five stars; only limited stocks).

Hungarian fruit spirits are famous and popular, especially barack pálinka, an apricot schnapps, szilva pálinka (plum schnapps) and cherry schnapps.

Spirits

In Budapest, foreign beers – especially Austrian and German ones – are increasingly available alongside local beers.

Beer (sör)

Typical Dishes

Hearty and savory – these attributes describe the Hungarian speciali-
ties, especially flavoured with paprika. As the heir to the Austro-
Hungarian monarchy Austrian desserts give the finishing touch.

Pörkölt: is the Hungarian name for the famous stew, braised in lard with onions, peppers, tomatoes, garlic, cumin and oregano and pieces of meat in a spicy sauce. This dish should not be confused with gulyás, a spicy stew with beef and cooked potatoes, peppers, onions, tomatoes, garlic and cumin.

Tokány: Very similar to pörkölt is the Tokány, stewed beef with a thick and hearty spiced sauce, seasoned with a dash of wine. In the preparation of both foods sour cream is usually used, which gives the sauce a creamy character. Nutritious, calorie-rich foods like stew and Tokány, seasoned with pepper and topped with whipped cream, care included under the term Paprikás.

Paprika chicken: Paprika chicken with pasta (Paprikás csirke galuskával) is a simple, nevertheless classic Hungarian dish. The chicken is steamed, fried with onions and served with a sour cream sauce.

Salami: Then there's the Hungarian hearty and spicy salami (szalámi), the frequent traveling companion on the way back from a vacation in Hungary. But only in Hungary does szalámi taste really good, they say. The sausage comes from the Italian »archetype« in 1883 and was further developed by the Hungarian Mark Pick Szeged.

Halászlé: Carefully prepared soups spiced with hot peppers, often with several fish such as carp or catfishs, flavored with a variety of vegetables, onions, roasted pieces of white bread and a little sour cream, called Halászlé. The Hungarian equivalent of the French bouillabaisse is very spicy!

Insider Tip

Pancakes à la Gundel: One of the most famous desserts, this pancake filled with walnuts and raisins, covered with sauce of cream and chocolate. Controversial is the question: to flambé or not. Apparently the fire spell is organized only for tourists.

Hungarian Wineries on the Rise

Hardly any restaurant in Budapest does without a Hungarian wine list. The times when quantity was more important than quality are gone. For more than 20 years, a dynamic wine scene has been developing that provides top-class whites and reds. Now the Hungarian viticulture is experiencing a remarkable renaissance – a tasting is a must.

Wine has a long tradition in Hungary: the Celts and Romans already cultivated it. The Magyars quickly took over the wine culture. A certificate of the southern Hungarian Abbey of Pécsvárad of 1015 already recorded 110 wineries on the lands of the abbey. The German settlers who flocked en masse into the depopulated country after the Turkish wars in the 18th century very quickly recognized the economic potential of viticulture.

Today, there are 22 historical wine regions in Hungary. In addition to internationally known varieties such as Chardonnay, Cabernet Sauvignon and Merlot, a number of typical Hungarian varieties exist. These include the white wines of Kéknyelű (Blue Stengler) from Lake Balaton, the Juhfark (lamb's tail), the Leányka Egri (Eger Leányka), the Cirfandli (Zierfandler) from the region of Pécs and the Ezerjó (Tausendgut). Popular white wines are also the Szürkebarát (Pinot Gris), the Olaszrizling (Welsch Riesling) and the Hárslevelű (Linden); among the reds are the Kékfrankos (blue Frankish), the Kékoportó (Blue Portugal) and the Kadarka very popular.

Magic Effect

Magical powers are ascribed to several varieties: in 1552 the famous Bull's Blood (Egri bikavér) lured the Turks from the siege of Eger because they assumed the wine was bull's blood and got scared. 200 years later it was said that the Somlói wedding wine caused male offspring when consumed in the wedding night. Even Maria Theresa allowed herself a sip – she is known to have had many children. In general, it was said about Somlói wine »Vinum somlainum omni sanum« (»Somlói wine heals everything«). A similar miracle effect was imputed to the red Kadarka from Szekszárd. The composer Franz Liszt sent the ailing Pope Pius IX some bottles for better recovery, which supposedly occured promptly.

King of Wines – Wine of Kings

No wonder that the crowned heads of Europe paid attention to the wine country of Hungary. Highly sought was the Aszú wine from Tokaj in the 18th century. None other than the French King Louis XIV actedas a marketing assistant. He decided that the Tokaji was »rex vinorum, vinum regum« (»king of wines and the wine of kings«). Because of the great success of the »liquid gold« the wine is celebrated in the Hungarian national anthem as a »gift from God«. Since 2002,

Tokaj is the king of Hungarian wines

the entire Tokaj wine region is a UNESCO World Heritage Site.

Renaissance

After the dissolution of the state wineries around 1990, winemakers restarted to produce superior quality wines. Even old traditions such as parades and wine festivals were revived. Awards for »Wine maker of the Year« or »Winery of the Year« provide an increase and recognition of quality wine. Especially in sunny Villány, there was a veritable renaissance of private quality wineries under the auspices of winemakers Ede Tiffán, József Bock and Attila Gere. In the North Hungarian Tokaj there have been, however, a strong presence of Spanish and French wineries that followed the royal reputation of the region. But around Eger and at Lake Balaton, Lake Neusiedl and even on the outskirts of Budapest ambitious young winemakers work to revive the old traditions.

Wines in Budapest

For several years, the rebirth of Hungarian wines in Budapest is clearly noticeable. Friendly wine bars opened, even the top restaurants rely on local products, and wine retailers are spoiled on account of the many choises. For many Westerners, the Hungarian wine market is still an undiscovered space. Therefore, choosing a wine can be a little exciting. Reliably good wines are served in restaurants such as Bock Bisztró or Klassz. The owner of the Book Café even has his own vineyard in Pécs. The House of Hungarian Wines may provide an initial overview, because not every visitor has the time and leisure to visit the wineries themselves. If you want to take a bottle home you can do so in the restaurants and cafes mentioned. The best wine merchant in the city is Bortársaság.

Gulyás is Not Goulash

Gulyás is the Hungarian national dish. The classic stew of the Maygars however didn't find its way into Hungarian civic culture until the 19th century. Many variations and receipts exist within and outside of Hungary - paprika however must be included. In Hungary such dishes are usually called »Pörkölt« or »Paprikás«.

▶ **The most common variants of Goulash**

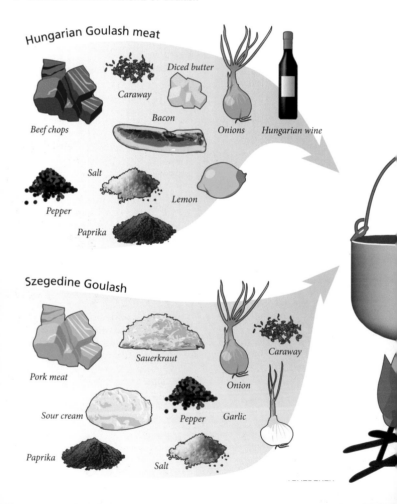

Hungarian Goulash meat

Beef chops
Caraway
Diced butter
Bacon
Onions
Hungarian wine
Pepper
Salt
Lemon
Paprika

Szegedine Goulash

Pork meat
Sauerkraut
Onion
Caraway
Sour cream
Pepper
Garlic
Paprika
Salt

▶ **Classical side dishes**

Bread

Bread rolls

Potatoes

Nockerl
(Austro-Hungarian »gnocchi«)

Dumplings

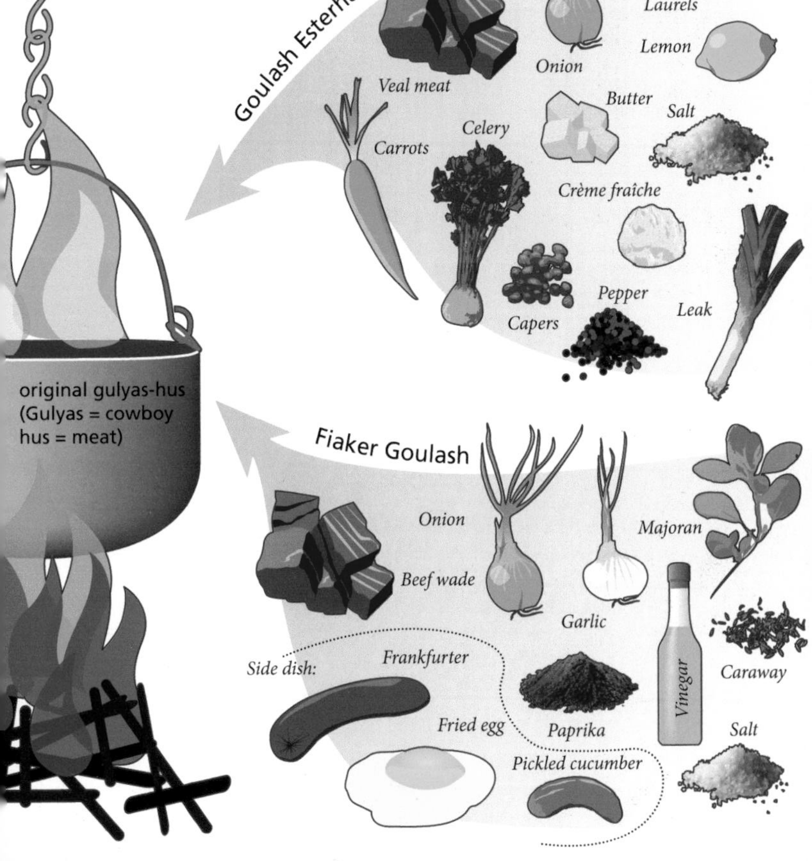

Goulash Esterhazy

Veal meat

Onion

Laurels

Lemon

Carrots

Celery

Butter

Salt

Crème fraîche

Capers

Pepper

Leak

original gulyas-hus
(Gulyas = cowboy
hus = meat)

Fiaker Goulash

Onion

Majoran

Beef wade

Garlic

Side dish: *Frankfurter*

Vinegar

Caraway

Fried egg   *Paprika*

Salt

Pickled cucumber

Recommended restaurants

❶ etc. ▶map p.94/95
No number: beyond the map

PRICE CATEGORIES
££££: over 5000 HUF
£££: 3500–5000 HUF
££: 2000-3500 HUF
£: up to 2000 HUF

TOP RESTAURANTS
CATEGORY **£££-££££**
❶ **Bock**
in Corinthia Hotel Budapest
VII., Erzsébet körút 43 – 49
Tel. 1 3 21 03 40
www.bockbisztro.hu
When it comes to fine Hungarian wines for dinner, the Bock Bisztró is the right address. The restaurant's name goes back to top winemaker József Bock from Villány who belongs to the pioneers of the Hungarian wine renaissance in southern Hungary. The chic Bisztró is headed by chef Lajos Bíró, who has already won several awards for his exquisite creations. A wine shop is attached.

❷ **Gundel ££££**
XIV., Állatkerti út 2
Tel. 14 68 4040
www.gundel.hu
In terms of renown at least, the top address in the Hungarian capital is Gundel (table reservations essential) near the Budapest Zoo. Founded by Ferenc Wampetics in 1894, it was taken over by the great master of modern Hungarian cuisine, Károly Gundel, in 1910. Today, the master chef and

his team conjure up almost all delicacies of Hungarian and international cuisine here, including of course the legendary Gundel pancakes with raisin and nut filling.

❸ **Onyx Étterem ££££**
V., Vörösmarty tér 7 – 8
Tel. 1 4 29 90 23
www.onyxrestaurant.hu
This exclusive restaurant, located in a side wing of Café Gerbeaud, has been serving food prepared by two-star chefs since 2011. The lunch menus are considerably more affordable.

❹ **Robinson £££ – ££££**
XIV., Városligeti-tó
Tel. 1 4 22 02 22
www.robinsonrestaurant.hu
The unique building and beatiful location on the lake in the city woods already make the Robinson worth a visit. The food is excellent; along with international dishes, we recommend the »authentic Hungarian recipes«. Terrace seating in the summer.

❺ Spoon Café & Lounge
£££ – ££££
V., Vigadó tér (pier 3)
Tel. 1 4 11 09 33
www.spooncafe.hu
What could be better: from the attractive restaurant ship the view wanders across the Danube up to the magnificent Castle. Also the Chain Bridge is illuminated in the evening. While the river promises pleasant cooling on deck in the summer, the cooking allures with modern light creations. The Spoon provides an attractive entertainment experience – definitely reserve in advance for the evening!

❻ Vadrózsa £££
II, Pentelei Molnár u. 15
Tel. 13 26 5817
www.vadrozsa.hu
A fine restaurant with a pretty seating area in the garden with a lovely location on Rose Hill, where many classy villas stand once again. Food and service are unmatched.

NATIONAL CUISINE
❼ Fatál ££ – £££
V., Váci utca 67
Tel. 1 2 66 26 07
Restaurant in the basement vault with almost huge servings. In the summer you can eat on the terrace

❽ Kéhli Vendéglö ££ – £££
III, Mókus utca 22
Tel. 250–4241, fax 387–6049
Lovers of exquisitely prepared game and fish dishes get their money's worth at Kéhli Vendéglö. The inn has a long tradition – you can even still catch a whiff of the Austro-Hungarian monarchy.

❾ Kék Rózsa ££
VII., Wesselényi utca 9
Tel. 1 3 42 89 81
www.kekrozsaetterem.hu
It is not glamorous in the »blue rose«. Solid Hungarian cuisine is served in a rather simple ambience. Reasonably priced set meals are offered at noon.

❿ Mátyás pince £££ Insider Tip
V, Március 15. tér7
Tel. 1 2 66 80 08
www.matyaspince.hu
The interior of this long-famous restaurant, established in 1904 on the Pest side of the Elizabeth Bridge, ist a listed monument. Paprikás in all variations are served here, accompanied by gypsy music.

⓫ Náncsi Néni ££ – £££
II., Ördögárok utca 80
Tel. 1 3 97 27 42
www.nancsineni.hu
Restaurant with cheap traditional food. In the summer you can enjoy seafood dishes in the garden.

HUNGARIAN AND INTERNATIONAL CUISINE
⓬ Aranyszarvas ££ – £££
I., Szarvas tér 1
Tel. 1 3 75-64 51
www.aranyszarvas.hu
The bistro serves haute cuisine with Hungarian influence in a historic building between the Castle and the Gellért Hill. One speciality is ham of the Mangalica pigs.

⓭ Fausto's Osteria ££ – ££££
VII., Dohány utca 5
Tel. 2 69 68 06
www.osteria.hu

Budapest Restaurants and Hotels

Where to eat

1. Bock
2. Gundel
3. Onyx Étterem
4. Robinson
5. Spoon
6. Vadrózsa
7. Fatal
8. Kéhli Vendéglő
9. Kék Rósza
10. Mátyás pince
11. Nánczi Néni
12. Aranyszarvas
13. Fausto's Osteria
14. Goriuda vega sarok
15. Karma
16. Klassz
17. Marquis de Salade
18. Muzeum
19. Pierrot
20. Pomo d'Oro
21. Rivalda
22. Wasabi

Where to stay

1. Budapest Marriot Hotel
2. Corinthia
3. Four Seasons Hotel Gresham Palast
4. Hilton
5. Inter-Continental Budapest
6. Kempinski Hotel Corvinus
7. Le Méridien
8. Sofitel Budapest Chain Bridge
9. Art'otel
10. Hungária
11. Margitsziget
12. Danubius Hotel Astoria City
13. Danubius Health Spa Resort Margitsziget
14. Gerlózy
15. K+K Hotel Opera
16. Korona
17. Radisson Blu Béke
18. Carlton
19. City Hotel Mátyás
20. Erzsébet City Center
21. IBIS Budapest Centrum
22. Peregrinus ELTE
23. Soho Boutique Hotel
24. Danubius Health
25. Benczúr
26. Connection Guesthouse
27. Medosz

Coffee Tradition in Hungarian

For non-Hungarians, the word is almost a tongue twister: cukrászda. What can be translated as »pastry shop« has a special tradition in Budapest, at least as old, if not older than that of the Viennese coffee house.

Let's start with the **Café Gerbeaud** at Vörösmarty tér. It was founded in 1858 and is still the best and most stylish cafe on the square and thereby an institution in Budapest. The popularity of the Gerbeauds has many reasons: for one person it is the interior of the house, which has not changed much since the 19th century; for others it is the overwhelming selection of cakes and pies, a mixture of Swiss and Austrian sophisticated diversity, although the large tourist crowds are accompanied with a loss in quality. And for others it is the coffee, which is of excellent quality.

Rich in tradition is also the family-owned pastry shop **Ruszwurm** on Castle Hill and much more intimate than the Gerbeaud, and has at least as good pastries and cakes. Part of the furniture dates back to the founding days of the cafés in the 1820s. An ideal place to recover from a tour of the Castle District with a good cup of coffee. Those who do not get a seat in Ruszwurm, should try the **Café Corona** on Dísz tér.

First Address

In the magnificent Andrássy út, on the way to Heroes' Square, there are two beautiful old coffee houses, the venerable Művész opposite the State Opera and the elegant **Book Café** in the former Terezín Casino. While the Művész formerly

Café New York: It can hardly get more fancy

The Gerbeaud is certainly the most popular cafe in Budapest

was one of the busy artist hangouts, the Book Café is an entirely new creation that was inserted absolutely true to style in the resurrected Lotz Hall of the former casino. Even the Lotz Hall was integrated into the Parisian department store, now the coffee house culture has made the noble address at the Andrássy út a magnet for visitors.

The former legendary literary **Café New York** on Erzsébet körút 9 – 11 is a class of its own. It attracts culinarys with the other houses. The neo-baroque, reveling in rich fabrics and lush stucco interior will certainly remain unsurpassed. The most important meeting place for the literary scene of Budapest until Communim, the **Café Central**, founded in 1887 in the Karolyi Mihaly utca near the Ferenciek tere, is also restored to its former splendor and style it appears more real than the New York. A little touch of the old world blows by the Astoria Mirror Café (Kossuth Lajos út). In the high hall time seems to stand still.

Confectioner Dynasties

A few meters further is the **Auguszt Cukrászda** with its lively atmosphere. The well-known long-established Budapest confectioner dynasty sold their treats, including the very rich Auguszt Cream, in this friendly, bright café. The Auguszt proves that you can run nice, welcoming cafes without much pomp.

When it comes to cakes, chocolates and marzipan in Budapest the name Szamos cannot be avoided. For generations they sweeten the resident's everyday life. The nice **Szamos Marcipán Cukrászda** is located on the main boulevard in the Corinthia Hotel, another branch in Szentendre.

Faustodi Vora is considered the doyen of exquisite Italian gourmet cuisine. Relatively cheap lunch and a creative diner menu beyond pizza and spaghetti.

⑭ Govinda vega sarok £
V., Papnövelde utca 1
Tel. 2 67 76 31
www.govinda.hu
The light-filled »vegetarian corner« is headed by Krishna followers and is one of the best places for vegetarian food in Budapest.

⑮ Karma £
VI, Liszt ferenc tér 11
Tel. 1413 67 64
www.karmabudapest.hu
A tasteful oriental interior and an international menu on which Thai dishes and Indian Tandoori predominate. The duck breast in apple and mustard sauce is delicious!

⑯ Klassz ££
VI., Andrássy út 41
www.klasszetterem.hu
The location on the boulevard Andrássy út is perfect, the kitchen is attractive and the list of fine Hungarian wines is superb – the Klassz is one of the best wine restaurants in the capital and correspondingly popular. But pay attention: this restaurant does not accept dinner reservations! So you have to bear a little waiting time in mind. Since the menu changes every two weeks, it is never boring in culinary matters. The wine is also available for sale in the back of the restaurant.

⑰ Marquis de Salade ££ – £££
VI., Hajós utca 43
Tel. 1 3 02 40 86
www.marquisdesalade.hu
In a tastefully decorated vault the Marquis serves Azerbaijani-Russian specialties, including vegetarian dishes – a pleasant alternative to the international mainstream.

⑱ Múzeum ££ – £££
VIII., Múzeum krt. 12
Tel. 1 2 67 03 75
www.museumkavehaz.hu
This tavern with a classical interior offers excellently prepared Hungarian and international dishes at moderate prices.

⑲ Pierrot ££ – ££££
I., Fortuna utca 14
Tel. 1 3 75 69 71
www.pierrot.hu
Among the restaurants in the Castle District, the elegant Pierrot is an haute address with delicious cuisine and Hungarian wines. In addition, the Pierrot is located away from the tourist track in the Castle District.

⑳ Pomo d' Oro ££ – ££££
V., Arany János utca 9
Tel. 1 302-64 73
www.pomodorobudapest.com
Although the prices are a bit higher than in a pizzeria, many Italians eat here. You should make a reservation in advance because the restaurant is very popular.

㉑ Rivalda ££ – ££££
I., Színház utca 5 – 9
Tel. 1 4 89 02 36
www.rivalda.net

Within sight of the castle the café/restaurant in the former Carmelite monastery is a splash of colour. The award-winning kitchen convinces with Hungarian and international creations.

㉒ Wasabi ££££
VI., Podmaniczky utca 21
f 374-00 08
www.wasabi.hu
A nice variety of sushi and wok dishes go around on a two storey conveyor belt through the restaurant. A fixed price has to be paid, then you can enjoy »all you can eat«. The Wasabi has two more branches in Buda.

COFFEE HOUSES
Art Nouveau Café
V., Honvéd utca 3
The Art Nouveau café in the house of the Hungarian Secession has only a small selection of cakes and pies.

Auguszt
V., Kossuth Lajos utca 14 – 16
www.augusztcukraszda,hu
The beautiful café is in possession of the Budapest confectioners dy-nasty. It offers fine candies and cream pies, including the Auguszt creams. In Buda is also a nice branch in the Fény ucta 8.

BookCafé
Insider Tip
VI., Andrássy út 39
The most elegant café in Budapest: The former casino hall is decorated with magnificent frescoes. It is beautiful to look at. In the afternoon, guests can enjoy the fine cake accomanied with soft piano music. Coffee prices are amazingly cheap for the Budapest city; in addition house wines of the owner Dezsö Matayi.

Gerlóczy
V., Gerlóczy utca 1
Tel. 5 01 40 00
www.gerloczy.hu
The small Old Town Square, which lies a little bit hidden, and the great elm provide a picturesque atmosphere. The terrace and the croissants are reminiscent of Parisian cafés, but otherwise Hungarian specialities are served – one of the most atmospheric cafés in the Hungarian capital. Attached is a highly recommended guest house.

Museums

Wide Range

More than 100 museums and numerous galleries make Budapest a very art-loving city. They range from small memorial rooms to internationally renowned museum palaces.

High above the Danube the castle with the Hungarian National Gallery and the Budapest History Museum has a dominant position. But the Museum of Fine Arts at Heroes Square, the Hungarian National Museum at Small Ring Road, the Museum of Decorative Arts and the Ludwig Museum inside the Palace of the Arts are further highlights of the museum landscape, which are absolutely worth visiting. These museums alone cover a wide range of topics from primeval discoveries to Hungarian and European painting to the artwork of Art Nouveau.

The opening of the Ludwig Museum in 1991 was groundbreaking for the commitment of private patrons of art in Budapest. Recent examples of interesting private exhibition halls are the House of Hungarian Secession, the Kogart House and the Gold Museum, opened in 2011. In times of scarce public funding these challenging projects set a new course in the city. The scene is completed by the private art dealers in the gallery street Falk Miksa ucta.

The museums in Budapest are open in general from Tue to Sun 10am to 6pm, smaller museums often close at 4pm in the winter months. However, some museums have different opening times. In many small museums the information is unfortunately available only in Hungarian, larger museums also offer information in English.

Opening times

At the Museum of Fine Arts, the Hungarian National Gallery, Budapest History Museum and Ethnographic Museum visitors with the Budapest Card receive free entrance. Other museums provide a discount on presentation of the card.

Budapest Card

A special highlight is the Night of Museums (Múzeumok Éjszakája) at the end of June, where many museums attract visitors with a free special program.

Night of Museums

List of museums

HISTORY/CULTURAL HISTORY
Apothecary Museum
▶p. 144

Banknotes and Coins Collection
V., Szabadság tér 8
Mon-Fri 9am – 4pm

The impressive, frescoed staircase of the National Museum

The exhibition of the Hungarian National Bank features coins and banknotes of Hungary.

Bible Museum
IX., Ráday utca 28
Tue – Sun 10am – 5pm
Cemprehensive exhibition about the Bible story in Hungarian and international context.

Stamp Museum
VII., Hársfa ucta 47
April – Oct.: Tue – Sun 10am – 6pm, Nov – March: Tue – Sun 10am – 4pm
Collection of all Hungarian and international stamps.

Ernst Museum
Nagymező utca 8
Tue – Sun 11am – 7pm
www.ernstmuzeum.hu
Changing exhibitions of artistic and cultural phenomena of the 20th century are presented.

Ethnographic Museum
▶p. 160

Protestant Museum
▶p. 189

Fire Museum
X., Martinovics tér 12
Tue – Sat 9am – 4pm
Sun 9am – 1pm
Covers the history of firefighting since Roman times.

Flag Museum
VIII., József körút 68
Tue -Sun 11am – 6pm
Official flags of countries and provinces, mostly presents of their respective presidents and rulers.

Gül Baba Tomb
▶p. 220

House of Terror
▶p. 134

Historical Museum
▶p. 229

Jewish Museum
▶p. 182

Crime Museum
VIII., Mosonyi ucta 7
Tue- Sun 10am – 5pm
Police objects and pieces of evidence of criminal cases since the mid 1960s are on exhibition.

National Museum
▶p. 208

Obuda Museum
▶p. 212

Post Museum
▶p. 132

Treasury of St Stephen´s Basilica
▶p. 233

Skanzen (open-air museum)
▶p. 240

ART/ARCHAELOGY
Exhibition of the Hungarian Monument Office
▶p. 142

Exhibition House of Budapest Gallery
III., Lajos ucta 158
Tue – Sun 10am – 6pm
National and international contempory art.

At the National Museum, the Turkish era comes alive

Exhibition Hall of the
Budapest Gallery
V., Szabadsjtó út 5
Tue – Sun 10am – 6pm
Painting, sculpture and photo art
from all over the world.

Frerenc Hopp Museum of
East Asian art
▶p. 134

Gold Museum
▶p. 134

György Ráth Museum
VI., Városligeti fasor 12
April – Oct. Tue – Sun 10am –
6pm, Nov – March Tue – Sun
10am – 4pm
The museum includes a collection
of Oriental and East Asian art.

House of Hungarian
Photographers
VI., Nagymező utca 20
Mon – Fri 2pm – 6pm
Sat, Sun 10am – 6pm
It presents an exhibition of works
by contemporary photographers.

House of Hungarian
Secession
▶p. 236

Kogart House
▶p. 134

Arts and Crafts Museum
▶p. 137

Art Exhibition Hall
▶p. 184

Ludwig Museum – Museum
of Contemporary Art
▶p. 215

Memento Park
▶p. 198

Museum of Fine Arts
▶p. 202

National Gallery
▶p. 225

Palace of Arts
▶p. 214

Pál Molnár Studio
Museum
XI., Ménesi út 65
April – Oct Tue – Thu 3pm – 6pm;
Sun 10am – 1pm, Nov – March
Tue – Thu 3pm – 6pm
Works of the »Roman school«
artist Pál Molnár (1894 – 1981)
are exhibited in his former studio.

VAM Design Center
VI., Király utca 26
Daily 10am – 6pm
The VAM is a modern art house,
presenting free shows around a re-
furbished courtyard and charged
special international exhibitions.

Vasarély Museum
▶p. 212

LITERATURE/
THEATRES/ MUSIC
Endre Ady Memorial
Museum
V., Veres Pálné utca 4 – 6
Wed – Sun 10am – 5pm
The museum is in the last home
of the poet Endre Ady
(1877 – 1919).

Josef Attila Museum
IX., Gát utca 3
Tue – Sun. 10am – 6pm
Documents and manuscripts give
insight into the life of the poet; in
his own apartment.

Béla Bartók Memorial
▶p. 220

Lajos Kassák Museum
▶p. 212

Mór Jókai Memorial
XII., Költő utca 21
March – Nov Wed – Sun 10am –
5pm
Personal belongings of the novel-
ist (1825 – 1904) are exhibited
here.

Zoltán Kodály Museum
▶p. 134

Franz Liszt Museum
▶p. 134

Petöfi Museum
▶p. 187

NATURE/TECHNOLOGY
Museum of Flight in the
Petöfi Hall
XIV., Zichy Mihály ucta 14
Mid-May – mid-Oct: Tue – Fri
10am – 5pm, Sat, Sun 10am – 6pm
You can see aircraft for passen-
gers, models and gliders as well as
a space capsule.

National Museum of
Geology
XIV., Stefánia út 14
Thu., Sat., Sun. 10am – 4pm
Minerals and fossils from Hungary
are shown.

Foundry Museum
▶p. 246

War Museum
▶p. 146

Agricultural Museum
▶p. 200

Museum Park of Trains
XIV., Tatai út 95   *Insider Tip*
www.miwo.hu/old_trains
Apr – Oct: Tue – Sun 10am – 6pm
Nov – Mar: Tue – Sun 10am – 5pm
Train fans can expect nearly 100
of yesterday's carriages and trains.

Science Museum
▶p. 67

Palace of Wonders
▶p. 67

Semmelweis Museum
▶p. 241

Telephone Museum
▶p. 146

Textile Museum
III., Lajos ucta 138
Tue – Sun 10am – 2pm
Old machine and the full establishment of a historic shoe factory
shed light on the history of the
textile industry in Hungary.

Metro Museum
▶MARCO POLO Tip p. 189

Transport Museum
▶p. 201

Zwack Museum
▶p. 178

Shopping

Modern Shopping City

Even though the »Paris of the East« cannot quite match the French original, for Central Europe Budapest is clearly the number one.

Since 1990, the shopping scene in Budapest has shifted dramatically. Until then the inner city areas of Pest with the Vaci utca in the center and the Great Ring were the main shopping district of the capital, the arrival of the glittering post-modern shopping centers has highly decentralized buyers currents to the suburbs. Similarly, as elsewhere, it is often common courtesy among young people to visit one of the malls on a weekend day. Since also restaurants and cinemas are included, the visit can expand until late in the evening.

Development of shopping areas

But the traditional shopping areas in the city center have been able to survive despite the strong competition. The Váci utca is quite touristy today as many designers have settled on the »Fashion Street« Deák Ferenc utca and in the first part of Andrássy út. It is always worth taking a look in the narrow backstreets, because they often feature small family businesses hawking their special wares. Very popular are, i. e. handmade shoes from Budapest. Smaller shops can also be found in the courtyards along the Great Ring road, especially between Blaha Lujza tér and Margaret Bridge.

Shopping streets

You should not miss the market halls of the capital, especially the Central Market Hall at the south end of Vaci utca. In the smaller markethalls of the districts, the residents buy fruits, vegetables, bread, cheese, sausage and meat. In the Chinese market in the Kőbányai út you can clearly see that many people in Budapest have only a little money. Cheap clothing is sold from the Middle Kingdom. For years, even customers from Ukraine, Romania and the former Yugoslavia came here to stock up cheaply.

Markets

Souvenirs of varying quality are offered at all tourist hot spots. Dolls in folk costume and bulky wine jars are popular. Hand-made textiles such as blouses, dresses, table cloths and bedding are often exquisitely embroidered and make pretty, unique holiday gifts. Kalocs blouses, Matyó embroideries, jackets with colourful cloth decorations and woven country ware find just as many buyers as Herend porcelain, Pécs ceramics, pottery after the style of puszta shepherds, and cutlery and vessels carved from different types of wood. Glass,

Souvenirs

A stroll on Váci utca is just part of a Budapest trip

leatherwear, elegant ladies' handbags, shoes, cravats, belts and natural remedies – especially flower pollen, propolis, honey and medicinal herbs – are very popular with tourists as they are relatively cheap. Popular holiday gifts are Hungarian salami, »Barack pálinka« apricot schnapps, and the popular Szilva damson schnapps, spirits made by Peter Zwack, wines from the various wine-growing regions – especially Eger and Tokaj – as well as creatively packaged paprika and garlic.

Galleries, antiques

In Budapest there are two neighborhoods with particularly many galleries and antique shops: on Falk Miksa utca in the Leopold town between Parliament and the Szent István körút the cream of the Hungarian gallery scene has settled during the past 20 years. But even in the city center around Váci utca some art dealers can still be found.

Made-to-measure clothing and shoes

Those who value the personal touch can have value-for-money clothes and shoes made to measure from high-quality materials by excellent craft workers in Budapest.

Opening hours

Shops are generally open Mon–Fri 10am–6pm, Sat 9am–1pm. In the Pest pedestrian zone shops often stay open till the evening, and shopping malls till 9pm. Market halls and markets are open weekdays from 6am to 5pm.

Vass produces bespoke shoes

Shopping adresses

ANTIQUES • GALLERIES
Antik Bazár
V, Váci utca 67
Large selection of antiques, especially dolls and jewellery.

Belvárosi Aukcióház
V, Váci utca 36
Auction house which sells valuable furniture, jewellery, art works and more every Monday from 5pm; previews are possible daily from 10am.

BÁV (Bizományi Áruház Vállalat)
V, Bécsi utca 1–3 (jewellery, paintings and gift items)
V, Semmelweis ucta 15 (weapons)
V., Szent István körút 3 (furniture, art and paintings)
www.bav.hu
The numerous shops of the state auction house BÁV are a good place for all kinds of antiques and great for bargain hunters

Csók István Galéria
V, Váci utca 5
Old and contemporary Hungarian art, also sculptures, prints and jewellery.

Kieselbach Galéria
V., Szent István körút 5
www.kieselbach.hu
The internationally renowned art collector Tamás Kieselbach regularly exhibits Hungarian paintings of the late 19th and early 20th century, intended for auction.

Nagyházi Galéria
V, Balaton utca 8

www.nagyhazi.hu
Budapest's largest gallery offers, next to its extensive selection of paintings, also furniture, porcelain and jewellery.

Polgár Galéria
V., Petőfi Sándor utca 16
V., Kossuth Lajos utca 3
Polgár offers in his two stores jewelry, silver, china and crystal.

Virág Judit Galéria
V., Falk Miksa u. 30
Hungary's leading gallery offers paintings from the Hungarian »Golden Age« at the turn of the 20th century.

BOOKS • SECOND-HAND BOOKSHOPS
Írók Boltja
VI, Andrássy út 45
www.irokboltja.hu
Bookshop with regular readings by authors and a café; those who haven't mastered Hungarian should head for the foreign language department

Libri Stúdium Könyvesbolt
V., Váci utca 22
Well-stocked bookstore, and foreign language books.

Alexandra Könyveshaz
VI., Andrássy út 39
www.alexandra.hu
Large bookstore in the elegant former Parisian department store, also DVDs and Hungarian wines. Passage to the fantastic Book Café. Alexandra now has many branches in the city.

Lovers of fine porcelain must go to Herend

Központi Antikvárium
V, Múzeum krt.17
Hungary's largest antiquarian bookshop has been trading since 1881, and also sells foreign language books and maps.

Párizsi Udvar
V, Petöfi Sándor u.2
Large selection of travel books, illustrated books and maps.

Sós Antiquárium
V, Váci utca73
In addition to books, there is a large selection of prints, maps and postcards.

FLEA MARKETS
Ecseri flea market
XIX, Nagykörösi út156
Huge flea market at which the bargain hunter can find virtually anything that the heart desires: watches, furniture, clothes, porcelain. Prices are always negotiable! (Opening times: Mon – Fri, 8am – 4pm, Sat, 7am – 3pm)

Flea market in Városliget Bolhapiac
On the area around the Petöfi Hall (XIV district)
www.bohalpiac.hu

Significantly smaller than the Ec-
seri flea market, but still worth a
visit. (Opening times: Sat – Sun,
7am – 2pm).

FOLKLORE • FOLK ART
Népművészeti Bolt
Insider Tip

V., Régi posta utca 12
Folklore clothes, colorful Haban
ceramics and black ceramics from
Nádudvar are just a few of the interesting displays in folk art shop,
a few steps from Váci utca.

GLASS • PORCELAIN
Ajka Kristály
V., József Attila utca 7
www.ajka.hu
Wide range of crystal and glass-
ware of the western Hungarian
company, along with fine porcelain from Zsolnay.

Haas & Czjzek
VI, Bajcsy-Zsilinszky út23
Large selection of Hungarian por-
celain.

Herend
V, József Nádor tér11
V, Kígyó utca5I, Szentháromság
utca5
www.herend.com
High-class Herend tableware.

Zsolnay/Hollóháza
V., Kálvin tér 1
The South-Hungarian manufactur-
er Zsolnay also stands for elegant
porcelain. The company from Pécs
created artistically challenging Art
Nouveau designs at the beginning
of the 20th century and with the
distinctive eosin glaze they developed their own trademark.
Hollóháza, the third Hungarian

> **MARCO POLO INSIGHT** ❓
>
> *Famous Manufactory*
>
> Herend is a synonym for fine por-
> celain. The factory was founded
> in the same place in 1826 north of
> Lake Balaton and in the 19th cen-
> tury it supplied the monarchs of
> Europe, including Queen Victoria
> and Empress Sisi. After the closure
> of the Viennese manufacturer
> Herend was the imperial court
> supplier. They got famous for
> their oriental style. Even today, all
> patterns are hand painted. The
> prices are accordingly high.

porcelain factory from the same
northern Hungarian town is also
represented here with attractive
pieces.

DEPARTMENT STORES • SHOPPING CENTRES
Corvin
VIII, Blaha Lujza tér1–2
You can get just about anything
here, and for a good price too;
this once state-owned chain still
has something of the socialist era
about it.

Mammut
II, Széna tér1–3
Popular shopping centre on Mosz-
kva tér; the original weekly market has been integrated.

Westend City Centre
VI, Váci út1–3
Central Europe's largest shopping,
commercial and leisure centre:
over 400 shops in an area of
90,000 sq m (100,000 sq ft). The
triangular building with sloping
glass roof is worth a visit alone.

The Central Market Hall is an inexhaustible treasure trove

MARKET HALLS
Central Market Hall
IX, Vámház körút1-3
Mon 6am – 5pm, Tue – Fri
6am –6pm, Sat 6am – 2pm
Elaborately renovated showpiece
of the Budapest market halls. Besides Hungarian specialties and
folklore articles, fresh fruit, vegetables and meat is offered. There
is always lots of activity. At the
end of the 19th century the market halls revolutionised the supply
of the residents.

Additional market halls
Just like the central market hall,
the following were also founded
in the late 19th century and offer
similar products:
V, Hold ucta 13
VI, Hunyadi tér 4
VII, Klauzál tér 11
VIII., Rákóczi tér 7 – 9

There are, of course, also modern
market halls in Budapest, which
are an established part of the
shopping experience. They are
located in:
I, Batthyány tér
II, Fény utca
XI, Fehérvári út
XIII., Lehel tér

FASHION / SHOES / LEATHER GOODS
International fashion brands are
mainly located in the Váci utca
and the Deak Ferenc utca. The lat-
ter may have been hyped up a bit
as »Fashion Street«.

Biró Eva
I., Dísz tér 16
The store in the Castle District has handmade leather bags and belts to offer.

Ékes
V., Régi posta utca 14
Those who feel cold, can buy elegant gloves at Ékes.

Kaczián
V., Régi posta utca 14
The family business right next to Ékes is known for its fashionable ties.

Tamás Náray
V., Károly Mihály utca 12
Elegant high quality clothes from one of the most famous haute couture fashion designers of Hungary, who was educated in Paris.

Retrock Deluxe
V., Henszlmann Imre utca 1
Designer clothes for men and women, also from young fashion designers.

V-50 Design Art Studio
V, Belgrád rakpart 16
V., Váci utca 50
Classic designer fashion, linen dresses, and hats for brave ladies.

Vass (▶ill. p. 108)
V, Haris köz 2
www.vass-cipo.hu
Made-to-measure shoes for those with plenty of time; the rest will have to buy the standard goods on offer.

WINE
Bortárság
I., Lánchíd utca 5
IX., Ráday utca 7
www.bortarsag.hu
Hungarian wines have reached international level. Bortársag, the »wine company,« holds a good selection of different wine regions, including several top wine makers.

Insider Tip

Tours · Guides

Many Possibilities

If you want to explore the city on a guided tour, you have a lot of possibilities. Guided tours are available by bus, by boat, by bike or on foot, and the spectrum ranges from introductory tours to special topics tours, which also present the hidden facets of Budapest. Walking is the best way to get through the city center.

If it is your first time in the city, it is worth buying a so-called hop-on-hop-off ticket. The provider of these bus tours allows unlimited dismounting and boarding at many of the main attractions on a circular route through the city. While a classic city tour only lasts 2 – 3 hours, you can spend more or less time at the respective highlights. It is up to you!

Hop-on-hop-off

Several providers have started to integrate a one-hour boat trip in addition to the bus tour. This is obviously a real bonus since a boat trip on the Danube should definitely be included in the tour programme. It is romantic at night, when the skyline of Budapest is illuminated and festive. A special feature are the amphibious buses from RiverRide, they dip from the road directly into the Danube.

Boat tours

There is extensive information material on city tours by bus, as well as on boat cruises on the Danube, air tours and, of course, walks around particular districts at the tourist information offices as well as at hotel receptions.

Organized tours

For holders of the Budapest Card (►Prices, Discounts), tram lines 2, 4 and 6 are a cost-effective way of getting an overview of sights around the Pest side of the city: a recommended tour begins at the Margaret Bridge, south of ►Margaret Island. Tram lines 4 and 6 travel along the ►Great Ring, past the West Railway Station, the Oktogon (►Andrássy út) and Café New York to the Petöfi Bridge, where you change to tram line 2 or 2A heading north. From here the journey goes along the Danube, with views of ►Fövám tér and the Central Market Hall, the ►Chain Bridge and ►Parliament, as well as ►Gellért Hill and the ►Gellért Bath, before ending back at the starting point. Not recommended during the rush hour (5–7pm) because of the crowded trams!

Tram tour

Many tour deals also include English-language comments. Tours by bicycle and on foot through the most interesting neighborhoods are

Guided tours

Even with the tram you can get to know the city

The evenings are especially impressive on the Danube

with an English-speaking guide as well. Very interesting are the tours of the Jewish Quarter. The guided tours of Budapest Tours are free for owners of the Budapest Card.

To the spas Those who need rest and relaxation after a day of visiting should definitely visit one of the magnificent spas, for which Budapest is very famous.

Excursions The Buda Hills are always worth a visit. The highest mountain of the city is an attractive destination, the 527 m high János-hegy, as well as a trip to the fascinating caves of the capital.

Danube cruise A boat trip on the wide river leads to the main attractions of the Danube metropolis: the ships glide under the Chain Bridge to the impressive Parliament and Margaret Island before it passes Castle Hill and Gellért Hill to the National Theatre. Some bus tour providers have added boat trips, while RiverRide offers amphibious boat tours. Evening boat trips are especially romantic when the Chain Bridge and the Castle are illuminated festively!

Sightseeing information

CITY WALKS

Information on the wide choice of escorted walking tours around the city can be found at tourist offices (►Information) and hotel receptions. Travel agents offering city tours include:

Absolute Walking Tours
Tel. 12118861
www.absolutetours.com

Beyond Budapest
Insider Tip
Tel. 0620 3 32 54 89
www.beyondbudapest.hu
Especially walking tours through District VIII in English. Dates available on request.

Budapest Tours
Tel. 1 3 23 07 91
www.budapest-tours.hu
Informative tours of Pest and Buda (in English); free for owners of the Budapest Card.

Hidden Treasure Tours
Tel. 1 5 33 56 96
www.greatsynagogue.hu
Guided tours to »hidden treasures« through the Jewish Quarter starting from the Dohány Street Synagogue.

BUS TOURS
Budatours
VI, Andrássy út 2
Tel. 06 20 3 53 05 58
www.budatours.hu

Cityrama
Báthori utca 22
Tel. 1 3 02 4382
www.cityrama.hu

Hop on Hop off
Tel. 1 3 74 70 70
www.citytour.hu

DANUBE CRUISES
DunaYacht
V., Belgrád rakpart (Petőfi tér)
Pier 10
Tel. 06 30 5 86 50 01
www.dunayacht.com

Legenda Ltd.
V., Vigadó tér
Pier 7
Tel. 317–2203
www.legenda.hu

Mahart PassNave
V, Belgrád rakpart
Tel. 318–1586
www.mahartpassnave.hu

RiverRide
Tel. 1 3 32 25 55
www.riverride.com
This company offers an exciting special: a floating bus which can drive on land and on water.

BICYCLE TOURS
Budapestbike
VII., Wesselényi utca 13
Tel. 0630 9 44 55 33
www.budapestbike.hu
Bike rental from April to September; tours by appointment only.

Yellow Zebra Bikes
VI., Lázár utca 16
Tel. 1 2 66 87 77
www.yellowzebrabikes.com
Bicycle rental; partner of Absolute Walking

TOURS

The highlight in the following tours are indeed grand. But don't pass up exploring quiet streets and alleys on your own.

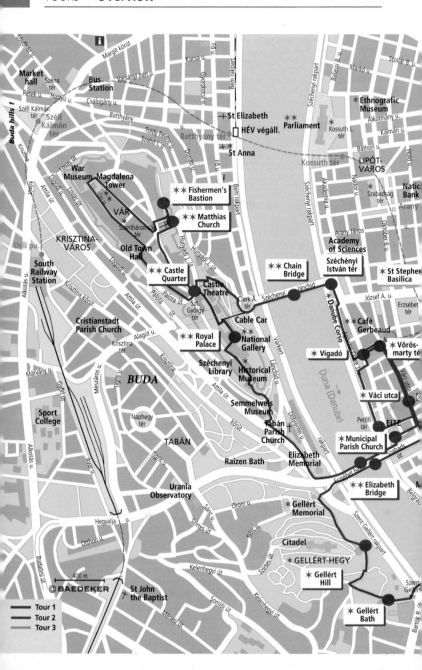

Tour 1
Tour 2
Tour 3

Tours Through Budapest

Three extended walks – those, who have time for all three will know all highlights of the city

Tour 1
Over the Chain Bridge to the Castle District
This walk leads to the Buda side of the Danube.
▶page 122

Tour 2
Gellért Hill
A combination of terrific views and urban activity
▶page 125

Tour 3
To Heroes' Square
Architecture, history, coffee houses and art: straight ahead on Budapest's magnificent street Andrássy út
▶page 127

Getting Around in Budapest

By public transportation

By plane it is just a short trip to Budapest from other European countries. In theory, even a day trip is feasible. Nevertheless, this city is so rich in sights that it really deserves at least three days. The good news for weekend visitors is that in Budapest the shops open on Sundays. If you extend the weekend to Monday, however, it would be a good idea to reserve Sunday for museums, since almost all of them are closed on Mondays. Much can be seen on foot in Budapest, but to save energy it is recommended to take a tram occasionally for longer distances. Driving a car in this confusing city is a challenge that non-residents should avoid. Car parks are few and far between, while traffic jams and road works are common! Accommodation in all price categories is available everywhere: due to their central location the fifth and ninth quarters on the Pest side are especially pleasant. On the other side of the Danube it is quieter, though noticeably less convenient. In any event, it is a good idea to consider local transport connections when choosing a base.

Metro, bus and train for free

The cost of public transport in central Budapest is already low compared with other major cities, but those in possession of a Budapest Card (▶Practicalities, Prices and Discounts) can travel as the mood takes them, without having the trouble of getting tickets. EU citizen aged 65 and older can use public transportation for free.

Tour 1 Across the Chain Bridge to the Castle District

Start and finish: Vörösmarty tér
Duration: One day

This day tour leads along the Danube Corso to the Chain Bridge and over to the Buda side of the Hungarian capital. The Castle District with its numerous sights, including the Matthias Church, Fishermen's Bastion and especially Royal Palace, can reached either by cable car or on foot, returning via the Elizabeth Bridge.

Still in Pest

On the north-west side of ❶*Vörösmarty tér Vigadó utca leads past the – in comparison with its spectacular frontage – drab side of the Vigadó concert hall and ballroom ❷*Vigadó to the Danube Corso, where the bronze princess by László Marton sits on the railings

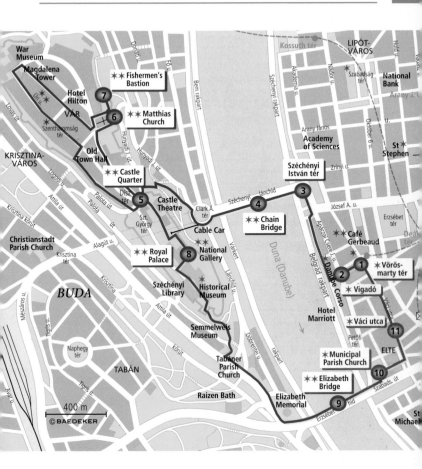

claiming the admiration due to her. The Danube Corso is Budapest's most popular and best-known promenade, lined by numerous street cafés and several architecturally nondescript five-star hotels on one side, and by the tramline, the busy Belgrád rakpart and the Danube on the other side. Stroll north on the Corso to Gresham Palace on ❸ **Széchenyi István tér**. Today this Palace houses the Four Seasons, probably the city's most stylish hotel. A peek into the lobby or a coffee and cake in the Gresham Kávéház is highly recommended.

From here the ❹ ****Chain Bridge** leads over the Danube to Clark Ádám tér on the Buda side, where a cable car (Sikló) covers the short distance up to the ❺ ****Castle District**. As an alternative to the Sikló,

Up to Buda

walk up to Dísz tér via the Royal Steps (Királylépcskö), which are north-west of the cable car's lower terminus. Beyond the square, a rather forlorn statue of a hussar awaits visitors. Between the bus stop behind the statue and a not particularly attractive café is the start of Tóth Árpad sétány, a pretty tree-lined promenade that leads along the south-west exterior wall of Castle District and offers beautiful views onto the lower Buda quarters of the city. Turn right to Szentháromság utca and arrive at the square that opens out by **Café Miró**. Friends of the Spanish artist can choose to visit the café designed in his surrealist style, while those with more traditional tastes take a few steps further and try to get a seat in **Café Ruszwurm**.

Buda attractions If you are interested, follow the atmospheric Úri utca with its Gothic architectural details all the way to the tower of the Magdalene Church, and then onwards to Szentháromság tér, either via Országház utca or alternatively via Fortuna utca. If you have less time, walk to the end of Szentháromság utca, past the former Buda town hall, directly to Szentháromság tér, where a visit to the ❻**Matthias Church** constitutes one of the main attractions of Budapest. Next door, the ❼** Fishermen's Bastion** is a wonderful place for enjoying a view of the Pester side of city. If you are lucky, a »gypsy band« plays in the cafe, then you can especially enjoy the view. Return to Dísz tér via Tárnok utca.

Like a castle of a fairy tale: Fishermen´s Bastion

Cross the square and follow Színház utca, past the Castle Theatre and Sándor Palace all the way to Szent György tér. On the south-eastern side a neo-Baroque archway – eyed suspiciously by the eagle Turul – which gives admittance to the forecourt of the ❽****Royal Palace** with an equestrian statue of Prince Eugene. A passage leads to another castle forecourt with the ***Matthias Well**. Walk through the Lion Gate to the inner court of the castle, with the main entrances to the Széchenyi National Library and the ***Budapest Historical Museum**, as well as the side entrance to the ****Hungarian National Gallery**, which presents the Hungarian art from the Middle age to the present day. Another passage by the Historical Museum leads to the south-facing medieval fortifications of the castle, with the castle tower at their south-western end. From the foot of the tower there is a wonderful view across the **Tabán quarter** of the city, with its parish church and the Danube flowing behind it, and the Elizabeth and Liberty Bridges.

Royal palace

Leave the castle fortifications via the steps at the castle tower. Walk down past the Golden Stag tavern to the bridgehead of Erzsébet híd, with its memorial to the Elizabeth, Empress of Austria and Queen of Hungary, better known as Sisi. Cross the ❾**Elisabeth Bridge** to the Pest side and pass the ❿***inner city parish church** on the left. An archway gives access to the busy Váci utca ***Váci utca**, which leads back to ***Vörösmarty tér**, where the cakes and coffee of the legendary **coffee house Gerbeaud**, along with an interesting interior, are a pleasant conclusion to the tour.

Back in Pest

On Gellért Hill

Tour 2

Start and finish: Vörösmarty tér
Length: At least six hours

This tour starts from Pest city centre, crossing the Elizabeth Bridge to begin a scenically attractive but quite exhausting walk up Gellért Hill. Returning past the Gellért Baths and reaching the Pest side once more via Liberty Bridge.

Just as on Tour 1, set off from ❶***Vörösmarty tér**, and follow Vigadó utca to the imposing frontage of the ❷***Vigadó** concert hall. Beyond Vigadó tér stroll along the ***Danube Corso** in a southerly direction with the tasteless Marriot Hotel to the left. A few steps further along the Danube Corso lies **Petöfi tér** with its bronze statue of the Hungarian poet and the Greek Orthodox Church on its east side. Immediately behind the memorial to Petöfi, take the newly reno-

Squares of Pest

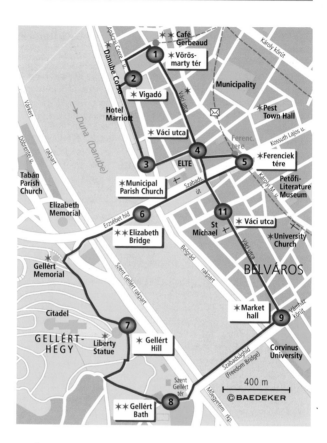

vated Március 15 th tér – with the remains of the Roman fort Contra
Aquincum – all the way to ❸*Inner City Parish Church. The passage Piarista köz leads to the new pedestrian street ❹*Váci ucta and
turns onto Kígyó ucta, which leads to the traffic junction ❺*Ferenciek ter. It would be a good idea to plan brief stops at *Parisi utca
shopping arcade and the Franciscan Church.

Back across
the Danube Past the Clotilde Palaces the Szabadsajtó út leads to ❻Elizabeth
Bridge, and the Buda side. From the bridge there is already a great
view of the *Gellért Memorial and the waterfall beneath. Beautifully designed steps lead to the memorial past both sides of the waterfall. From there choose the path in a south-east direction for wonderful views of the city. After a few minutes the highest point of
❼*Gellért Hill is reached, with its imposing Liberation Monument

and Citadella. To get to the famous ❽****Gellért Bath**, descend through Jubilee Park. A few step along from the Citadella, it is worth visiting the Rock Chapel, a quiet place in a natural cave. Liberty Bridge leads back to Pest and Fövám tér, where the lively scenes of the ❾**central market hall** await. A variety of spices, fruit and vegetables, meat and sausages, spirits and much more can be found here. Return to the starting point of the tour via the much quieter, though no less attractive southern part of Váci utca and then the livelier northern section of the shopping street.

Along Andrássy út to Heroes' Square   Tour 3

Start and finish: Vörösmarty tér – Heroes' Square
Length: At least three hours

This tour follows the busy Andrássy út, designed as a fine boulevard in 1872, to Heroes' Square and the wooded Városliget Park. Return to Vörösmarty tér and the starting point of this extended walk with the historic underground railway (M 1), a cosy and bumpy version of a city metro line.

Leaving ❶***Vörösmarty tér** follow Deák Ferenc utca to Deák Fe-   First, a church renc tér (►Little Ring). Then take Bajcsy-Zsilinszky út in a north-   tour erly direction and turn right onto ❷****Andrássy út**. Before turning off, however, it is worth strolling a bit further along Bajcsy-Zsilinszky út, in order to give ❸***St Stephen's Basilica** the attention it deserves.

There are several significant sights along Andrássy út. After just a few   Follow An-steps the imposing ❹***State Opera House** appears on the left. Past   drássy út the traditional art café Müvész you pass the arts district Nagymezö utca, also known as the »**Pest Broadway**«, a little bit further. Here several nice cafes are located. Highlight is the **BookCafé** decorated with frescos of the former Parisian department store (Andrassy út 39). A little bit further to the right the ❺**Liszt Ferenc tér** branches off, which is completely lined with cafes and invites to have a break. Passing the Great Ring at the Oktogon, you notice immediately the House of Terror. Several interesting museums follow, including the ❻**Franz Liszt Museum** inside his last Budapest home to the right. ❼***Heroes' Square**, you have walked the entire length of Budapest's show street. If the pedestrian route along Andrássy út is too far, it is always possible to shorten the distance by taking metro line 11,

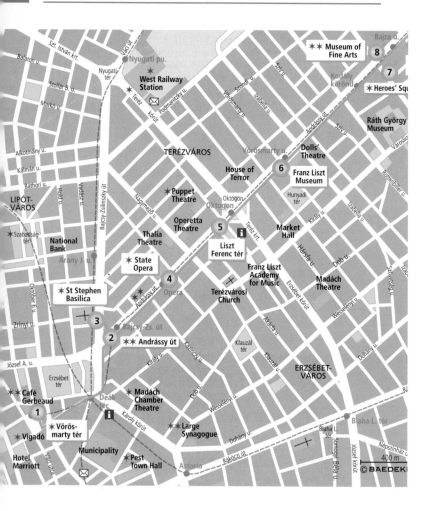

which runs underneath the street. The ⑧ **National Museum of Fine Arts** on the north-west side of Heroes' Square exhibits Budapest's most important art collection.

To the city woods

From the northern end of the square Állatkerti körút leads past Budapest's gourmet restaurant Gundel and the art nouveau entrance of the Zoological and Botanical Gardens to wooded park of ⑨ *** Városliget**. Immediately behind the *Széchenyi Baths** a path leads off to the right to Kós Károly sétány, on which a right turn will take you to ***Vajdahunyad Castle**. For the return to Heroes' Square, cross the castle island – not forgetting to take note of the expressive Anonymous Memorial – to the bridge beyond, and take a right turn along the shores of the lake. From the square there is a direct metro connection (line m1) back to Vörösmarty tér.

SIGHTS FROM A TO Z

Budapest's golden age was during the time of the Habsburg dual monarchy, when most of the sights were built. Castle Hill, Parliament, the Danube Promenade: there is much to discover …

* Andrássy út

━━━━━━━━━━━━━━━━━━━━━━ ✳ C – E 4 – 6

Location: VI district
Metro: M 1 (Bajcsy-Zsilinszky út - Hfsök tere)
Bus: 4, 105

Budapest's glorious boulevard is part of the UNESCO World Heritage since 2002. City mansions, monumental houses as well as important cultural institutions, such as the opera building, cluster along this main artery.

Showpiece The glorious boulevard Andrássy út runs for a distance of approximately 2.5km/1.5mi in a north-easterly direction out of the city, from Erzsébet tér to Hösök tere (Heroes' Square), with the Millennium Column as the visual endpoint. Two spacious squares, the Oktogon and the Kodály körönd, interrupt its course.
Continental Europe's oldest underground railway, affectionately called the »Little One« by Budapest's inhabitants, has been running underneath Andrássy út since 1896. The oldest carriages can be viewed at the Underground Museum on Deák Ferenc tér (▶MARCO POLO Tip, p.189).

Museum of the Hungarian postal service The museum of the Hungarian postal service (Postamúzeum, no. 3) is housed in a mansion that was built for the businessman Saxlehner by Gyözö Czigler in 1886. The staircase of this former apartment block is embellished by a ceiling fresco by Károly Lotz. The museum on the first floor contains, in addition to documents on the development of the Hungarian postal service, a few items of equipment, including the telephone of Emperor Franz Joseph I.
❶ April–Oct Tue–Sun 10am–6pm, Nov–March Tue–Sun 10am–4pm); www.postamuzeum.hu; admission 750 HUF

Pest's Broadway Andrássy út passes the state opera building and crosses the Nagymezö utca, which is also called »Pest's Broadway« due to the many theatre houses and night clubs; the highlight is the elegant Budapest operetta house. Directly on the opposite side the renowned House of the Hungarian Photographers regularly present sophisticated exhibitions in the original photo studio of Manó May, photographer of the kings' court between 1855–1917.

Insider Tip

Back on the Andrássy út the fabulously renovated, formerly **Parisian department store** is the next building in line. The façade is a jewel of art nouveau architecture. There is a large bookstore and one of the nicest Budapest coffee houses in its interior. The **Book Café** is decorated with voluptuous frescos as well as huge mirrors, because this formerly was the festive hall of the Theresiatown Casinos. Now the

Vivid life on the Franz Liszt Square with the statue of the pianist

love for pomp of the late 19th century is revieved within this marvellous café.

House of the Hungarian Photographers: Mon–Fri 2pm–7pm Sat–Sun 11am–7pm

The nicest place for drinks in the evening is the green Liszt Ferenc tér, which directly borders the Andrássy út. Despite the high density of cafés on mild summer nights it often is quite hard to find a free table here. At the end of the plaza lies the ▶Franz Liszt University for music. It is the most important address for concerts and the art nouveau interior is impressive. The house is closed at the moment due to renovation.

Liszt Ferenc tér (Franz Liszt Square)

The Great Ring crosses Andrássy út at the Oktogon. Even though this eight-sided square has been re-named several times throughout its history, it has always been the Oktogon for the people of Budapest. It is uniformly lined by tall apartment blocks and businesses in historicist style, which give it both architectural unity and a sense of space. Andrássy út becomes a boulevard after the Oktogon. Narrow streets running parallel, originally riding paths, flank the main traffic artery.

Oktogon

House of
Terror
Originally head office for the national socialist Arrow Cross Party and, after the war, seat of the Communist state security services, **Andrássy út no. 60**, with its interrogation rooms and prison cells, was a notorious address in the 1940s and 1950s. Today the »House of Terror« is not so much a museum as a multi-media memorial (unfortunately almost entirely in Hungarian), recalling Hungary's grim era of totalitarian rule however only the crimes of the communist regime are touched.

❶ Tue–Fri 10am–6pm Sat–Sun 10am–7.30pm; www.terrorhaza.hu; admission: 2000 HUF

Liszt museum
Liszt Ferenc
Emlék
múzeum
The most noteworthy building on the section between the Oktogon and the roundel Kodály körönd is the magnificent building (no. 67) on the corner of Andrássy út and Vörösmarty utca, built in the style of an Italian renaissance palace by Alois Lang, in 1879. The Academy of Music founded by the composer Franz Liszt had its original home here (▶Franz Liszt Academy of Music), and since its restoration in the 1980s the academy has used it once more. The composer's former apartment in this building is now a museum on the first floor (entrance: Vörösmarty utca 35). The reconstructed interior of the three rooms – bedroom and office, dining room, and sitting room – in part with Liszt's own furniture, is augmented by books, scores, memorabilia and a few musical instruments, including the small glass piano in his office, Liszt's favourite Bösendorfer piano, as well as his Chickering concert grand piano.

❶ Wen–Fri 10am–5pm, Sat 10am–5pm, closed during the first three weeks of August: www.lisztmuseum.hu; admission: 900 HUF.

Kodálv
körönd
At Kodálv körönd, build at a nicely planed rondel, stands the former **house of composer Zoltán Kodály** (no.1), which unfortunately is temporarily closed due to renovation.

Kogart
House
From this point on the Andrássy út expands to a wide avenue, which is dappled with freestanding estates. Here the art-collector Gábor Kovács opend an art collection, the Kogart House, in no.112, which now frequently hosts various art exhibitions well worth seeing.

❶ Mon–Fri 10am–4pm, Sat–Sun 10am–8pm

Museums
This area of the Andrássy út slowly is emerging as a small art quarter. On the opposite side the **Ferenc Hopp Museum** (no.103) displays East Asian art and right next to the Kogart a new **Gold Museum** (No. 100) will open its doors, its emphasis being Southeast Asia.

Ferenc Hopp Museum: April– Oct. 10pm–4am, Nov–Mar 10am–4pm
Gold Museum: daily: 9 am–7pm

* Aquincum

⟡ Excursion

Location: Óbuda, Szentendrei út 135
Suburban train HÉV: Aquincum
Bus: 42, 106

❶ 15–30 April, Oct, Thu–Sun
10am–5pm, May–Sept Thu–Sun
10am–6pm
www.aquincum.hu
Admission: 1300 HUF

Traces of the Roman past can be found at various places in the Budapest district of Óbuda, but they are especially impressive at Aquincum, where the foundations of a civil settlement have been excavated since the 1870s.

Today the excavation site is open to the public and the most valuable finds are exhibited in a small museum (▶see below). The remains of the garrison, which preceded the civil settlement, lie a little closer to the city centre, near Flórián tér (▶Óbuda). The garrison and settlement extended almost all the way to Gellért Hill, and also covered the Danube island at Aquincum, as well as the east bank of the Danube, where the Romans built the fortification Contra-Aquincum close to today's Elizabeth Bridge (▶Március 15. tér). The Romans conquered Transdanubia around the year 10 BC and established the province of Pannonia. A few years after the birth of Christ, they founded a garrison on the terrain of Budapest's present-day district of Óbuda, around which the city of Aquincum soon developed. This flourishing settlement was already the provincial capital of Pannonia Inferior by the beginning of the 2nd century AD. During its heyday in the first half of the 3rd century AD, around 50,000 people lived in Aquincum. Emperor Septimius Severus raised the city to the status of a Colonia in AD 194. Aquincum's decline came after the defeat of the Roman legions at Hadrianopolis and Roman withdrawal from Pannonia in AD 378, and was accelerated by increasingly severe invasions by the Huns.

Roman settlement

Statue of Jupiter

The excavations of the civil town were already transformed into a museum during the 19th century. The history of Aquincum is vividly displayed by means of frescos, murals and masonry within the exhibition building. One of the sights is the water-organ dating back to 228. Also the annual exhibitions which present the contemporary findings from Budapest and the surrounding areas are very intriguing.

Museum

Aquincum

Amphitheatre

City Wall

100 m

©BAEDEKER

City Gate

City Wall

Keled utca

Entrance

Keled utca

Aqueduct

Large
Shrine

Law
Court

Residences &
workshops

Baths

Large Bath

Archaeological
Museum

Aqueduct

Meat market

Baths

Mithras
Shrine

Residences &
workshop

Residences &
workshop

Celtic
Shrine

Aqueduct

Tavern

Mithras
Shrine

Baths

The excavation site gives an idea of the planned Roman city, around 400m x 600m in size, which in addition to numerous, mostly one-storey private homes encompassed several baths, a market hall, a Mithras sanctuary and a basilica. The remains of the ancient water and sewage system, including water pipes, canals and heating installations, are interesting not only for experts. An aqueduct was exposed during the extension of Szentendrei út, a broad arterial road that leads all the way to the small town of Szentendre. Individual sections can still be seen along the side of the road or on the central reserve between traffic lanes.

Excavation site

Diagonally across from the excavation site, on the other side of Szentendrei út and very close to the HÉV Aquincum station, remains of the Roman city's amphitheatre were revealed during excavations in 1880 and 1937. Originally, it measured around 80m x 90m (90yd x 100yd) and could hold 7500 spectators. A restored section of the ancient city walls can also be seen here.

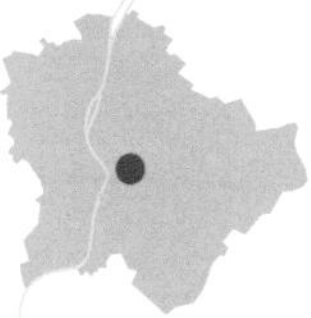

Amphitheatre

✶✶ Arts and Crafts Museum
(Iparművészeti Múzeum)

✦ D 8

Location: IX Üllői út 33 - 37
Metro: M 3 (Corvin-negved)
Tram: 4, 6

❶ Tue–Sun
10am–6pm
www.imm.hu
Admission: 2000 HUF

The Budapest Arts and Crafts Museum is one of the oldest of its kind. Not just the collection, but also the architectural surroundings in which it is presented, make a visit worthwhile.

Ödön Lechner (1845–1914), the most important proponent of Hungarian art nouveau, designed the two-storey building at Üllöi út, which opened its doors in 1896. In contrast to his work on the later ▶Post Savings Bank building, Lechner still had recourse to past – especially oriental – architectural forms for the Arts and Crafts Museum, and melded them with national elements from Hungarian folk art into a new style. Granite tiles and roof tiles in colourful patterns from the Zsolnay factory in Pécs enliven the façade. To the right of the main entrance stands a statue of the architect, created by Béla Farkas in 1936. The central inner courtyard, which is covered by a glass roof, and the ticket hall in front of it almost appear like a fairy tale with their mixture of Indian and Moorish designs. The construction with its unclad steel support was highly modern at the time.

Art nouveau building

The Arts and Crafts Museum is inspired by oriental architecture

Exhibitions The museum offers a wide thematic scope because various special exhibitions run parallel to each other. On the first floor a permanent exhibition »collectors and treasures« presents some of the most beautiful objects of the museums fund.

Batthyány tér

✳ B 5

Suburban train HÉV: Batthyány tér
Metro: M 2 (Batthyány tér)
Tram: 19, 41
Bus: 11, 39, 60, 80, 260

This square, named after the first prime minister of the independent Hungarian Republic, Count Lajos Batthyány (1806–1849), has always stood at the heart of Watertown (▶Vízi-város), the district between Castle Hill and the Danube.

The heart of Watertown
Batthyány tér used to be a marketplace. Today it is the end of the line for the suburban HÉV train coming from ▶Szentendre to Budapest, as well as for the underground station and several bus routes. A few of the old houses on the square lie below street level, which emphasizes even further the height of St Anne's Church on the south side of Batthyány tér, making it appear even taller in relation to its surroundings.

Batthyány tér is dominated by the building of St Anne's Church, whose imposing double-tower frontage occupies the southern side of the square. This church, built between 1740 and 1758 to plans by Christoph Hamom and Matthäus Nepauer, is one of the most beautiful Baroque buildings in Budapest. It was restored in the late 1950s, after severe damage in the 19th century and especially during the Second World War. The three-bay main façade has impressively balanced proportions. St Anne and the Virgin can be seen in the framed niche above the main entrance. The tympanum bears the coat of arms of Buda and a symbol for the Holy Trinity. The ground plan of the church – typically for Baroque architecture – only becomes apparent in the interior. It consists of an oval nave and choir and two chapels. The tall, extravagantly decorated high altar and the pulpit, which was later redesigned, belong to the original interior of the church and presumably derive from the workshop of the sculptor Carlo Bebo. The marble panelling and the frescoes on the central dome are 20th-century additions by Pál Molnár and Béla Kontuly. The fresco in the choir illustrating the Holy Trinity was done by Gregor Vogl in 1772. The sculptures by Anton Eberhard by the side altars, as well as altar panels by the Viennese painter Franz Wagenschön, are worth seeing.

St Anne's Church

Compared to St Anne's Church, the other buildings – except for the market hall dating from 1902 to its right – appear rather small. This also goes for the former inn called The White Cross (no/no. 4), which sinks into the street and now has a less impressive appearance. The house grew out of the combination of two buildings in 1770; while the right half displays Baroque forms, the left one is Rococo in style. Another wing was additionally constructed between the two courtyards behind the arched gateway in the 19th century. Here theatrical performances and balls were held.

The White Cross

Hickisch House (no. 3) was built in late Rococo style in 1795 and is named after its former owner, the mason Christoph Hickisch. The relief on the façade represents the four seasons of the year.

Hickisch House

** Buda (Castle district)

✦ A/B 5 – 7 ●

Location: Castle Hill
Funicular: Clark Adám ter - Szent György tér
Bus: 16, 16 A, 116

For visitors a stroll along the almost entirely pedestrianized streets and lanes of Buda is one of the most pleasant experiences the Hungarian capital has to offer.

Baroque
quarter

With its predominantly Baroque buildings, the old centre of Buda on Castle Hill has managed to maintain its charm to this day. It is not just the highlights, such as the Matthias Church and Fisherman's Bastion that make the Castle District a prime destination, but also the numerous architectural details, niches and courtyards that can be discovered here. Buda's Castle Hill, consisting of the Castle District and the castle, is listed as a **UNESCO World Heritage site**, along with Budapest's Danube panorama,

History

The Hungarians recognized the strategic significance of the solitary club-shaped hill (168m/551ft) on the right bank of the Danube in the 13th century under King Béla IV, and built Buda Castle at its south-eastern tip, which soon became the residence of Hungarian kings. To the north-west, on the Castle Hill plateau, a city developed in tandem and was to be for a long time the glittering heart of the country. It was largely destroyed during the Turkish wars and the city was rebuilt in the Baroque style during the 17th and 18th centuries. Buda, which rapidly also expanded downwards, merged with the neighbouring small town of Óbuda to the north, and with Óbuda and Pest in 1873 became the capital city of Budapest. The Castle District suffered heavy destruction once more during the Second World War. During reconstruction after the war, the medieval foundations and several beautiful details, such as the Gothic seat niches, were revealed in numerous houses.

MAIN STREETS AND SQUARES OF BUDA

Tour

The following description of the Castle District is designed as a tour that begins in the north, at Bécsi kapu tér (the Viennese Gate) and covers the most important sights.

Viennese
Gate

One of the main access points to Castle District is the northerly Bécsi kapu which was built to plans by Jenö Lechner in 1936 on the occasion of the 250th anniversary of Buda's liberation from the Turks in 1686. A memorial tablet on the inside of the gate recalls the event. Behind the Viennese Gate lies Bécsi kapu tér (Viennese Gate Square), on which the Saturday market was once held
Directly opposite Bécsi kapu square, on the tapering plot of land between Táncsics and Fortuna utca, stands the **Lutheran Church** (**Evangélikus templom**) built in 1896, in which organ concerts are held throughout the year.
To the right, adjacent to the Viennese Gate, is the neo-Romanesque **National Archive**, built between 1915 and 1918. Several late Baroque and classical apartment blocks on the western side of Bécsi kapu tér deserve a look, especially the Lobner House (no. 5) with a beautiful

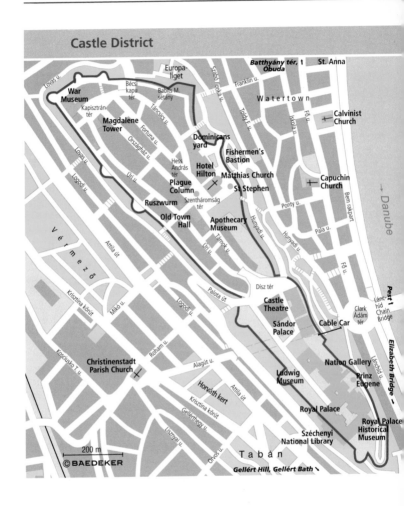

Castle District

stairwell in Hungarian late Rococo style, and the house at no. 7 built around 1800 with a façade adorned by portrait medallions of poets from antiquity.

West of the Viennese Gate, behind the National Archive, is the **Anjou Bastion**, the north-western section of the castle fortifications, which was fiercely contested during the liberation battles of 1686. There is a wonderful view over the western districts of Budapest and the Buda Hills from the bastion. In 1936, the Hungarians set a memorial to the

Anjou Bastion

Beautiful façades in scenic Buda

last Turkish pasha of Buda, who fell here in 1686, on the second semi-circular protrusion of the Anjou Bastion.

Táncsics
Mihály utca From Bécsi kapu tér, Táncsics Mihály utca leads in a southerly direction towards Szentháromság tér (Holy Trinity Square). One of the oldest streets on Castle Hill, it was formerly called the Jewish Lane, but was then renamed after the author Mihály Táncsics.

The **Hungarian National Monuments Office** presents a remarkable **exhibition** in the building at no. 1 Táncsics Mihály utca including, among other things, illustrations on the life and work of Hungary's most important master builders and architects are shown.

The **Museum of Music History** has found a worthy home in the house at no. 7, an elegant Rococo mansion built between 1750 and 1769 to plans by Matthäus Nepauer where the Museum for Music History occasionally holds various special exhibitions. There is no permanent exhibition at the moment.

The history of the Jewish community of Buda, which lived in this part of the Castle District from the second half of the 14th century, is recalled in the small **exhibition in the Gothic house** at Táncsics utca 26. This former Jewish prayer house was restored a few years ago. Fragments from the synagogue. Fragments from the synagogue built in 1461 are shown in the courtyard, whose foundations were revealed in the garden building behind house number 23.

From Táncsics Mihály utca, a passage between house numbers 17 and 21 gives access to the north-eastern part of the fortifications, leading to **Mihály Babits Promenade**, which extends all the way to the Viennese Gate (Bécsi kapu) to the north. There is a beautiful view of the city from here. At the foot of the walls lies the Europa Park, which was established in 1972 on the occasion of the centenary of the unification of Buda and Pest.

National Monuments Office: daily 9am–4:30pm
Jewish prayer house: May–Oct, Thu–Sun 10am–6pm, admission: 600 HUF

Hess András tér, which was named after the bookbinder Andreas Hess, lies at the junction of Fortuna utca and Táncsics utca. Hess was recalled to Buda in 1472 after having studied in Italy. In 1473, Hungary's first printed book, the *Chronica Hungarium*, was produced in his house at no. 4, now the Fortuna Restaurant. A memorial to Pope Innocent XI, made by József Damkó in 1936, decorates the square in honour of the man who instigated the Holy League against the Turks in 1686. The house with the red hedgehog (Vörös sün ház) as an emblem above its gate was one of the oldest taverns on Castle Hill. It was built on medieval foundations in the 17th and 18th centuries and was later given a classical façade. The commanding building of the plaza next to the ▶Matthias Church is the luxury Hilton Hotel opened in 1976. Here the Hungarian architect Béla Pinter proved that it is possible for tradition and modernity to exist in close proximity. Fragments of buildings that stood at this spot in the Middle Ages were also incorporated into the new building in such a way that they too come into their own. These sections are parts of a former Dominican monastery, which already existed in Buda in the 13th century. The most significant remnant of the monastery is the late Gothic tower (Miklós-torony) of **St Nicholas' Church**. On its west wall, a copy of a 15th-century relief of Matthias Corvinus was fixed. It shows the Hungarian king with sceptre and royal orb in an architectural frame. In the summer the Dominican courtyard is transformed into an open stage hosting klezmer, jazz, dixieland and classic concerts.

Hess András tér

MARCO ⊕ POLO TIP

House of Hungarian Wine   Insider Tip

There is undoubtedly no better opportunity to get to know the numerous wines of Hungary than at the House of Hungarian Wine (Magyar Borok Háza; daily: 12 noon until 8pm) at Szentháromság tér no. 6. Some 50 wines are available for tasting daily, and quality and fine wines from 22 historic wine regions can be purchased. You can learn more about Hungarian wine in ▶ MARCO POLO Insight, p. 88.

The main square of Castle District is Szentháromság tér, which is bordered by the ▶Matthias Church to the east, Fisherman's Bastion to the northeast and the former Ministry of Finance, built by A. Fell-

Szentháromság tér

ner between 1901 and 1904, to the north. In the middle of the square stands a magnificent Baroque plague column designed in 1714 by Philipp Ungleich from Würzburg to commemorate the epidemic of 1691. A representation of the Holy Trinity forms the tip of this 14m/46ft-high memorial, while the base is surrounded by saints. The emblems and reliefs on the pedestal are the work of the sculptor Antal Hörbinger. This plague column is a copy of the original monument, which was badly damaged during the Second World War.

The wide two-storey Baroque building on the corner of Szentháromság tér and Szentháromság utca was once **Buda town hall**, recognizable by the beautiful bay on the top floor. Today it is the seat of the language institute of the Hungarian Academy of Science. The Italian architect Venerio Ceresola supplied the plans to which the building was constructed in 1710, incorporating the medieval wall fragments of previous constructions. Later, an extension was built on Úri utca. The courtyard and the stairwell are also architecturally noteworthy. The statue of the Greek goddess Pallas Athene underneath the corner bay displays the coat of arms of Budapest on her shield. The figure, which dates from 1785, is the work of the Italian Carlo Adami.

Pastry shop Ruzwurm

On narrow **Szentháromság utca**, which leads west from Szentháromság tér all the way to the western wall of Castle Hill, a visit to Café Ruszwurm (no. 7) is recommended. In business since 1827, its original Empire interior is still largely intact. The selection of cakes and pastries can certainly match those on offer at the Gerbeaud coffee house on ▶Vörösmarty tér.

The broad **Tárnok utca** (Treasurer Street), a lively shopping street in the past as well as now, leads from Holy Trinity Square to Dísz tér. Historic buildings mix with modern houses. This is where most foreign exchange booths and souvenir shops, as well as antique shops, taverns and boutiques, are to be found. The house with its eaves facing the street at Tárnok utca no. 14 and a façade covered with colourful geometric patterns is a typical example of the Gothic merchants' houses that once characterized Tárnok utca. At Tárnok utca 18, the ground floor rooms housed the Arany Saspatika (Golden Eagle Pharmacy) in the 18th century. A merchant's house built in the 15th century, today it is home to the **Apothecary Museum**. This exhibition on the history of modern pharmacy from the 16th and 17th centuries occupies just four small rooms, but is nevertheless well worth seeing.

Apothecary Museum: 15 Mar–Oct Tue–Sun 10.30 am–6pm, Nov–14 Mar till 4pm; www.semmelweis.museum.hu; admission: 500 HUF

At the southern end of the Castle District lies the spacious Dísz tér, once a showpiece square. In the Middle Ages, this square now lined by imposing buildings in the late Baroque and classical styles, such as the Batthyány Mansion (no. 4), was a marketplace. On the spot where a church burnt down, the Honvéd statue by György Zala has stood since 1893, recalling the liberation battles of 1848/49. The Italian architect Venerio Ceresola built the Kremsmünster House at Dísz tér 4–5, so-called because Kremsmünster Abbey owned the property. The Gothic seating niches dating from the 13th century, over which Ceresola built his new building, can still be seen in the entrance. The post office building next to Café Korona also contains medieval architectural fragments in its Baroque structure.

Dísz tér

South of Dísz tér, on Színház utca stands the **Várszínház (Castle Theater)**. The long building complex once housed a Carmelite nunnery which was dissolved by decree of the Austrian Emperor Joseph II in 1786. The commission to convert the convent and church into a theatre was given to Farkas Kempelen. The first drama for the stage in the Hungarian language was performed in this theatre on 15 October 1790 – an important event for Hungarian national consciousness. Today the National Theatre resides here with a highly sophisticated program.

The classical **Sándor-palota (Sándor Mansion)**, with its main façade facing towards György tér, stands next to the Castle Theatre. It was built for Count Vincent Sándor by Mihály Pollack in 1806, and has been home to the Hungarian president since 2003. Every day at noon a changing of the guards in historic uniforms takes place for tourists.

Next are two important residencies. The archbishop of Budapest-Esztergom resides in nr. 62. He also is the traditional head of the catholic church in Hungary. In no. 64-66 the German embassy has its quarters.

Archbishop's residence

Úri utca is characterized by Romanesque, Gothic and Baroque buildings whose origins reach back to the 13th century. Nobles and wealthy merchants built their town houses here, in close proximity to the royal castle, in the 14th and 15th centuries. After the devastations of the Turkish wars, Baroque and classical houses were built over the originals. Úri utca is a very atmospheric scene as the buildings have been carefully renovated in recent years, the colour of their façades

**Úri utca

carefully matched and their Baroque decorations restored. The most interesting and oldest buildings are to be found in the section north of the junction with Szentháromság utca. Gothic seating niches under pointed arches can be discovered in, for example, the entrances to the buildings at nos. 32, 34, 36, 38 and 40 on Úri utca. The Hölbling House (no.31), dating mostly from the 15th century, is the only surviving Gothic home. A courtyard surrounded by Gothic arcades opens up beyond the entrance gate. The house at no. 32 contains a cross-vaulted columned arcade between the gate entrance and the courtyard, a typical feature of most buildings. The classical façade of the house at no. 40 conceals the remains of two Gothic residential houses, of whose splendour the cross vaulting in the gateway and the filigree tracery above the seating niches still testify. Field Marshal András Hadik (1710–90), whose equestrian statue stands at the crossing of Úri utca and Szentháromság utca, lived at house no. 58. The hussar from Buda was made a field marshal by regent Maria Theresa because of his considerable daring and is remembered for his temporary conquest of Berlin during the Seven Years' War. Touching the gold testicles of the horse is said to bring students luck for imminent exams.

Insider Tip

The Hungarian Telephone Museum is housed at Úri utca 49, and not without reason: the world's first functional telephone exchange was built in Budapest. The branch exhibited at the museum is still in working order today. The reconstructed west tower of the Church of Mary Magdalene rises at the northern end of Úri utca. Originally dating from the 13th to 15th centuries, the church was destroyed during the Second World War and the ruins were later removed.

Telephone Museum: Thu–Sun 10am–4pm; www.postamuzeum.hu
Admission: 700 HUF

Tóth Árpád sétány

A short detour to Tóth Árpád sétány, which was part of the castle fortifications extended in the 17th century, is worthwhile. Today it makes for a pretty promenade with four bastions as popular viewpoints.

Kapisztrán tér

Kapisztrán tér, at the extreme north-western corner of Castle District, is named after Johannes Capistranus, an Italian Franciscan monk and travelling companion of the conqueror of the Turks, János Hunyadi. József Damkó created a memorial to Capistranus that has adorned the square since 1922. The northern side of Kapisztrán tér is occupied by the former Ferdinand Barracks, which is today the **War Museum** (Hadtörténeti Múzeum). However, the entrance to the museum is not here, but on Tóth Árpád sétány. Documents and diverse exhibits on the history of Hungary's wars from the 16th century onwards are shown here, with emphasis on developments since 1848.

War Museum: Apr–Sep Thu–Sun 10am–6pm, Oct–March Tue–Sun 10am–4pm; www.militaria.hu; admission: 800 HUF

The Castle Hill offers wonderful views on Pest

Historic Országház utca turns south from Kapisztrán tér and is the main street of Castle District. The northern section of the alley is mostly characterized by Baroque buildings while the southern section is mainly classical. Occasionally there are still Gothic and Renaissance details to be spotted, for example on house no. 10. The house at no. 2 was built as a city mansion in the second half of the 13th century. However, only a few individual fragments, such as the seating niches under the arched tracery in the entrance gate, recall its Gothic origins. The houses at nos. 18–22 date from the 15th century and have been remodelled several times. The Gothic quatrefoil moulding on the first floor of house no. 20 is beautiful. The convent of the Poor Clares at no. 28, founded in the Middle Ages, was redesigned by Franz Anton Hillebrandt, who supervised the building works at the Royal Palace in the 18th century. After that, the buildings housed the parliament and the Hungarian capital's highest law courts. From time to time, it is possible to attend high-quality musical performances in the Great Hall, which has been restored to its original design.

*Országház utca

A widely branched, 10km/6mi long cave system branching out in many directions that has given shelter and storage space to the population of Buda many times during war runs beneath the palace. The tunnels were consecutively connected with each other throughout the Middle Ages and during the second wold war they were again used by

Cave system

the German Wehrmacht. The highly secret military hospital and fall-out shelter, the Rock Hospital (Sziklakórhaz; entrance: Lovas út 4/c), was later opened for visitors. At the end of the Second World War and during the revolts of 1956 injured people were treated here and during the Cold War the facility was expanded to a fall-out-shelter. Original furniture enhanced with wax figures are on display here.

❶ Thu–Sun 10am–8pm: guided tours: hourly; tel. 1 7 07 01 01 01; www.sziklakorhaz.hu

*Fortuna utca

The Országház and Fortuna utca cross at Matthias church, where it is best to follow Fortuna utca north. Here the artisans who participated in building the castle lived during the Middle Ages. Today the alleys are dominated by beautiful Baroque buildings.

Buda Hills

———————————————— ✳ **A / B 1 – 11**

Location: western suburb

The Buda Hills (Budai-hegység) form a natural western border to the Hungarian capital. The heights, which are mostly wooded, have long been a popular destination for short excursions. The hills consist of dolomite and chalk, as well as clay and marl, which may be especially intriguing for people interested in geology.

Underneath the Buda Hills a wide **cave system** (cave = barlang) can be found. Two of the caves have ben made accessible to the public: the **Pálvölgvi cave** (Szépvölgvi út 162) was discovered in 1904 and offers a 500m/650ft long walkway along enchanting dripstone formations. With its total length of 19km/11mi this cave is the second longest cave system in Hungary.

The **Szemlőhegyi cave** (Puszta-szeri út 35) doesn't contain any dripstones on its 300m/1000ft walkway, but for that pure, clean air, which is even used for medical purposes.

Pálvölgvi cave: Thu–Sun. 10am–4pm

Szemlőhegyi cave: Wen–Mon 10am–4pm

Hármashatár-hegy

The Hármashatár-hegy (497m/1640ft) rises on the northern border of Budapest and offers a beautiful view of Óbuda from its almost bare summit. Just over one mile north-west of Hármashatár-hegy, as the crow flies, good views are also to be had on Csúcs-hegy (445m/1470ft).

János-hegy

János-hegy rises to the west of Buda. At 527m/1739ft it is the Hungarian capital's highest elevation, and from the high Elisabeth observation tower, completed in 1910, a magnificent panorama can be enjoyed. One can comfortably ride the chairlift Libegō from the quarter Zugliget up the north flank of the hill or enjoy the view on the Donaube on the way back into the valley. John Hill has also become attractive for winter sports enthusiasts since the installation of a ski jump and slope with t-bar lift.

The Száb-hegy (»Swabian Hill«) rises to the west of the town. Its name derives from the Turk wars as two armies were camped at this place. The soldiers predominantly came from the southwest of Germany. In time wealthy Budapest citizens settled on the slopes of the hill. Today it is a favoured residential area with 19th century mansions and architecturally remarkable bungalows.

From Városmajor Park a cog railway runs up Szabadság-hegy, and also Széchenyi Hill behind it (439m/ **Széchenyi Hill** 1448ft), which is topped by a transmitting station of the Hungarian television company. The children's train (Gvermekvasút) also starts its 12km/7mi long tour from this hill. It runs through the woody slopes down to the suburb of Hűvösvölgy (www.gyermekvasut.hu).

> **!** MARCO ⊕ POLO TIP
>
> *Tour of the Buda Hills* ^Insider ^Tip
>
> A pleasant relaxing tour through the Buda Hills begins and ends at Széll Kálmán tér. From there walk to the valley station of the cog railway at the western edge of Városmajor Park, and ride up Széchenyi-hegy. A few metres from the summit station, one can get onto the children's railway, ride to »János-hegy« station, where a great view can be enjoyed by climbing to the top of the hill. The route passes the hill station of the chairlift below János-hegy (St John Hill); but to take the chairlift it is first necessary to descend from the summit (daily, 9.30am–4pm, closed on every Monday within an uneven week of the calendar). Near the valley stop, bus route 158 returns to the starting point.

Cemeteries

KEREPESI TEMETŐ

❶ VIII. 126, Fiumei út a E/F 6/7; metro: M 2 (Keleti pu.), tram: 24, 28, 37

Kerepesi Cemetery (Kerepesi temető) is one of the Hungarian capital's largest; it has numerous impressive tomb monuments that make it well worth seeing. Leading figures of the country and city have been buried here from the mid-19th century onwards, among others János Arany, Mór Jókai, Alajos Hauszmann, Ödön Lechner, Ferenc Erkel, Loránd Eötvös, Tivadar Puskás and many more. Several highly positioned people who died abroad and whose remains have been returned to their homeland in recent decades also lie here; among others, Mihály Graf Károlyi, who was the president of the first Hungarian Republic. Today burials in this cemetery only occur in exceptional circumstances. The mausoleums for the politicians Lajos Kossuth, Lajos Batthyány and Ferenc Deák testify to the special honour accorded to them. The monumental pantheon to the Hungarian Workers' Movement (Munkásmozgalmi Pantheon) can be seen.

NEW MUNICIPAL CEMETERY

❶ X. (Kőbánya), Kozma út 8; tram: 28, 37

The New Municipal Cemetery is located far beyond the city centre in the district of Kőbánya. At plot number 301, those executed after the 1956 uprising, among them their leader **Imre Nagy** (▶Famous People p. 51) were buried in a mass grave. On 16 June 1989, the 31st anniversary of Imre Nagy's execution, the time had come to rehabilitate them. A state ceremony took place on Heroes' Square, as well as a ceremonial re-burial in newly created graves, an event of great significance for Hungarians, which forced a renewed confrontation with their own history. On the wishes of his daughter, Imre Nagy, who was prime minister of a free Hungary for just a few days during the uprising, was re-interred at plot 301.

Jewish cemetery
A memorial of quite a different kind awaits the visitor at the small Jewish cemetery, which adjoins the new municipal cemetery to the north (no connecting access). This is the unusual mausoleum for the Schmidl family, for which Ödön Lechner and Béla Lajta supplied the designs in 1902/03. Already characteristic for Hungarian art nouveau are the decorations on the façade, with their turquoise tiles; but the flower patterns taken from Hungarian folk art also point in that direction

** Chain Bridge

✦ B 6

Bus: 16, 86, 105
Tram: 2, 2 A, 1941

One of the emblems of the Hungarian capital, the Chain Bridge (Széchenyi lánchíd) was Budapest's first permanent bridge across the Danube. Today it provides the shortest connection between Castle Hill and the shopping streets of Pest.

Atmospheric: the Chain Bridge

The bridge was designed by the English engineer William Tierney History Clark and built between 1839 and 1849 under the supervision of the Scottish architect Adam Clark. The 375m/1230ft long and almost 16m/52.5ft wide bridge is suspended from chains that are fixed to massive pillars 48m/157ft in height. The stone lions resting on pedestals at the bridgeheads are the work of János Marschalkó. Whether or not the lions had tongues or not was long a matter for discussion in Budapest: their creator claimed – perhaps as a joke – that you had to stand directly opposite the animals in order to see their tongues. Along with all of Budapest's other bridges, the Chain Bridge was blown up by German troops in January 1945, but was already re-opened to traffic in 1949, exactly 100 years after its first inauguration.

On Clark Ádám tér at the Buda bridgehead stands the zero stone de- Clark Ádám tér signed by Miklós Borsos in 1971 to mark the spot in Budapest from which all distances on outgoing Hungarian long-distance roads are measured.

At Clark Ádám tér, an entrance designed in classical style leads into the approximately 350m/1155ft long road tunnel that connects Buda with Krisztinaváros. The tunnel completed in 1857 was also the work of the bridge builder Adam Clark.

From the Buda bridgehead of the Széchenyi lánchíd it is possible to take the nostalgic-looking **funicular** up to the Royal Palace which was built in 1870. It was returned to service after decades of neglect. To save time or money when there are long queues at the Sikló, head for the Royal Steps that cover the few metres of elevation from the roundabout at Clark Ádám tér to the Castle District.

A Technical Masterstroke

Chain bridges are suspension bridges which use chains instead of ropes to hold the carriageway. This building technique had its grand age in the 19th century. The famous Budapest Chain Bridge (Széchenyi Lánch) was one of the most modern bridges in Europe as it was opened for traffic in 1849.

▶ **Data**

Length	375m/1230ft
Width	16m/52.5ft
Support width	202m/662ft
Duration of building	1839–49

Two pillars
resembling to
triumphal arches
carry the bridge.

▶ **Material and reconstruction**

Original construction 1839–49
The Chain Bridge was advanced technology as it was built. The largest chains worldwide were used.

Total weight
in tons

2146

Major material

Extension 1913–15
The bridge was extended with a steel construction in order to meet the increasing traffic needs. The pillars stayed unchanged.

5194

Reconstruction 1947–49
After the blasting during the retreat of the German troops the bridge was rebuilt and reduced in weight due to the usage of new material and new technology.

5000

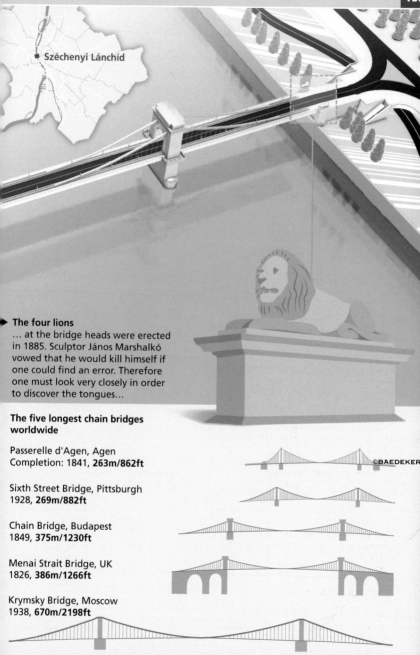

Széchenyi Lánchíd

► The four lions
… at the bridge heads were erected in 1885. Sculptor János Marshalkó vowed that he would kill himself if one could find an error. Therefore one must look very closely in order to discover the tongues…

The five longest chain bridges worldwide

Passerelle d'Agen, Agen
Completion: 1841, **263m/862ft**

Sixth Street Bridge, Pittsburgh
1928, **269m/882ft**

Chain Bridge, Budapest
1849, **375m/1230ft**

Menai Strait Bridge, UK
1826, **386m/1266ft**

Krymsky Bridge, Moscow
1938, **670m/2198ft**

©BAEDEKER

Danube Bend (Dunakanyar)

✳ Excursion

Location: 20–50km north of Budapest
Long distance route: 10/111, 11 and 2/12
Buses: from Metro Újpest-Városkapu to Visegrád and Esztergom
From the Metrostation Árpád híd directly to Esztergom
Train: from the west train station to Vá-nagymaros-Szob
Suburban train: from Batthyány tér to Szentendre

The Danube Bend is the name given to the roughly 60km/35mi stretch of the river which runs through particularly attractive scenery between Esztergom and Szentendre, where the Danube winds its way through the Visegrád mountains and turns in a southerly direction to Budapest (▶MARCO POLO Insight, p. 156).

Popular excursion and leisure destination
The Danube Bend is one of the most popular excursion and leisure destinations in the region around the Hungarian capital. On the right bank, parts of the Bakony forest reach to the river and the Pilis Mountains (Pilis-hegység) rise to a height of 757m/2484ft. From the north, the up to 938 65m high Börzsöny Mountains (Börzsöny-hegység) push towards the river. The Danube takes a winding passage dictated by the rocky terrain with a notable loop at Visegrád, and it splits into two arms shortly before Vác to embrace the island of Szentendre. The beautiful towns of Esztergom, Visegrád and Vác, as well as the artists' town of Szentendre are especially appealing to visitors. Hiking enthusiasts and nature lovers are particularly drawn to the back country of the Danube Bend, to the Pilis Mountains and the Visegrád Hills to the south of the river, as well as to the Börzsöny Mountains or to the Cserhát hill country to the north and east.

ESZTERGOM

Location: Approx. 60km/45mi north-west of Budapest

One of Hungary's oldest towns
Esztergom (pop. 32,000), located on the southern terraces of the Danube, at the entrance to the Danube gorge through the central Hungarian highlands, is one of Hungary's oldest towns, with noteworthy buildings and historic monuments. The Magyars settled the area of Esztergom as early as the 9th century. During the Middle Ages, Esztergom rose to become one of the most important royal residences in the Hungarian empire alongside Székesfehérvár, as well as seat of the archbishop. King Béla III had the castle of Esztergom extended into a magnificent residence. Occupied during the Turkish wars, the town flourished once more in the 18th century. After the Second World War, several larger industrial companies were also set-

tled here. Crossing the river to the Slovakian side the Mária Valéria Bridge, which was destroyed during the war, has been rebuilt. The view from the bridge offers the best view on the castle hill and the cathedral.

Begun in 1822 by János Páckh and completed in 1856 by József Hild, the cathedral with its massive dimensions dominates the townscape of Esztergom. While an antique-style portal highlights the east entrance, the crossing is flanked by towers and crowned by a dome in the style of the Italian Renaissance. A cool, classical sobriety reigns in the marble-clad interior. The most significant parts of the cathedral, which remain from the preceding building, are the 16th-century tomb chapel for Archbishop Tamás Bakócz and the **cathedral treasury**, with its unusually rich collection of sacred art from the 9th till the 19th century,

*Cathedral

The remains of the palace built in the 10th and 11th centuries and extended in the 12th century – and therefore Hungary's oldest royal palace – can be found to the left of the cathedral. The János Vitéz Hall with its Renaissance frescoes, the room in which King Stephen was probably born, and the **early Gothic castle chapel**, which is a gem of religious architecture at the transition from Romanesque to Gothic, deserve special mention. At the southern and western side of the royal palace wall remains from the 14th and 15th century fortifications still survive.

*Palace

The dome dominates the view of Esztergom

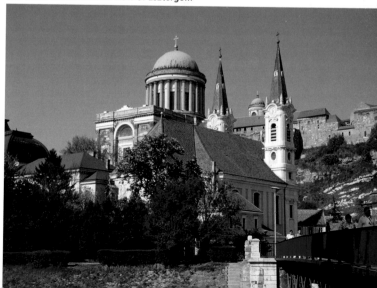

Hungary's Lifeline

With its length of 2857km/1775mi the Danube is the second longest European river after the Volga. 596km/370mi flow through Hungary. For the country as well as for Budapest, the largest city on the Danube, it is an economical factor of primary importance.

▶ **Foreign trade via domestic shipping**

■ Export   ■ Import
in 1000 TEU (standard container)

Austria
298
317

Hungary
158
224

Slovakia
93
56

▶ **Port sizes**
Important Danube ports in comparison

Vienna
3.50sq km/1.35sq mi

Budapest
1.52sq km/0.59sq mi

Bratislava
1.43sq km/0.55sq mi

Belgrade
1.10sq km/0.42sq mi

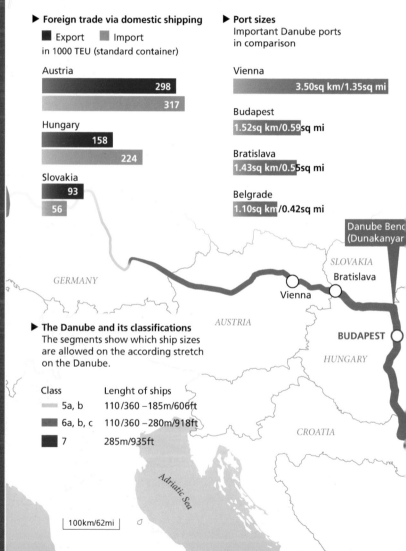

Danube Bend
(Dunakanyar)

SLOVAKIA
GERMANY
Bratislava
Vienna

AUSTRIA

BUDAPEST

HUNGARY

▶ **The Danube and its classifications**
The segments show which ship sizes are allowed on the according stretch on the Danube.

Class	Lenght of ships
5a, b	110/360 –185m/606ft
6a, b, c	110/360 –280m/918ft
7	285m/935ft

CROATIA

Adriatic Sea

100km/62mi

▶ **Csepel, the port of Budapest**
After the Freeport Budapest Logistics Ltd. took over the port in 2005 it became a public trading port. Today it encompasses three basins, storage facilities as well as a roll-on roll-off terminal.

Port area 1.52 sq km/0.6sq mi	
Number of wharfs	18
Warehouse area 0.092sq km/	
0.036 sq mi	

Margaret Island
Thanks to its extensive park the island is very popular with tourists. Besides taxis, busses and rickshaw-like crafts, motorized vehicles are banned on the island.

Danube Corso
The promenade is especially recommendable during the evening hours when the majestic buildings and bridges are illuminated.

5km/3.1mi

▶ **Domestic shipping on the Danube**
The importance of the Danube as a water way is increasing from year to year – one major reason is the lesser staining of the streets, as the comparison with lorries shows.

©BAEDEKER

JOWI class container ships

Length	**135m/443ft**	Draught	**3.7m/12ft**
Width	**17m/55ft**	Tonnage	**470 TEU**

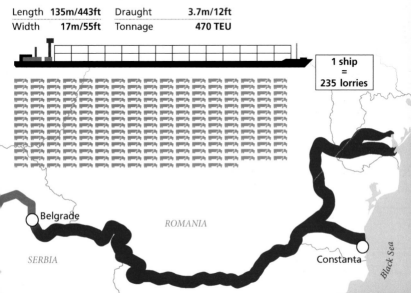

1 ship
=
235 lorries

Christian Museum	In the former palace of the archbishop, in the Watertown district beneath the castle hill, the Christian Museum (Keresztény Múzeum) today presents its treasures. This provincial collection, famous far beyond the national borders, contains an extensive display of old Hungarian and early Italian Renaissance painting, as well as a high-quality collection of sculptures from the 14th to 18th centuries and historic crafts. The dual-towered late Baroque church directly next to the museum was built for the Jesuit order between 1728 and 1738.
Széchenyi tér	Széchenyi tér, then as now the former market square of Esztergom, surrounded by lovingly restored houses from the 18th and 19th centuries, stands at the heart of the town's life. The town hall (Városháza) decorated by arcades and a Rococo façade on the south side is worth a look.

VÁC

Location: 34km/21mi north of Budapest

Baroque town	Vác (pop. 35,000), on the north bank of the Danube Bend, has retained the charm of a pretty Baroque town despite industrial development on its periphery. Fortuitously located at a Danube crossing, Vác was the seat of a bishop from the 11th century onwards and, at the height of the Middle Ages, a regional trading centre protected by a royal castle. The town was severely ravaged during the Turkish wars in the 16th century and the Baroque town was built north of the medieval castle in the 18th century. The first Hungarian railway line, inaugurated in 1846, ran from Pest to Vác.
Historic centre	The historic centre of Vác lies along the eastern bank of the Danube between Konstantin tér, which is dominated by the cathedral, and Március 15 tér (March 15 Square) to the north, which is lined by beautiful town houses.

Designed by the Viennese architect Isidore Canevale between 1763 and 1777, the *cathedral with an antique-style columned portico in front of its west façade is as an early example of the classical style developed in France. The dome fresco of 1771 is the work of Franz Anton Maulbertsch. The two-storey bishop's palace, built between 1768 and 1775, is opposite the cathedral.

The pre-eminent building on Szentháromság tér (Holy Trinity Square) is the former Piarist church of St Anne, dating from 1745. The area in front is adorned with a magnificent Baroque Holy Trinity column (1755), and opposite is an entrance to the thermal baths of Vác. The triangular *Március 15. tér with its decorative fountains and sculptures was the heart of the historic town. With its surrounding Baroque and late Rococo houses, it forms an atmospheric ensem-

The baroque town of Vác offers delightful scenery

ble. The former Dominican church on the south side has a beautiful Rococo interior.

A few streets north of Március tér, at the former edge of town stands an early classical triumphal arch, which was built to designs by Isidore Canevale in honour of a visit to Vác by queen regent Maria Theresa in 1764.

VISEGRÁD

Location: 42km/26mi north of Budapest

Visegrád (»high fortress«; pop. 2100) has an extremely picturesque site at the end of a loop in the Danube Bend and is a popular place for excursions because of the royal palace ruins and the high citadel with great views. The strategically important site above the Danube was already used to advantage by the Romans, who established a garrison here. Under King Béla IV, the lower castle was built on the banks of the Danube. It was connected to the mighty upper castle on the hill by a wall. Visegrád developed into a highly significant town politically and culturally under the regency of Charles I of Anjou, who moved his residence there in 1316. It experienced its final flowering in the second half of the 15th century, when King Matthias Corvinus I had the royal palace on the castle hill remodelled in the style of the Italian early Renaissance.

Residence

Salomon torony	The most impressive remnant of Visegrád's lower castle is the hexagonal, originally 31m/102ft high Salomon torony dating from the 13th century. After successful renovation, it now houses a museum with valuable finds from the former royal palace, including the red marble Hercules fountain.

The water bastion (Vízibástya) on the banks of the Danube was part of the lower castle and served to guard the waterway and the water supply to the palace. This Romanesque building was reconstructed in 1937.

Royal palace	The site of the royal palace above Fő utca (entrance at house no. 27), which was built in the first half of the 14th century and magnificently remodelled in the style of the Italian early Renaissance by King Matthias, was buried by earth slips over the course of centuries, and has been excavated and gradually exposed only since 1934. So far, the northern part of the palace, which was the royal residence, has been uncovered. The heart of the grounds, which extend over several terraces and once included numerous magnificent buildings, a court garden, baths, and around 350 sumptuous rooms, is the late Gothic court of honour lined by arcaded walks.

Upper castle	A serpentine road signposted from the centre of town leads to ruins of the upper castle at a height of 315m/1039ft. It is possible to chose a beautiful walkway from the town centre up to the castle, however the climb is quite exhausting. A small path marked with blue-white signs leads from the ferry dock past the church then turning left afterwards. A small chapel lies on the way and in 50 min one reaches the castle.

Several circular walls with gates and drawbridges surround the core of the castle; the best-preserved tower gate is the eastern one, an interesting example of Hungarian castle architecture. Up on the castle the visitor may enjoy the best view on the Danube Bend.

Ethnographic Museum

✦ **B / C 5**

Location: Kossuth Lajos tér 12
Bus: 15, 70, 78
Metro: 2 (Kossuth tér)
Tram: 2 A

www.nepraiz.hu
❶ Thu–Sun
10am–6pm
Admission: 1400 HUF

A visit to the Ethnographic Museum, the Néprajzi Múzeum, is recommended not only for its collections but also for its architecture. This is exactly the right place to find out about Hungarian culture.

The gorgeous entrance of the Ethnographic Museum

The museum is housed in the former building of the Supreme Court at »Kossuth Lajos tér« which was completed in 1896, just in time for the millennium jubilee. The designs were drawn up by the much-employed architect Alajos Hauszmann, who united elements of Renaissance, Baroque and classical style for this monumental building. The sculptural decorations on the façade are focused on the former function of the building as a palace of justice: above the six high columns carrying the tympanum the »Goddess of Justice« drives a three-horse chariot, a work in bronze by Károly Senyei. The interior is also lacking in pomp.

Building with lots of styles

The museum rooms are grouped around an extensive hall, whose broad dual staircases leading up two storeys, elaborate marble cladding and gold-leaf stucco details are worthy of the building's original purpose. This is also recalled by the allegorical representation of Law and Justice on the ceiling fresco by Károly Lotz. The room above the entrance hall, which is used for lectures and concerts, is also worth viewing.

Collection
The extensive collection on Hungarian national culture and art is shown on the first floor. The theme-based exhibition has explanations in Hungarian and English. In the first room, the various national groups of the Pannonian basin are introduced by means of their folk costumes. The next room is dedicated to institutions that shaped life in the country, such as the church and the village community. Common crafts and trades are presented in the following rooms, and there are also two rooms dedicated to Hungarian building skills and domestic culture. The following room exhibits traditional products from local art and craftwork. The typical Hungarian farmhouse is the topic of a further exhibit. The exhibition ends with a representation of the different stages of life, such as birth and death, and the customs and festivals associated with them, which provide a vivid picture of rural life in Hungary.

Ferenciek tere

✦ C 7

Location: V district
Metro: M 3 (Ferenciek tere)
Bus: 5, 7, 7A, 8, 15, 112, 173

Ferenciek tere on the southern edge of central Pest is one the squares of Budapest with the heaviest traffic, it is still one of the most interesting squares, a place of pulsating city life.

*Párisi Udvar (Parisian Court)
The department stores around Ferenciek tere represent the most diverse styles of late historicism. On the north-western side of the square, at the beginning of Kigyó utca, the Parisian Court (1911) displays its somewhat faded but fantastically designed art nouveau shopping arcade with shops and cafés that hold a particular nostalgic attraction. The stairwells, which have old-fashioned elevators, are worth exploring. This is also an opportunity to get a little closer to the interesting roof construction of the shopping arcade.

*Clothilde Palaces
The west side of the Franciscan square is framed by the two mirror-image Clothilde Palaces which open up a view of the Elizabeth Bridge. These buildings were constructed as apartment blocks in 1902 by Kálmán Giergl and Floris Korb, by order of the Habsburg Duchess Clothilde. Their magnificent, though in the meantime blackened, façades with their curved gables and turrets were inspired by Spanish Baroque architecture.

Franciscan church
In the northwest Fernciek tere opens into a small square that is encapsulated by the Franciscan church and the attached house of the

Franciscan order next door. After Turkish rule, during which it was turned into a mosque, the Franciscan church was demolished and replaced by a new Baroque building in the mid-18th century. The master builder Ferenc Wieser designed the historicist spire of the choir of the church in 1858.

Figures of St Peter of Alcantara, St Francis and St Anthony, as well as the coat of arms of the Franciscan order (above the portal) form the sculptural decoration of the main façade. A bronze relief on the northwestern exterior wall (on Kossuth Lajos utca) recalls Baron Wesselényi, who saved many people from drowning during the catastrophic floods of 1838.

A magnificent high altar has survived from the original **interior** of the church. The richly embellished side altars, as well as the wooden pulpit with its 12 apostles, were brought into the church in the 19th century. The walls are decorated by paintings by Károly Lotz (1895) and V. Tardos-Krenner, (1927).

Március 15 tér (15 March Square)

The square at the Pest bridgehead of the Elizabeth Bridge recalls 15 March 1848, when civil war broke out. The Romans left their mark here. The dominant building on Március tér is the inner city municipal church with its sweeping Baroque façade facing the Danube. Long before the building of the church the Romans had a camp here, Castrum Contra Aquincum, so called because it was located on the opposite side from the Aquincum garrison, on the unsecured side of the Danube at that time. Contra Aquincum therefore formed a forward defence post intended to protect the Danube crossing. The remains of this fortification, which were exposed and conserved during several excavation campaigns, along with historical documentation can be seen in the lower area of the square.

Petöfi tér

Március 15 tér to the northeast is named after the Hungarian poet Sándor Petöfi (▶Famous People p. 52), and serves as a stage for annual patriotic festivities on 15 March. A bronze memorial made by Adolf Huszár in 1882 commemorates Petöfi with some pathos in the middle of the square.

On the eastern side of Petöfi tér stands the **Greek Orthodox Church**, which was built to designs by József Jung in 1790 and remodelled by Miklós Ybl in the 19th century. The interior is memorable for an iconostasis by Miklós Jankovich and a painting by Anton Kochmeister.

❶ Mon–Thu 12 in the noon–4pm

*Danube Corso

The promenade along the Pest bank of the Danube, which begins between Március 15 tér and the ▶Chain Bridge, is called the Danube Corso (Dunakorzó). Particularly when it is illuminated in the evening, there are wonderful views of Fishermen's Bastion, the Matthias

The banks of the Danube for strolling and enjoying

Church, the Royal Palace and the Liberation Memorial on Gellért Hill from here. All in all, the Corso is a very busy place with much to do and see. Many of the top-class hotels in Budapest are located here; excursion boats stop on their trips up and down the river and quieter streets run into Pest. On level with the Vigado, a bronze princess with her back to the Danube by László Marton has watched the crowds go by on the promenade since 1990.

Below the Danube Corso the landing stages for the sightseeing ships (►Tours and Guides, p.116) are located. Various organizers offer either one-hour tours or longer excursions on the Danube. Between the Vigadó tér and the Chain Bridge a few restaurant boats have dropped their anchors.

Erzsébet-híd At Március 15. tér the modern Erzsébet híd crosses the Danube. The present bridge replaces a predecessor constructed from 1898 to 1903, which for many years was the largest arched bridge in the world. It was destroyed in the Second World War. The suspension bridge was built to designs by Pál Sávoly between 1961 and 1964, and is 378m long and almost 30m wide. Its rather sombre, modern design forms an attractive contrast to the Chain Bridge with its massive bridge posts. The bridge received its name from the Austrian Empress and Hungarian Queen Elizabeth (Sisi) who promoted the Compromise between Austria and Hungary. A memorial to the monarch, who is deeply honoured by Hungarians and was assassinated in 1898, by György Zala is today located north of the Buda bridgehead, in the middle of a small green space.

* Fishermen's Bastion

(Halászbástya)

A / B 6

Location: Szentháromság tér
Bus: 16, 16 A, 116

Fishermen's Bastion, next to Matthias Church, is probably one of the most visited and photographed buildings in Budapest by tourists from around the world. Visitors have a breathtaking view from the observation deck on the Danube and the riverside of Pest.

The bastion is one of the emblems of the Hungarian capital whose creation – like so many of Budapest's memorials – was closely associated with the jubilee celebrations in 1896. The name of the structure originates in the former purpose of this place: in the Middle Ages there was a defence post here for the Budapest guild of fishermen who used to hold their market on Castle Hill. The Budapest architect Frigyes Schulek (1841–1919), who had given the Matthias Church its present-day neo-Gothic appearance, seemed the best architect for the Fishermen's Bastion, which was built between 1895 and 1902. For the mighty bastion he chose Romanesque style, which he effectively mixed with designs inspired by other historic building eras. The picturesque ensemble of the old-style fortifications of the Fishermen's Bastion and the Gothic Matthias Church are typical of the romanticized picture of the Middle Ages that emerged during the course of the nationalist movement in the 19th century, to which architects such as Frigyes Schulek also paid tribute. The Fishermen's Bastion viewing platform commands a breathtaking panorama of the left bank of the Danube with Parliament and the Pest side of the city.

Romanticized castle

Popular Fishermen's Bastion

In 1906, Alajos Stróbl, one of the most popular sculptors of his day, created the bronze equestrian statue of the holy monarch Stephen (Szent István), who went down in history as the first Christian ruler of the Hungarians, for the southern courtyard at the Fishermen's Bastion. The plinth with its four lions and the reliefs around its sides showing scenes from the life of Stephen, was designed by Frigyes Schulek as well.

Equestrian Statue of Stephen

From the bastion, a magnificent double stairway leads down Castle Hill towards Víziváros, past a bronze sculpture of St George. At the foot of the staircase stands a bronze memorial to the statesman and military leader János Hunyadi (1905) by István Tóth.

Fővám tér (Customs Square)

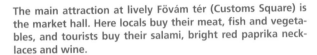

C 7

Tram: 47, 49
Trolley bus: 83
Bus: 15

The main attraction at lively Fővám tér (Customs Square) is the market hall. Here locals buy their meat, fish and vegetables, and tourists buy their salami, bright red paprika necklaces and wine.

Main customs house/ Corvinus University

The square at the Pest bridgehead of Freedom Bridge, the Szabadság híd, marks the south end of Váci utca. The two-storey main customs house in neo-Renaissance style, which stands side-on to the square, was built onto Fővám tér between 1871 and 1874 from designs made by Miklós Ybl, the architect of the Budapest opera house. The University of Business Sciences, today's Corvinus University has used the building since 1951, and the magnificent gala courtyard of the 170m-long building has been remodelled into an auditorium.

Central market hall (Központi vásárcsarnok)

The central market hall near the University was built by Samuel Pecz in 1896. Of the five market halls that were opened in Budapest at the end of the 19th century, this was the largest. Next to the West Railway Station (p. 177), it is a further example of an iron and glass construction in Budapest. The combination of a contemporary construction with traditional architectural forms is typical for these buildings at the transition to the modern age. In the case of the market hall, with its elevated centre joined to low aisle-type extensions, the architect has recalled the form of medieval churches. The locals appreciate the market hall most for the wealth of provisions on offer, from fresh fruit and vegetables, to spices, meat and sausages, as well as fish and baked goods. Even craftwork, textiles and basketwork are available here.

Popular: the market halls

❶ Mon 6am–5pm, Tue–Fri 6am–6pm, Sat 6am–2pm

The steel Freedom Bridge (Szabadság-híd) was opened to traffic in 1896 and connects Fővám tér with Gellért tér on the Buda side of the Danube. This 331m/362yd-long and 20m/22yd-wide metal construction was the first Danube bridge to be rebuilt after its destruction at the end of the Second World War, and was already re-opened by 1946.

Freedom Bridge

Franz Liszt Academy of Music

⬥ D 6

Location: Liszt Ferenc tér 8
Metro: M1 (Oktogon)
Tram: 4, 6
Bus: 4
ⓘ temporarily closed

The Academy of Music has a delightful foyer, while concerts in the large hall with its superb acoustics provide a veritable treat for the ears.

This musical educational facility named after Franz Liszt (▶Famous People p. 50) the founder of Budapest's first music school and initiator of a higher college of music, is today an academy that is known far beyond Hungary's borders. After Franz Liszt, famous music personalities such as Béla Bartók (Famous People p. 47) and Zoltán Kodály (p. 49) worked here. Furthermore, the academy owns the most important collection of Hungarian music literature. Built between 1904 and 1907, the building of the Franz Liszt Academy, an imposing mansion on Liszt Ferenc tér, is rightly considered a masterpiece of art nouveau in Budapest. The plans were drawn by the two architects Flóris Korb and Kálmán Giergl who had already collaborated on the Clothilde Palaces (Ferenciek tere). The seated bronze figure of Franz Liszt by Alajos Stróbl looks down from the main entrance; in the foyer the composers Béla Bartók and Frederic Chopin are honoured with a bust and a statue.

Famous music school

It is not absolutely necessary to attend a concert to view the **foyer**, though considering the superb acoustics in the large hall, this pleasure is highly recommended.. Not only the richly ornamented walls and columns are worth a look. The **large hall** is on the ground flour. With its two galleries it can hold an audience of up to 1200 and has unusually good acoustics. Attractive reliefs by the artists Groh and Telcs decorate the corners of the hall.

*Interior

The **small hall** on the first floor can hold an audience of around 400 and is less grand. The enchanting art nouveau wall painting *The Fountain of Youth* by painter Aladár Körös-fői-Kriesch portrays the origin of art.

✶✶ Gellért Bath (Gellért fürdő)

✦ C 8

Location: XI district, Kelenhegyi út 2–4
Tram: 18, 19, 41, 47, 49
Bus: 7, 86, 173
🕑 daily 6am–8pm

The famous medicinal spa and hotel is one of the most beautiful of its kind. Not only is it a wonderful swimming pool but also an important art nouveau monument in the Hungarian capital

One of the most beautiful spas in Budapest

A spa that already existed here in the 13th century used the thermal waters of Gellért Hill for healing treatments. According to a report by the chronicler Evliya celebi from Istanbul, the Turks turned the spa into a luxurious bathhouse, but the spa on Gellért Hill also enjoyed great popularity under the Habsburg rulers. After

The part of the Gellért bath restricted to men only

that building was demolished around the end of the 19th century, the present building, which has been restored to its former splendour, was created between 1911 and 1918 to designs in late Secessionist style by Ármin **Hegedűs**, Artúr Sebestyén and Izidor Stark that united the hotel and thermal baths under one roof. The opulently designed entrance to the thermal bath lies on the narrow Kelenhegi út, while the hotel and café face onto Szent Gellért tér. The spa installations, such as the thermal bath, the jacuzzi and saunas, as well as the exterior facilities with the wave pool, have all been modernized.

Gellért Hill

(Gellért-hegy; Witches' Citadel)

✴ **B / C 7 / 8**

Location: I and XI district
Tram: 18,19, 41, 47, 49
Bus: 27

Gellért Hill is probably the most notable feature of the Hungarian capital and offers fine views. The eastern flank of this chunk of dolomite drops steeply down towards the Danube. At its peak stands the Liberty Statue built in 1947: the 14m/46ft high figure with a palm frond is visible from far and wide.

The western side of the hill, on the other hand, consists of stepped terraces that were once vineyards. Several medicinal thermal springs rise along its geological fault line and feed the ▶Gellért Bath and the Rudas Bath. The hill is named after Bishop Gellért, who served during the time of King Stephen I (around 974–1038). There are various legends regarding his death in 1046: one of them says that the martyr was rolled down the hill in a barrel; another says that he was harnessed to a wagon, stoned, and his heart pierced by a lance. In earlier times, another legend held that Gellért Hill was a witches' citadel. The Turks kept a small fortification on Gellért Hill and the Habsburg troops occupied the excellent observation post during the liberation wars in 1848–49. Since the end of the 19th century a well-to-do villa district has developed on the slopes of Gellért Hill, which is considered one of the city's best residential areas.

Observation hill with healing springs

? *Witches Hill*

MARCO ● POLO INSIGHT

In past times Gellért Hill was considered to be meeting point for witches. This mirrors the Budapestians liking for the supernatural. This is why fearful souls avoided being on Gellért Hill after dusk.

Bathing in Style

What can be more relaxing than enjoying recuperation from the city's hectic in a Turkish thermal bath or an art nouveau swimming pool? This is exactly the purpose of these institutions. The Romans as well as the Turkish Pashas already enjoyed the thermal baths. The Danube metropolis can be considered an Eldorado for wellness fans (▶MARCO POLO Insight p. 174).

Budapest is favoured by nature as is the entire Carpathian Basin. The crust of the earth is especially thin, which is why thermal water easily finds its way to the surface. No less than 123 thermal springs bubble in Budapest, some natural, others were made accessible by drilling. No matter where you drill into the earth in Hungary, sooner or later you will strike thermal water. The hot springs were already known to the Celts. They called the region ak inc (rich water). Later the Roman city name Aquincum derived from it. The garrison, which camped on the site of what now is Óbuda became the nucleus of Budapest. Because the Romans always enjoyed their thermal baths they constructed large bathing facilities in Aquincum, which still can be admired today.

Hamams

After the Romans left the hot springs apparently weren't used actively until the late Middle Ages. The Renaissance King Matthias supposedly was a friend of bathing but it wasn't until the Turks arrived that bathing culture established itself once more. As they conquered Buda in the mid of the 16th century they made themselves at home. The Paschas were delighted about

the richness of thermal springs in the city and therefore created sublime Hamams.

The most impressive example is today's **Rudas Spa** at the fool of Gellért Hill, which was expanded by Pasha Mustafa Sokollu in 1566. The exterior may seem unimpressive but upon entering the visitor steps into an oriental world. The central dome is supported by eight pillars. Only the sounds of the murmuring of the guests and the soft splashing of the 36° warm water can be heard. Surrounding the central pool are smaller ones with various water temperatures between 16 and 42° C.

Another Turkish spa is the **Király Spa**. Here Mustafa Sokollu was involved as well after his predecessor Arslan had started the construction. Arslan had an underground pipeline laid from today's Lukás spa because he did not want to miss his bath in thermal waters when the city was under siege. The Hungarian name of the bath »Király« (»King«) derives from the family name König. They remodelled the spa in a neoclassicistic style at the beginning of the 19th century.

The third Turkisch spa is the **Rácz Spa**. It is part of a luxurious hotel with the same name that will reopen shortly. The classicist expansion

Hardly any bathing desires cannot be fulfilled in the large Széchenvi bath

from the 19th century by Miklós Ybl was restored in the process as well.

Palaces of the 19th Century

Thermal baths became en vogue once more in the 19th century. They also spawned a growing popularity of the bathing culture. This becomes evident through two wonderful bathing palaces, which are further landmarks of the city. On the edge of Gellért Hill a true bathing temple was erected together with the Gellért Hotel. With its swimming pool framed by pillars and the art nouveau thermal area **Gellért Bath** (►p. 168) represents one of the architectural highlights of Budapest. The pool area is open to everyone while there are seperate, identical thermal areas for men and women. An open-air pool is connected to the premesis and open in summer, here the first wave machine of Hungary was installed.

Another bathing palace was built on the Pest side of the Danube. The **Széchenvi Spa** represents an accomplished mixture of a family-friendly open air pool and relaxing thermal bath. The chess players are famous. Withstanding the 37° C hot water they serenely play along for hours, analyzing the moves of their opponents. Széchenvi Spa is especially pleasant in the winter. When it is freezing cold outside and foggy steam floats across the water the experience becomes particularly relaxing and an excellent cure for possible winter depression.

Many thermal baths also include a medical department and can offer a healing massage on the spot.

MARCO ◈ POLO TIP

!

A marvellous view   Insider Tip

From the observation deck at the access road to Gellért Hill there is an overwhelming view on the Royal Palace, the Danube and the banks of Pest. It is especially recommendable in the night time when everything is illuminated.

On the north-eastern slope of Gellért Hill, above the bridgehead for the Elizabeth Bridge, stands the monumental bronze sculpture of the bishop and martyr St Gellért. It was created by Gyula Jankovits in 1902 and is bordered by a semi-circular colonnade. An artificial waterfall splashes beneath the memorial. The best view of the memorial is from the Elizabeth Bridge, which leads directly towards the pointed cliff that gives the saint's statue its dramatic site. In order to see the saint from close up, it is necessary to climb up the steps from the bridgehead. It takes about 20 minutes to continue from the memorial to the summit of the hill and its citadel (see below), an enjoyable walk with wonderful views of the city and the Danube.

Citadella   The Citadella, built at the highest point of Gellért Hill between 1850 and 1854 is still in good condition. The fortification was militarily unnecessary at that time and its intended function was probably to remind the population of Buda and Pest, who had risen up against Habsburg rule in 1848, of Austrian hegemony and to warn against further liberation attempts. Part of the fortress, which is over 200m/650ft long and up to 60m/200ft wide, is today open to tourists. A large firework display is held here every year on the Hungarian national holiday of 20 August.

❶ mid March–mid Oct daily 8am–10pm, mid Oct to mid March, daily 9am–4pm www.citadella.hu; admission: 1200 HUF

Liberation   The Liberation Memorial, also known as Liberty Statue, was erected
Memorial   on the southeastern tip of Gellért Hill in 1947 to honour the Soviet soldiers who fell during the fight against fascism during the Second World War, and despite a revised view of history, has emerged as one of Budapest's emblems. It is made up of a colossal 14m/46ft-high female figure standing on a limestone pedestal and holding a palm frond in her raised arms. The two heroic male figures at the feet of the triumphant Goddess of Victory embody progress and destruction. Originally, there was also a flag-carrying Soviet soldier between them, who can today be viewed with the other monumental statues of the Soviet era at the ▶Memento Park.

Jubileumi   Jubileumi Park has attractive promenades and fine statues, among
Park   them also the work by István Kiss. With its generously proportioned children's playground and green spaces, this park attracts many visitors on nice days.

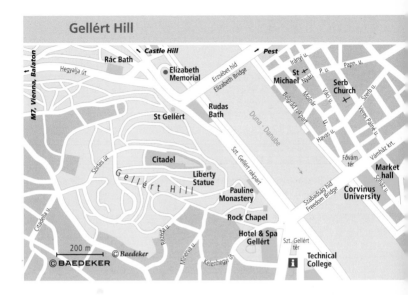

The old Rudas Bath (Rudas fürdö) lies at the foot of Gellért Hill, close to the Buda bridgehead of the ▶Elizabeth Bridge (Döbrentei tér 9). The thermal springs here were already in use during the Middle Ages and the first bath house was built at that period. The Turks extended the facilities in the 16th century and the typical dome construction with the octagonal central room survives from that time. In addition to the steam bath, it is possible to enjoy the medicinal waters of the Juventus and Hungária springs in a drinking hall. While textile-free bathing in the Turkish bath was the preserve of men until 2006, there is now a visiting day reserved for women 6am–8pm.

Rudas Bath

At the main entrance to the Géllert Cave lies the cave or cliff chapel (Sziklaká-polna), based on the grotto at Lourdes and founded by the Pauline order in 1931. The Pauline order was active in Hungary from the 14th century onwards, but was dissolved by Joseph II in 1786 and only readmitted in 1931. The grotto was blocked off after the Communists dissolved the order once more at the beginning of the 1950s, but it has been accessible again since 1992. The chapel is almost always open, except during mass.

The Pauline monastery (Szent Gellért rakpart 1/a) nearby dates from 1932 and can only be viewed from outside. It was home to students of the Budapest ballet institute from the dissolution of the order by the Communists until 1989. After that, the building was returned to the Pauline order.

Pauline monastery

Europe's Thermal Capital

Nowhere else on the European mainland do so many thermal springs emerge to the surface than in Budapest. More than 120 thermal springs rise along a fault line which stretches from Gellért Hill in the southwest to Margaret Island on the north tip and supply a daily amount of 70 million litres of mineral water.

The 20–78 °C warm waters contain broad varieties of hydro-chemical mixture. 21 baths and pools, 10 healing spas with drinking fountains and balneological departments included, are supplied by these waters.

Pünkösdfürdői

Csillaghegy
Római

Újpe

Dagály

Palatinus
Lukács
Király
Szécheny

Rudas   Budapes
Gellért
Dandár

Pesterzsébeti

Csepeli

▶ **Janos Molnár Cave**
(Molnár Janos barlang)
The millpond (Malom-tó) lies opposite of Lucas Bath where a Turkish powder mill used to stand. This pond supplies the neighbouring spas Lukás fürdő and Király fürdő. The pond is also the source for the thermal water cave system, one of the largest of its kind. It is only accessible for divers.

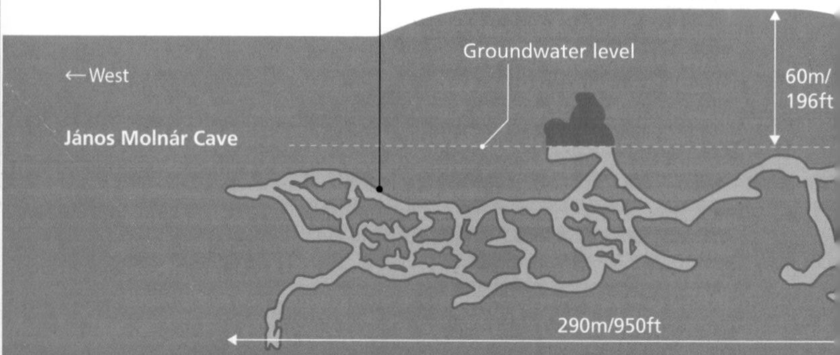

Buda Hills (Budai-hegység)

Groundwater level

60m/
196ft

←West

János Molnár Cave

290m/950ft

▶ **Gellért Bath**

The thermal healing waters of Gellért Bath rise from the inner of Gellért Hill. They contain calcium, magnesium, hydrogen carbonate, sodium, sulphate, chloride and fluoride. The water helps with joint and back pains, rheumatic aches, neuralgia, circularly disorders and diseases of the respiratory organs.

▶ **Water components**

Only one thousandth of a litre results in other components of water. The average in chemical composition of the thermal water of the spa on Margaret Island is:

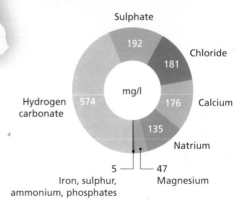

Sulphate 192
Chloride 181
Calcium 176
Hydrogen carbonate 574
mg/l
Natrium 135
Magnesium 47
Iron, sulphur, ammonium, phosphates 5

Strand-/Freibad
Heil-/Thermalbad

Paskál

©BAEDEKER

Turkish powder mill, millpond (Malom-tó)

Lukács Bath

Danube

Margaret Island/ Margitsziget

East →

▶ **Formation of mineral water**

Mineral water results from rainfall that seeps into the earth. The water percolates through various geological layers and thereby collects minerals and trace elements. With increasing depth the temperature rises. Especially underneath Budapest the water accumulates carbon dioxide which rises from the deeper earth's crust along the fault line as a result of magmatic processes.

Gödöllő

──────────────────────────── ✳ Excursion

Access: with the car via M 3
Metro: 2 to Örs vezér tere, then switch to Tram HÉV 8 to
Gödöllő Szabadság tér

The attraction of a trip to Gödöllő is its palace in which Empress Elizabeth liked to stay. Extensive restoration work has restored the building to its former glory.

**Gödöllő
Palace

An extensive park surrounds the Baroque palace in the middle of town, which Prince Antal Grassalkovich built in close proximity to his estates between 1744 and 1748. The building plans for the princely residence were drawn up by the famous architect Andreas Mayerhoffer. First a building including three wings and a chapel was built. This design became an archetype for other castles in Hungary, known as the Grassalkovich type. Later further additions in the form of more wings were made. Hungary gave the palace – Europe's largest Baroque palace after Versailles – to its ruling couple after the Austro-Hungarian Compromise of 1867. Empress Elizabeth (»Sisi«) loved to spend time here. Magnificent halls, salons and princely quarters, including Sisi's dressing room, are today part of the **palace museum**, which offers an interesting insight into the luxurious life of the nobility of the 18th and 19th centuries. A memorial exhibition covers the life and death of the empress so deeply cherished in Hungary. The **Baroque theatre** in the south wing, which still contains unique original stage sets, can be viewed during performances and tours.

❶ April–Oct Thu–Sun 10am–6pm, Nov–Mar Thu–Sun 10am–5pm; www.kiralyikastely.hu; admission: 1800 HUF

Great Ring (Nagykörút)

──────────────────────────── ✳ B 4 – D 8

Tram: 4, 6

The Great Ring Road (Nagykörút) arcs around Pest city centre in a semi-circle over 4km/2.4mi long from the eastern bridgehead of the Margaret Bridge (Margit hid) to the eastern bridgehead of Petöfi Bridge. The West Railway Station designed by the Parisian firm Eiffel is an outstanding building here.

»Imperial«
boulevard

With the exception of Szent István körút, the individual sections of the Great Ring are named after members of the Austrian imperial house: Teréz körút (Theresa), Erzsébet körút (Elizabeth), József körút

(Joseph), Ferenc körút (Franz). Opened to traffic in 1896, the Great Ring follows a drained arm of the Danube. Numerous significant buildings from the fin-de-siècle era line the Nagykörút.

Szent István körút is the northernmost section of the Great Ring. It begins at Jászai Mari tér, which is named after Mari Jászai (1850–1926), who was one of the greatest European actresses of her day. The highlight of this section of the ring is the Comedy Theatre no.14, built to plans by Fellner & Helmer from Vienna in the 1890s and re-built after severe war damage.

Szent István körút

Extended at great cost after 1978, Nyugati tér (West Square) also acts as a forecourt to the West Railway Station (Nyugati pályaudvar), a protected monument which, next to the market hall, is the most important and perhaps most beautiful example of cast-iron architecture in the Hungarian capital. The first trains in Hungary departed from the site of the West Railway Station as early as 1846. It is a terminus comprising two brick side-buildings with superimposed brick walls and a glass-roofed hall above the railway tracks at the centre. The platform hall is supported by filigree cast-iron supports, like the ones developed for the Crystal Palace in London. The Eiffel firm in Paris produced the designs for what at the time was a highly modern construction. It is well worth taking a look into the interior of the platform hall: everything appears to be as in the old days. Being at the end of the line, the Nyugati pályaudvar is only significant for local transport.

*West Railway Station

From the West Railway Station, Teréz körút (Theresa Ring) leads to **Erzsébet körút (Elizabeth Ring)**. Several noteworthy buildings stand along Erzsébet körút. The Madách Theatre (Madách Színház) opened in 1961 and evolved out of a tavern built in the 19th century. The wall mosaics by Eszter Mattioni are an attractive feature of this much-frequented venue.

> **!**
> MARCO POLO TIP
>
> *The former meeting place* — Insider Tip
>
> In the first three decades of the 20th century the famous and opulent café New York (Erzsébet körút no. 9 – 11) was the meeting place of the trendy scene par excellence and renowned far beyond Europe. It was reopened after thorough renovation in 2006. It is located in the ground floor of an ostentatious neo-Renaissance house that was originally built for the New York insurance company from 1891 until 1893 and now functions as a luxury hotel.

The last section of the Great Ring runs right through District IX, formerly known as Francistown (Ferencváros). Like the district, the street was named after the Austrian Emperor Franz I. Like so many other southeastern districts, Ferencváros is characterized by industrial settlements and workshops.

Francistown

SOUTH OF THE GREAT RING

Holocaust Museum
The first Holocaust Museum of eastern Europe (2003) lies in Ferencváros (Franz Cizy) south of the ring on the corner of Tözelto/Páva utca. It consists of the modern, mostly underground exhibition rooms, designed by the Hungarian architect István Mányi, and a synagogue from 1924 by architect Leopold Baumhorn. A black memorial was set up in the courtyard where the names of the Hungarian Holocaust victims are engraved.

❶ Thu–Sun 10am–6pm; www.hdke.hu; admission: 1400 HUF

Zwack Museum

Insider Tip

The history of the businessman Zwack in Ferencváros goes back to an exclamation of Emeror Joseph II. The emperor supposedly proclaimed: »This is a Unicum!«, after he had taken a dose of bitters from Zwack, doctor of the royal court. This became the name of Hungary's most famous herbal liqueur. The family-run business has been selling it since the mid 19th century. In the old manufacturing buildings an exhibition as well as a movie show the firm's varied history. The grownups may enjoy a taste later on.

❶ Soroksári út 26; Mon–Fri 10am–6pm; www.zack.hu

National Theatre, modern and controversial

South of the Great Ring the so-called Millenial City was developed in recent years on the banks of the Danube between Petõfi bridge and Rákóczi bridge (until 2011: Lágymánvosi bridge). The area was originally planned to become the site of the World's Fair, which was supposed to be held together with Vienna. Today high-rises for business and living space dominate the north. In the south part the arcitecturally interesting National Theatre (Nemzeti Színház) was opened in 2002 while the ▶Palace of Arts (Komor Marcell utca 1) opened in 2005. The National Theatre of Dance has its headquarters in the National Theatre, designed by architect Mária Siklós. Concert halls – including the National Concert Hall with its marvellous acoustics – and the renowned Ludwig Museum are located in the Palace of Arts.

Millenial City

National Theatre: www.nemzetiszinhaz.hu

** Great Synagogue

✦ C 6

Location: VII, Dohány utca. 2
Metro: M 1, M 2, M 3
Trolley bus: 74
Bus: 5, 7, 7A, 78, 173
Tram: 47, 49

The Great Synagogue (Dohány utcai zsinagóga) on Dohány utca (Tobacco Lane), also known as Tobacco Synagogue, is one of the most significant and historically important monuments in Budapest.

The greatly increased Jewish community inaugurated its new synagogue in 1859 at the border between the old city of Pest and the newer district of Elizabeth Town (VII district), which was soon to become a ghetto. It was constructed in the Moorish-Byzantine style of romantic historicism to plans by the architect Ludwig Förster. Two polygonal towers over 30m/100ft high dominate the façade. The interior of the synagogue, which can hold around 3000 people, was designed by Hungarian artists and craftsmen, including the famous architect Frigyes Feszl. Delicate columns of cast iron form the filigree supporting structure for the broad triple-aisled room. The two side aisles have galleries for the women. The magnificent organ has been played in the past by such renowned musicians as Franz (Ferenc) Liszt and Camille Saint-Saëns.

Historically significant structure

A cemetery for the martyrs of the Budapest Ghetto can be found in the garden of the Great Synagogue. Several thousand Jewish victims of fascism are buried here in two mass graves.

On Survival

The Jewish community has made its mark on Budapest for centuries. Especially on the eve of the 19th century their influence was important for the cultural and economic prosperity of the metropolis on the Danube. In Elisabethtown, which was named after the Austrian and Hungarian queen Sisi and was the larges ghetto during the Second World War, Jewish culture and way of life - withstanding the attempts of the Nazis to eradicate it – are still vivid.

The entirety of the horror of the Holocaust is also revealed by the numbers, which unravel terrible efficiency of the national socialist killing machinery. More than 500,000 of the 820,000 Hungarian Jews were murdered in Auschwitz. Approximately 200,000 lived in Budapest, which was attractive for Jews at the end of the 19th century because of its liberal laws in real estate acquisition, practising a profession and also its cosmopolitan flairs.

The new residents soon adapted to city life. As in other European cities Jews influenced the development of their hometown in a unique way. The city's climate still was relatively free of resentment at the beginning of the 20th century. Jews worked as craftsmen, businessmen, were restaurant and café owners and managed cultural institutions.

Life in the Ghetto

As in most of Europe most of them could hardly believe what was going on. In November 1944 however the Nazis made a ghetto out of Jewish quarter Elisabeth town, enclosed with a board fence. 2600 buildings were marked as »star houses« and assigned to Jews from the whole city. As the Red Army freed the ghetto on the 18th of January 1945 65,000 people were living here.

A further ghetto existed in District XIII of New Leopoldtown.

Thousands of Budapest Jews owe their lives to Swedish diplomat Raoul Wallenberg. He issued a pass of protection to every family that could somehow prove some kind of connection to Sweden, even if it was only a random address, copied a Swedish telephone book.

Wallenberg himself, who arrived in Budapest on the 9th of July 1944 with two backpacks, a sleeping bag and a gun, was arrested by the Soviets. His fate never was resolved.

The Great Synagogue

A Long History

Judaism may look back on a long history in Budapest. In the 11th century Jews received the certified right to practice their religion freely by Béla IV. From the 13th century onward they were in charge of the financial matters of the monarch as treasurers. The coinage was then located in the Royal Palace, which became the heart of the developing Jewish quarter. At the end of the 18th century the Jewish community moved to Pest where the Great Synagoge was built between 1854 and 1859 in today's Dohány utca.

A Thora shield in the Jewish Museum

Judaism Today

Today approximately 80,000 Jews live in Budapest. Many of those in Elizabethtown, the quarter of the city with the highest population density, District VII. Hardly anything was undertaken under Soviet rule to preserve the bourgeois buildings. The apartments and buildings were divided into smaller and smaller entities in order to fit double, later three or four times more people than originally intended. Nevertheless the quarter enfolds its unique atmosphere due to the interlacing and intertwining backyards and alleyways. Kosher restaurants and butchers, festivities like the Jewish Culture Festival and the synagogues are proof of a vivid and lovingly preserved culture. The Jewish Museum keeps the memory of the most prosperous times alive.

The Great Synagogue is the religious centre of the liberal Jewish community. It was restored a few years ago with the financial support of the American actor Tony Curtis who is the son of a Jewish emigrant. A few steps away in Rumbach Sebestvén utca stands the so-called Status quo Synagogue, which was built after a split in the Jewish community. The orthodox community settled in Kazinczy utca at the beginning of the 20th century and built a wonderful art nouveau synagogue. The rabbi seminar (VIII., József körút) is unique in Middle Eastern Europe. The rabbinic education survived all repressions and proves that Jewish life in Budapest and in the region has a future. Jewish cook shops around Klauzál Square, the former central square of the ghetto, and its side streets enable a direct experience with Jewish culture. Here you can find all kinds of specialties such as »gefilte fis« or »sólet« a stew with beans and goose meat , and »pászka« a bread with unleavened dough. Finally have some almond bread for dessert.

Great Synagogue

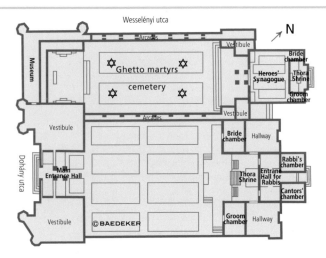

In front of the martyrs' cemetery stands the smaller **Heroes' Synagogue**, also built in oriental style, which was erected in the 1930s for the Hungarian Jewish soldiers who fell in the First World War.

❶ Mar–Oct Mon–Thu, Sun, 10am–5.30pm, Fri till 2.30pm; 2 Nov–Feb Mon–Thu, Sun 10am–3.30pm, Fri till 2.30pm; www.greatsynagogue.hu; admission: 2250 HUF (incl. Jewish Museum)

*Jewish Museum

The Jewish Museum has been built on the spot where Theodor Herzl's (▶Famous People) birthplace stood next to the Great Synagogue, on the corner of Dohány utca and Wesselényi utca. It houses one of the most extensive collections of Central European Jewish sacred art, including many valuable items, such as old Torah and Talmud scripts, Hanukkah candlesticks, as well as other items used during celebrations and also in daily life. The Holocaust is recalled in a separate room.

Holocaust Memorial

In the small garden at the back of the Great Synagogue, a memorial by the artist Imre Varga to the victims of the Hungarian holocaust was inaugurated in 1992: a weeping willow, whose leaves – small metal plates – are each engraved with the name of a Jewish victim of fascism.

Orthodox synagogue

Budapest's orthodox Jews built their main art nouveau synagogue (orthodox zsinagógx) on Kazinczv utca between 1911 and 1913. The

blue orthodox synagogue by Béla and Sándor is one of the largest in Europe; the community however is quite small today. (The entrance can be found in a backyard next to Dob utca no. 35.)
❶ Mon-Fri, Sun 10am–12:30pm

The Jewish ghetto was located on Wesselényi utca. A relatively high percentage of Budapest's Jews were saved from the abuses of fascist thugs, not least because the Swedish embassy and its legate Raoul Wallenberg bought dozens of houses in Budapest, which it considered its sovereign territory. The Budapest ghetto was the only one of its kind liberated (by Soviet troops) in time to prevent the planned deportation of its inhabitants (▶MARCO POLO Insight p.180).   **Jewish ghetto**

Lively trade has sprung up in this quarter once more. Especially around Klauzál tér it is now possible to buy kosher food, sample excellent wine and enjoy other kosher specialities.

** Hősök tere (Heroes' Square)

E 4

Metro: M 1 (Hősök tere)
Trolley bus: 75, 79
Bus: 4, 20, 30, 105

Spacious Heroes' Square on the western edge of the ▶Városliget Woods forms the imposing finale for ▶Andrássy út, which leads directly to this square from the city centre. Skateboarders do their turns under the stern gaze of the Hungarian national heroes while traffic buzzes all around.

The occasion for creating a monumental memorial for the heroes of Hungarian history was the celebration of the 1896 millennium jubilee. The architect Albert Schickedanz and the sculptor György Zala were entrusted with the design of the square. Heroes' Square was only completed in 1927, three decades after building began.   **Historic square**

Over the past hundred years, Hősök tere has again and again been a stage for decisive moments in Hungarian history. During the 1918–19 revolution, the sculpture of Emperor Franz Joseph was smashed as a symbol for the break with the Habsburgs, the entire square draped with red cloth, and the statues of Árpád replaced with a sculpture of Marx and a monument to workers and farmers. Hősök tere was also repeatedly the stage for political demonstrations after 1945, as well as in 1989, when Imre Nagy (▶Famous People) and his companions were posthumously rehabilitated in a solemn ceremony of state.

Heroes Square has consistently been the stage for important events

*Millennium Memorial (Millenniumi emlékmü)

The Millennium Memorial is the dominant monument on the square. Visible from afar, the 36m/118ft-high column crowned by a bronze figure of the Archangel Gabriel – a work by György Zala – rises between the two semi-circular colonnades. The bronze equestrian group at the base of the monument represents the seven Magyar chieftains of the Árpád dynasty who are credited with conquering the land in 896. Hungarian kings from the Árpád dynasty to the Anjou dynasty were placed in the left colonnade; on the right, statues honour Hungary's revolutionary heroes. Sculptures by György Zala crown the corner pillars of the colonnades. The bronze figures embody work and wealth, war and peace (the chariot to the left of the column is war, the one to the right is peace), and also science and fame. On the square in front of the millennium column there is a memorial stone for the national heroes who have fought for Hungary's freedom and independence.

Art Exhibition Hall

The building to the right of the Millennium Memorial is also part of the construction activities for the 1896 jubilee. The magnificent building completed in 1895 was built as an art exhibition hall in neo-classical style to plans by Albert Schickedanz. Today the works of contemporary Hungarian artists, including works by famous craftsmen, designers and photographers, are presented in this large exhibition hall.

❶ Tue–Sun 10am–6pm

✳ Inner City Parish Church
(Belvárosi plébániatemplom)

✦ C 7

Location: Március 15 tér
Tram: 2, 2 A
Bus: 7, 8, 15

The inner city parish church (Belvárosi plébanis-templon) is the oldest religious building in the Pest quarter of the city. It stands on the remains of the Roman Castrum Contra Aquincum, at the Pest bridgehead of the Elizabeth Bridge. In time it underwent a plenty of change in its architectural structure.

A small church, in which Bishop Gellért was interred in 1046, existed on the site in the 11th century. The building received a semi-circular choir in the 12th century, when the church was already under the patronage of the royal family. A major extension in the French Gothic style took place under King Sigismund, and Pest's main church received its side chapels in the second half of the 15th century. Under Turkish rule the inner city parish church was used as a mosque. Relics of a Turkish mihrab (prayer niche) still survive on the south-eastern wall of the choir today.

Church with varied history

The church was badly damaged during a fire in 1723 and received its present-day appearance during the Baroque reconstruction undertaken by Georg Paur, who began with the erection of the south tower in 1726 and completed the work with the northern tower in 1739–40. Jòzsef Hild undertook a restoration of the church in classical style during the years 1805–08. However, this was altered four decades later by Imre Steindl, who remodelled it in Gothic style. After the church was badly damaged during the Second World War, rebuilding began in 1948; but with the reconstruction of the ▶Elizabeth Bridge from 1961 onwards, an urban planning problem emerged at the Pest side of the bridgehead. The inner city parish church was simply in the way, a problem that was solved by leaving a truly breathtakingly narrow space between the bridge and the church.

Two building styles, Gothic and Baroque, characterize the church: the nave and the double-tower façade have survived in the Baroque

Exterior

style, whereas the choir, which is almost as long as the nave, retains its Gothic appearance. There is a beautiful Holy Trinity statue by Anton Hörger over the main portal on the west. Hörger, a sculptor from Buda, also created the figure of St Florian behind the choir, which was erected to honour the patron saint after the great fire of 1723.

Interior The interior is that of a vaulted hall church without aisles but with four chapels on each side. Adjoining to the east is the wonderful Gothic ambulatory choir, which is clearly separated from the nave by its narrow supports. Also of note are the two Renaissance epitaphs of red and light yellow marble in the northern chapels. The pulpit of 1808 is the work of the Pest master carpenter Philipp Ungnad. Fragments of 15th-century Gothic frescoes can be admired in the spaces between the pointed arches in the polygonal southern chapel. The present high altar is the work of Károly Antal and Pál Molnár and dates from 1948.

Municipal Parish Church

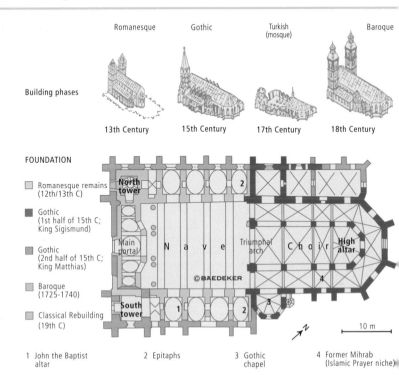

Building phases

Romanesque	Gothic	Turkish (mosque)	Baroque
13th Century	15th Century	17th Century	18th Century

FOUNDATION

- ☐ Romanesque remains (12th/13th C)
- ■ Gothic (1st half of 15th C; King Sigismund)
- ■ Gothic (2nd half of 15th C; King Matthias)
- ■ Baroque (1725-1740)
- ☐ Classical Rebuilding (19th C)

North tower

Main portal

N a v e   Triumphal arch   C h o i r   High altar

©BAEDEKER

South tower

10 m

1 John the Baptist altar

2 Epitaphs

3 Gothic chapel

4 Former Mihrab (Islamic Prayer niche)

Károlyi Palace

✦ C 7

Location: VI district, Károlyi Mihály utca 16
Underground: M 3 (Ferenciek tere)
Bus: 15

Károlyi Palace, a mansion with a colourful history, today houses the Petőfi-Museum.

The building named after its last owner, the Hungarian politician and first president of the republic Mihály Károlyi (1875–1955), was built as a single-storey townhouse at the end of the 17th century. An 18th-century Rococo façade had to give way to renovation in the new classical style in 1832–34. Hungary's first prime minister, Count Lajos Batthyány, was arrested here in 1849. There is a memorial room in honour of Mihály Károlyi. **History**

The literature museum carries the name of Hungary's most famous poet from the revolutionary era, Sándor Petőfi (▶Famous People). It contains exhibits from Hungarian literature and collections of texts by the country's outstanding poets and writers. Manuscripts, books and magazines, an audio archive and works by various artists make a visit to the museum worthwhile. Changing exhibitions complement the main presentation. **Petőfi Museum**
❶ Tue–Sun 10pm–6am

In the back of the palace a small space of green stretches onward. The downtown area of Pest is not exactly spoilt with parks, which is why the former private gardens of the Károlyis represent a welcome opportunity of rest and relaxation. **Garden**

✶ Kossuth Lajos tér

✦ B 5

Location: V district
Metro: M 2 (Kossuth Lajos tér)
Tram: 2, 2A

The large Kossuth Lajos tér (Laios Kossuth Square), framed by monumental showpieces, is one of the most impressive squares of the Hungarian capital.

On its western flank stands the former Palace of Justice which today houses the ▶Ethnographic Museum, as well as the Agricultural Min- **Opulent square** istry (Földmüvelésügyi Minisztérium), built in the neoclassical style in 1885. The southern side of Kossuth Lajos tér is taken up by the modern building of the Hungarian Chamber of Commerce, which was completed in 1972.

Memorials A memorial recalling the Battle of Independence in 1848 has stood on the northern side of the green square since 1952. **Lajos Kossuth** (▶Famous People), who went down in history as the man who proclaimed Hungarian independence, stands at the highest point of the memorial. The figures on the lower pedestals represent the Hungarian people taking up Kossuth's call to resistance against Austria. There were already uprisings against Habsburg rule 150 years earlier. They are remembered on the opposite, narrow side of the square, with an equestrian statue of Prince **Ferenc Rákóczi II**, created by János Pásztor in 1935. He is honoured as the most important leader of the fight for independence in the early 18th century. On the small green space at the entrance to Vecsey utca stands a small bridge as a memorial to Imre Nagy (▶Famous People), whose reforming policies cost him his life in 1956.

Imposing buildings The roads north and east of Kossuth Lajos tér are characterized by imposing buildings, whose façades reflect the stylistic variety of late historicism. Several of these are seats of ministries, including the buildings at Honvéd utca 13–15, in which the Ministry for International Economic Relations resides, and those at Honvéd utca 26–30, which house the Ministry of Defence. The continuation of Honvéd utca has lovely art nouveau townhouses.

Falk Miksa utca From Kossuth Lajos tér the narrow Falk Miksa utca leads to the ▶Great Ring. This alley has developed into the centre of Hungarian art trade. Here antique shops and galleries reside door to door.

Little Ring (Kiskörút)

✳ C 6 / 7

Location: V district
Tram: 47, 49
Bus: 7, 8, 9, 109, 173

The Little Ring, between the ▶Chain Bridge and the Freedom Bridge (▶Fövám tér), encompasses the old city centre of Pest, which is today referred to as Budapest city centre. This ring road traces the old city walls of Pest.

Sections The individual sections of the Little Ring have their own names: József Attila utca, Bajcsy-Zsilinszky út, Deák Ferenc tér, Károly körút,

Múzeum körút, Kálvin tér and Vámház körút. Erzsébet tér also counts as part of the Little Ring.

Erzsébet tér was once a cemetery. Today, the Danubius Fountain, designed by Miklós Ybl, stands in the middle of the green space of the square. Copies replaced the fountain figures by Leó Feszler in 1959, after severe damage during the Second World War. They symbolize the Danube and its great tributaries, the Drava, Tisza and Sava. A marble memorial by György Kiss in honour of Mrs Veres (1815–95), who dedicated herself to the provision of education for women, was erected on the eastern side of the square in 1906. On the north-western side of the square the bronze shepherd by J. Horvay has been playing his pipes since 1929.

Erzsébet tér

Ferenc Deák Square (Deák Ferenc tér), which adjoins Erzsébet tér, is one of the most important traffic junctions in the city centre. The three underground lines meet here. The **Lutheran Church** (Evangélikus templom) on the south side of the square is a monument of a special kind. The building of this church was begun ten years after Emperor Joseph II's religious toleration edict in 1781, which permitted membership of the Protestant churches and the building of Protestant places of worship. It was completed by Mihály Pollack in 1809. The church received its classical entrance portal crowned by a pediment during the renovation by József Hild in 1856. The altar is notable for its copy of Raphael's *Transfiguration*.

Deák Ferenc tér

> **MARCO ⊕ POLO TIP**
>
> ! *On the beginnings of the Metro* Insider Tip
>
> The Underground Museum (Földalatti Vasút Múzeum) is located in a tunnel underneath the Deák Ferenc tér. The first electric underground train drove through this tunnel. The documents, modules and explanation signs are only moderately interesting. The wagons and trains of the pioneering days of the public transportation are very well worth the visit. Opening times: Tue–Sun 10am–5pm

Mihály Pollack also designed the building adjacent to the church, a parish office and Protestant secondary school, which today houses the small **Protestant National Museum** (Evangelikus Országos Múzeum). Diverse liturgical objects and many important documents of the Hungarian Protestant Church can be viewed in this museum. The absolute highlight of the exhibition is the will written by Martin Luther in 1542.

Protestant National Museum: Tue–Sun 10am–6pm

Rákóczi út is one of the Hungarian capital's liveliest shopping streets. It is lined by several large department stores and a wide selection of small but exclusive shops and major cultural facilities. This traffic artery named after the leader of the independence movement of the

*Rákóczi út

early 18th century, Prince Rákóczi, is a continuation of Kossuth Lajos and leads to the East Railway Station. Rákóczi út was already an important transport route in the Middle Ages, when it led to the eastern Pest city gate (Hatvan Gate), which stood at the present-day junction of Rákóczi út and the Little Ring. After the construction of the East Railway Station in 1884, many high-rise office and department stores were built here. This is also where the College for Theatre and Film Arts (Színmüvészeti Föiskola) and the adjoining Odry Theatre (Odry színház) are based. The Uránia cinema with its oriental design is also connected to the building complex. It frequently hosts grand premieres of Hungarian films.

Múzeum Körút

Two leading Hungarian educational and cultural institutions can be found on **Museum Ring**. Imre Steindl, builder of the parliament, and Antal Weber designed the buildings of the natural science faculty of the Eötvös Loránd University in neo-Renaissance style. The design for the Hungarian ▶National Museum is by Mihály Pollack. The house at no. 7, completed by Miklós Ybl in 1852, is also noteworthy. Fragments of the Pest city wall were found in the courtyards of houses no. 17 and 21.

Kálvin tér

Kálvin tér marks the southern edge of the Pest city centre. Remains of the former Kecskemét Gate of old Pest's fortifications were found here during building works and incorporated into the new Hotel Korona building. An outstanding example of the old cityscape, partly destroyed during the Second World War, is the former tavern »The Two Lions« at no. 8, dating from 1818. This **Reformed Church** in classical style was erected between 1816 and 1859 by Josef Hofrichter and with the assistance of József Hild, who created the façade. Its has a noteworthy portal, whose four columns carry a tympanum. In the interior note the fine coffered ceiling and the organ by Hild. The tomb of Countess Zichy designed by Frigyes Feszl is abdorned with a figure of the deceased originating from the workshop of the sculptor Raymond Gayard (1854). The treasury contains valuable gold forged items from the 17th till the 19th centurie.

Szabó E. tér

The dominant building on Szabó E. tér is the apartment block built to designs by Arthur Meining in 1887. Today it houses the municipal Ervin Szabó Library, named after the Hungarian sociologist Ervin Szabó (1877–1918).

Ráday utca

To the south the restaurant street Ráday utca branches from Kálvin tér. Here numerous restaurants and cafés have established themselves, adding a further impulse to Budapest's nightlife.

Vámház körút

Vámház körút has developed into a very busy shopping street in recent years, not least because of the ever-lively central market hall in close proximity at ▶Fővám tér. One of the most beautiful buildings on this section of the ring road is the house at no. 12, built in the classical style. There is a pretty sculpture of a dancer in its courtyard.

Margaret Island
(Margit-sziget)

╋ B / C 2 – 4

Tram: 4, 6
Bus: 26

With its baths and gardens, Margaret Island, almost 2km/1.2mi long and up to 0.5km/0.3mi wide, with its spas and gardens is Budapest's top leisure and recreational centre close to the city.

Many visitors of Margaret Island are drawn to the thermal springs, the spa and exercise pools, the restaurants, sports pitches and playgrounds, as well as well-kept gardens and promenades, not to mention a few historically important urban architectural remains. By car the island is accessible only at the northern end, on a ramp that branches off the Árpád Bridge. Vehicles are only allowed as far as the

Popular recreational park

This is how summer is enjoyed: bathing in the beautiful Palatinus bath on Margaret Island

spa hotel car parks. In the south, Margaret Island can be reached on foot, by boat or via public transport across Margaret Bridge (Margit híd), from whose central pier there is access to the island.

History   The Romans used the thermal springs at the northern end of the Danube island. Premonstratensians, Dominicans and Franciscans built their monasteries here in the 12th and 13th centuries. At the end of the 18th century, the Habsburg Archduke Johann, who lived as palatine in Budapest, had the island gardened. Between 1868 and 1870, a spa (Margit fürdő) was constructed to plans by Miklós Ybl. It was destroyed during the Second World War. The Grand Hotel (Margit-szigeti Nagyszálló), also designed by Ybl, opened its doors in 1873. A spa centre was created on the island with the thermal spa hotel added in 1978.

Name   During the time of Arpád rule, the island was a popular hunting ground known as Rabbit Island (Nyulak sziget). The Danube island received its present name in the 14th century in memory of the canonized Princess Margaret (1252–1271), a daughter of the Hungarian King Béla IV. She became a nun in the Dominican nunnery in accordance with a vow made by her father.

Unification Memorial   The petal-shaped metal work by István Kiss was inaugurated in 1972 on the occasion of the centenary of the unification of Óbuda, Buda and Pest. The insides of the petals record various episodes from the Danube capital's recent history. A colourful spectacle on summer evenings is to be seen next to the Unification Memorial, when the water jets of the large fountain are illuminated by coloured lights.

Remains of Franciscan monastery   Only a few little fragments survive from the 13th/14th-century church of the Franciscan monastery, including a section of its western side, and parts of the north wall, the apse, and the tower.

Palatinus lido
Insider Tip
   Fed by thermal waters, the facilities of the Palatinus lido (Palatinus strandfürdö) include a wave pool, diverse swimming pools, medicinal baths and children's pools which can take up to 20,000 visitors. Opposite the lido there is a pretty rose garden.

Remains of Dominican convent   The remains of a Dominican convent that became derelict during the Turkish era were discovered on Margaret Island after the catastrophic floods of 1838. The nunnery church was erected in the 13th century, rebuilt in the 14th and extended in the 15th century.

Water tower   The 52m/170ft high water tower with viewing platform was built in 1911 and has been carefully restored. Next to the tower, an open-air theatre holds 3500 spectators.

Several foundations still survive of the Premonstratensian monastery built in the 12th century. The monastery church was rebuilt in Romanesque style in 1930–31. A bell cast in the 15th century hangs in the tower, which is one of the oldest bells in Hungary.

Premonstratensian monastery

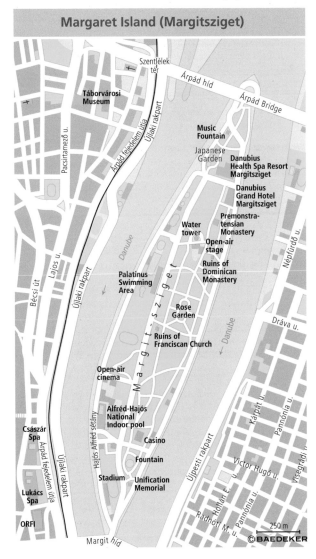

Margaret Island (Margitsziget)

Szentlélek tér

Árpád híd

Árpád Bridge

Táborvárosi Museum

Parcsirtamező u.

Árpád fejedelem útja

Újlaki rakpart

Music Fountain

Japanese Garden

Danubius Health Spa Resort Margitsziget

Danubius Grand Hotel Margitsziget

Lajos u.

Danube

Water tower

Premonstratensian Monastery

Open-air stage

Népfürdő u.

Bécsi út

Újlaki rakpart

Margit-sziget

Palatinus Swimming Area

Ruins of Dominican Monastery

Rose Garden

Ruins of Franciscan Church

Danube

Dráva u.

Open-air cinema

Császár Spa

Árpád fejedelem útja

Hajós Alfréd sétány

Alfréd-Hajós National Indoor pool

Casino

Fountain

Stadium

Unification Memorial

Újpesti rakpart

Kárpát u.

Pannónia u.

Victor Hugó u.

Visegrádi u.

Lukács Spa

Újlaki rakpart

ORFI

Margit híd

Hollán E.

Radnóti M. u.

Pannónia u.

250 m

©BAEDEKER

Grand Hotel
Margitsziget

In its day, the Grand Hotel Margitsziget was the top hotel of the recently united capital. Built in 1873, it has been repeatedly renovated and remains a popular high-class hotel, not least because of its unique location in the middle of a park on Margaret Island, yet it is close to the city. It gained its present appearance after being taken over by an international hotel chain.

Next to the hotel the small Japanese Garden is an isle of silence. Even turtles feel comfortable in the small pond, which is provided with warm water from the thermal springs.

** Matthias Church
(Mátyás-templom)

A 6

Location: Szentháromság tér
Bus: 16, 16A A. 116
www.matyas-templom.hu
Admission: 9000 HUF

The Matthias Church stands directly in front of the Fishermen's Bastion. Its painted interior today attracts admiring visitors from all over the world.

Top sight

Buda's Church of the Blessed Virgin is one of the Hungarian capital's top sights and has its origin in a sacred building which was erected between 1255 and 1269, during the time of King Béla IV. It has been remodelled numerous times since then. In the second half of the 14th century, the basilica was converted into a hall church, the aisles extended to the east and given polygonal endings, and a magnificent Gothic portal with a representation of the Virgin Mary's death in the tympanum erected on the southern façade. Charles Robert of Anjou was crowned King of Hungary in the Church of the Blessed Virgin in 1309. Side chapels, an oratory for the royal family and a new south tower were added under King Matthias, after whom the church is now named. The church fell victim to a fire in 1526 and fifteen years later, when the Turks occupied the city, it was turned into a mosque. After the expulsion of the Turks by the Austrians, the Jesuits took over the Matthias Church and renovated it in the Baroque style.

Frigyes Schulek gave the Matthias Church its present form between 1874 and 1896. The Baroque architecture fell victim to his puritanical intention to restore the building's Gothic appearance. The church suffered heavy damage at the end of the Second World War and was painstakingly rebuilt during the post-war years. At the moment a total restoration of the interior and exterior is in progress.

The interior walls of Matthias church are painted magnificently

The western façade facing Szentháromság tér, with its portal and wonderful rose window, is largely the result of Schulek's remodelling. Schulek had a low building with pointed roof and patterned roof tiles built around the lower section of the northern Béla tower, originally dating from the 13th century; whereas the southern, 80m/260ft-high Matthias Tower remains square at its base and then becomes octagonal from the second floor. The most important remnant from the Gothic church is the portal of the Virgin Mary on the south side, today protected by Schulek's porch. The wonderful relief in the gable illustrating the Virgin Mary's death dates from the 14th century. The entrance is flanked on either side by statues of the canonized kings Stephen and Ladislaus. **Exterior**

The interior of the Matthias Church is decorated with geometric patterns and plant ornamentation that recalls the decoration of a mosque. Bertalan Székely and Károly Lotz designed the frescoes as well as the stained glass in the choir, done in the 1890s. The neo-Gothic main altar and the pews are by Schulek. **Interior**

** *Matthias Church*

*Matthias Church is a landmark, which can be recognized from afar due
to its colourful roofing. The true beauty and atmosphere however can
only be grasped if one visits the interior. Every inch of the huge nave is
painted with frescos and ornaments. In the dimmed light of the coloured windows church glows festively.*

❶ Mon–Fr 9am–5pm
Sa 9am–12 in the noon
Sun 1pm–5am

❶ Béla Tower
The founder of the church was King
Béla. The tower with its original Gothic
elements was named after him.

❷ Matthias Tower
This high, slender tower holds the
imitation of the raven coat of arms of
King Matthias.

❸ Main Portal
In the tympanum of the main portal,
which is in westward direction, a Madonna with child watches between
two angels. Lajos Lontai crafted them
in the 19th century.

❹ Baroque Madonna
The legend has it that this statue was
deeply encapsulated in the walls of
the church during the Turkish siege.
As the church was destroyed in 1686
the Madonna reappeared miraculously
– for the Turks an obvious omen for
their loss.

❺ Portal of Mother Mary
The Portal of the mother Mary is a bril-
liant example of Gothic sculpturing.

❻ Pulpit
Four fathers of the church and four
apostles decorate the pulpit.

❼ Glass Window
The marvellous stained glass windows
date back to the 19th century.

Matthias Church

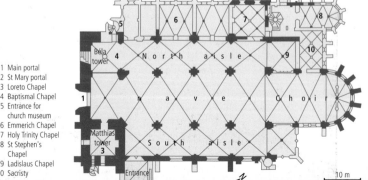

1 Main portal
2 St Mary portal
3 Loreto Chapel
4 Baptismal Chapel
5 Entrance for
   church museum
6 Emmerich Chapel
7 Holy Trinity Chapel
8 St Stephen's
   Chapel
9 Ladislaus Chapel
10 Sacristy

© BAEDEKER

The centre of the impressive
sanctuary is the neo-gothic main
altar.

Romy Schneider and Karlheinz Böhm in the movie
»Sissi«: In 1867 Franz Joseph I. and his wife Sissi
were crowned as the Kings of Hungary in Matthias
church.

The crowning mural:
Franz Joseph I and
his wife Elisabeth bid
the blessing of
mother Mary

©BAEDEKER

In the Matthias Tower there are two important items from the Baroque era: the red marble Madonna and the ebony carved Madonna on the altar panel. The columns of the baptismal chapel in the Béla tower have retained their medieval capitals. The north choir is a chapel dedicated to St Ladislaus; the frescoes by Károly Lotz show scenes from the saint's life. Behind railings in the Holy Trinity Chapel in the north aisle are the sarcophagi of King Béla III and his wife, which were originally in the cathedral at Székesfehérvár. They were moved to the Matthias Church in 1848. An altar painting by Mihály Zichy from 1894 adorns the chapel dedicated to St Emmerich.

The crypt, the royal oratory with its flags that were raised on the occasion of the coronation of King Charles IV and Queen Zita on 30 December 1916, the sacristy and the side galleries all serve as the Church Museum today. Relics, vestments and other sacred art are shown here, as well as copies of the royal crown and orb, which are kept in ▶Parliament.

Memento Park

✴ **Excursion**

Location: XXII, Ballatoni út/Szabadkai utca
Bus: 150 from Újbuda-központ (terminal station of Tram 4)
● daily 10.00pm till dawn
www.mementopark.hu
Admission: 1500 HUF

A »museum« of the more special kind can be visited in district XXII at the south-west outskirts. Here all monuments are collected which were banned from streets and squares after the fall of socialism.

More than 40 communist statues and monuments found a new home after the political turnaround in Memento Park, which was opened 1994. The dual portrait of the founding fathers of communism Marx and Engels greet the visitor at the entrance of the park. Until the fall of communism the work of sculptor György Segesdy stood on Jászai Mari tér in Pest. A reconstruction of Stalin's Tribune, which was used by the communist rulers, can be seen as well. It was however already removed from the city in 1956. The collection is also complemented with the exhibition »Stalin's Boots«, which recollects the freedom movement of 1956 and 1989/90. Also the Stasi instruction movie »The life of an agent« is on display, which shows the tips and tricks for government undercover work.

★ Municipal Forest (Városliget)

$\diamondsuit$ D – F 4 / 5

Location: XIV district
Metro: M 1 (Hfsök tere, Széchenyi fürdŐ)
Trolley bus: 70, 72, 74, 75, 79
Bus: 20, 30

With its zoo and castle, park and pool, green spaces and options for drinking coffee, the wooded park known as Városliget is deservedly one of the most popular nearby recreational areas – and of interest to tourists as well.

The park known as Városliget spreads across north-east of Budapest's city centre. An area of over one square kilometre was turned into a park with a lake according to plans by the French landscape gardener Nebbion in the 19th century. The broad Károly Kós promenade (Kós Károly sétány) – open to traffic – cuts across the northern sector of the park. Numerous recreational and cultural facilities have evolved on the municipal park's terrain over time, including two large art museums, the Museum of Fine Arts and the Palace of Art (▶Heroes' Square); it is also the site of the zoological and botanical garden, the capital's large circus, the Széchenyi Bath, as well as the magnificent Vajdahunyad Castle. One of Budapest's oldest and finest restaurants, **Gundel**, spoils its guests here in a neo-Renaissance building.

On entering the park across from Hösök tere, a castle-like building on the island in the lake immediately confronts the visitor. It has a castle gate, pointed towers, as well as gables and turrets, yet the medieval impression is misleading, for this complex was built for the millennium jubilee in 1896, just like the neighbouring Heroes' Square and many of Budapest's other buildings. Ignác Alpár, the builder of Vajdahunyad Castle, tried to combine numerous building styles characteristic for Hungary in one building in his project. The pseudo-medieval castle that forms the heart of the property copies the fortification of Hunyadi, the conqueror of the Turks, which today stands in Hunedoara in Rumania. The Gothic gate is flanked by a copy of a Hungarian tower to the left and, to the right, by a tower whose model stands in Sighisoara in Rumania.

*Vajdahunyad Castle

MARCO ● POLO TIP

! *Summer Concerts* Insider Tip

In July and August evenings in Budapest usually are pleasantly warm. The courtyard of the Vaídahunvad castle and the square in front of the palm house in the zoo are used as open air stages for opera performances, klezmer, jazz and classic concerts. Definitely worthwhile are performances of the Budapest Klezmer Bad as well as the Benkó Dixieland Band, two institutions in Budapest.

Municipal Forest (Városliget)

A chapel lies behind the Romanesque wing on the eastern side of the castle courtyard. Its portal is an exact copy of the one at the monastic church in Ják, which numbers among Hungary's most important medieval sacred buildings. The appearance of the section to the right behind the castle gate is characterized by stylistic elements from northern Hungary and Transylvania. It begins with a Gothic wing that leads to an imposing building with Renaissance and Baroque elements. The interior of the entire building complex to the right of the castle gate is accessible only during the course of a visit to the **Agricultural Museum** (Mezőgazdasági Múzeum) which provides insights into the different spheres of Hungarian agriculture and forestry. Farming tools and agricultural machinery are displayed, as well as exhibitions on the theme of animal husbandry, especially the breeding of horses, cows, sheep and pigs; other sections are devoted to winegrowing and viticulture, forest conservation and management, as well as hunting and fishing. Special exhibitions augment the programme.

Agricultural Museum: mid Feb–mid Nov Tue–Fr, Sun 10am–5pm, Sat until 6am; otherwise Tue–Fri 10am–4pm, Sat–Sun untill 5pm

Opposite the entrance to the Agricultural Museum stands a memorial created by Miklós Ligeti in 1903 in honour of the anonymous 12th–13th-century scribe who wrote Hungary's first chronicle (Gesta Hungarorum), presumably on the orders of Béla.

Gesta Hungarorum Memorial

The Széchenyi thermal bath (Széchenyi fürdő) is not one of Budapest's oldest – it was opened in 1881 – but it is among the most popular. Located in the northern section of the Városliget park, its extensive grounds include three open-air pools and one indoor pool in the neo-Baroque style with steam baths and hot tubs. A stylistically matching entrance hall was added to the buildings on the northern side in 1927. The whole complex has been restored to its former glory, and a glance into the entrance hall is recommended to non-swimmers as well! The pool is fed by a thermal spring at a temperature of over 70 °C (▶MARCO POLO Insight, p.174).

*Széchenyi thermal bath

The Budapest Zoological and Botanical Garden lies on the northwestern side of the Városliget park. It was created on a private initiative in 1866, and ownership passed to the city at the end of the nineteenth century. Enclosures and animal houses were built in 1911–12. Of the buildings from that time, the elephant house, which is reminiscent of a mosque, is particularly worth seeing, as well as the bird house built and designed by Károly Kós. The zoo's other attractions include an aviary for birds of prey, a rock garden, a pool for polar bears and sea lions, a baby animal enclosure, the monkey house, lion and bear caves, and the Africa House. The species-rich flora of moderate latitudes can be studied along outdoor footpaths, while tropical plants grow in the architecturally interesting palm house, as well as in the terrarium and aquarium for animals from warm climates.

Zoological and Botanical Garden

❶ daily from 9am. Closing time depends on the time of year, either between 4pm and 8pm, www.zoobudapes.com, admission: 2100 HUF

The building for the Metropolitan Circus (Fővárosi Nagycirkusz) at the eastern edge of the zoo was completed in 1971. It is one of the most visited institutions of its kind in Europe. The world's most renowned circus companies have performed here and continue to do so.

Metropolitan Circus

Vidám Amusement Park, which draws thousands of visitors annually, is located at the northern corner of the Városliget and has a Ferris wheel, a roller coaster, an enchanted castle, carousels and other attractions.

Vidám Amusement Park

❶ April–Sep daily 10am–8pm, Mar–Oct 10am–7pm

The exhibits of the Hungarian Transport Museum are housed in a purpose-built property on the eastern edge of the Városliget, which

Transport Museum

originated in a show for the 1896 millennium jubilee. It is an attractive presentation of the development of transport from ancient times to the present is given: models of old ships from the Danube and Lake Balaton are represented as well as various locomotives and flying machines.

❶ May–Sep Tue–Fri 10am–5pm, Sat, Sun until 6pm, Oct–April Tue–Fri 10am–4pm, Sun untill 5pm

✱✱ **Museum of Fine Arts**

✦ E 4

Location: XIV, Hösök tere
Metro: M1 (Hösök tere)
Trolley bus: 75, 79
Bus: 4, 20, 30
❶ Tue–Sun 10pm–5.30am, Thu also 6pm–10pm
www.szepmuveszeti.hu

Next to the National Gallery (▶Royal Palace), the Museum of Fine Arts (Szépművészeti Múzeum) is the most important and extensive art collection in the Hungarian capital and one of the great European galleries with works of old masters.

Collection in a historic setting

This large collection of Italian, Spanish and Dutch paintings enjoys international renown. The presentation of the collection in a historic 19th-century museum building is interesting, with long corridors for the large-scale paintings, cabinet rooms for the smaller formats and intimate subjects, as well as individual rooms, such as the Renaissance hall, where the architectural setting and the exhibits complement each other.

History of the collection

The history of the collection begins in the year 1870, when the Hungarian state purchased a collection of paintings, drawings and prints from Count Miklós Esterházy. The National Museum – as it was called then – originally found a home in the building of the Hungarian Academy of Sciences (Széchenyi István tér). Through a systematic buying policy, as well as the incorporation of various private collections and gifts, including a row of painted panels from the estate of János László Pyrke, Archbishop of Eger, and paintings from Archbishop Arnold Ipolyi's collection, the museum collection expanded rapidly. Soon sculptures were also bought, in addition to paintings and graphics. The departments created most recently are the antiquity collection (1908) and the Egyptian collection (1934). The plan for an imposing new museum building developed out of the preparations for the millennium celebrations of 1896. The monumental building, designed by Albert Schickendanz and Fülop Herzog, was finally opened to the public in 1906. Numerous quotes from Greek antiquity and the Italian Renaissance embellish the façade and the interior. The entrance side is dominated by the mighty portal, whose Corinthian pillars carry a tympanum relief of the *Battle of the Centaurs*, a copy of the sculptures from the pediment of the Temple of Zeus in Olympia.

At present some of the departments are closed due to redecoration. This is why no definitive location for the various collections can be given.

The **basement** is reserved for the Egyptian section, art of the 20th century as well as varied temporary exhibitions. The Egyptian department housed in the right wing of the basement includes monuments from the Old, Middle and New Kingdoms, as well as from antiquity. The especially outstanding pieces are the tombs from the various epochs, a diorite pharaoh's head, a limestone male head, as well as animal statues

The marvellous Renaissance hall in the Museum of Fine Arts

and other small figures of bronze that show the high standard of casting techniques in ancient Egypt. The stone relief from a Ptolemaic temple is also remarkable.

The other departments offer a cross section through the artistic trends of the turn of 19th/20th century. Works by Oskar Kokoschka, Hans Arp, Marc Chagall, György Kepes, Pablo Picasso and Victor Vasarély attract many admirers.

Egyptian department: temporally closed

The ground floor of the museum holds sncient art, the graphic col-   **Ground floor**
lection as well as paintings and sculptures from the 19th century. Objects from the first, second and third millennia BC are shown here, including gold and bronze works, and also terracotta. The art of the fourth and fifth millennia BC includes the bronze Grimani jar (mid-5th century BC), vases, and an Attic tomb relief. Among the items from the first millennium BC are Etruscan, Roman and Greek

objects; a lovely marble dancing figure (mid-3rd century BC), as well as a Tyche statue are of particular interest here. A beautiful example of sculpture from late antiquity is the relief on the Attic marble sarcophagus from the 3rd century AD.

The two-storey neo-Renaissance hall recalls an Italian palazzo with its surrounding galleries. It provides a suitable setting for sculptures and frescoes of the 14th to 16th centuries by Girolamo Romanino, Giulio Campi and other Italian Renaissance artists.

The exhibition room for the graphics collection, which contains about 10,000 drawings and around 100,000 prints, is reached from the Renaissance hall. All important schools and epochs of European art are represented in this collection. Periodic exhibitions are mounted from the extensive collection to illuminate individual aspects, or highlight schools or outstanding artists and their circle. Studies by Leonardo da Vinci, Raphael, Tintoretto and Veronese are part of this collection, as well as drawings by Dürer, Cranach, Rembrandt, Manet, Cézanne, Gainsborough and numerous other renowned artists. Temporarily closed.

The entrance to the most important special exhibitions is on the left side of the neo-Renaissance hall. Here frequently exhibitions of international acclaim are held.

First floor Galleries with works from the 13th till the 19th century from all European schools can be found on the first floor.

The collection devoted to Old Masters on the first floor begins with Tuscan panel painting from the 13th to 15th centuries, including Maso di Banco's *Coronation of the Virgin*. The collection is particularly rich in the art of the quattrocento (15th century) and the cinquecento (16th century). With the so-called Esterházy Madonna by Raphael, named after its former owners, the Esterházy family, the gallery owns an outstanding work of the Italian Renaissance. By the same artist, the collection also contains a youthful portrait of the humanist Pietro Bembo (around 1504).

Art of the 15th and 16th centuries from central Italy is represented by works from the school of Giovanni Santi, as well as by Domenico and Rodolfo Ghirlandaio, while northern Italian painting from the 14th to 16th centuries is well covered by works of Gentile Bellini of Venice, and Michele Pannonio, an artist of Hungarian origin, among others. The cinquecento is illustrated by the works of numerous renowned artists, among them Giorgione, Sebastiano del Piombo, Lorenzo Lotto, Filippino Lippi, Correggio, Jacopo Bassano, Jacopo Tintoretto and Veronese. Lombard painting, which was lastingly defined by Leonardo da Vinci – himself only represented by drawings in the graphics collection – can be discovered through many works of lesser-known masters. There is the *Portrait of the Doge Marcantonio Trevisani* (after 1553) by Titian. Of the representatives of Italian Baroque painting,

Museum of Fine Arts

First Floor

1 Italian Painting
2 British Painting
3 Romanticism to
   Post-Impressionism
4 German and Austrian
   Painting
5 Early Dutch painting
6 Flemish Painting
7 Spanish Painting

Second Floor

   Dutch painting

Ground Floor

1 Changing exhibitions
2 Baroque hall
3 Shop
4 Antique art

Lower Ground Floor

4 Café
2/3 Changing exhibitions
4 Art from the turn of the
   20th century
5 Egyptian department

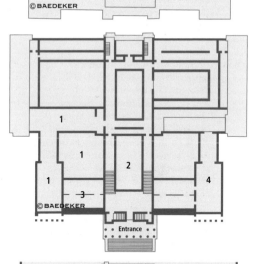

! *Art and music*   Insider Tip

Special treats are the Múzeum evenings every Thursday, which offer thematic guided tours with accompanying music.

special mention should be made of Bernardo Bellotto, Bernardo Strozzi, Giovanni Battista Tiepolo and Canaletto.

In the department of paintings and sculptures of the 19th century especially French and German artists are represented.

The museum's sculpture collection encompasses predominantly French artists such as Meunier, Rodin and Maillot. Paintings of German-speaking artists such as Achenbach, Waldmüller, von Stuck, Böcklin, Leibl, Menzel and others with their works are represented. The development of French painting from Romanticism via Realism to Post-Impressionism is made very understandable by selected works of Delacroix, Courbet, Corot, Manet, Monet, Pissarro, Renoir, Toulouse Laut rec and Cézanne.

Highlights of 15th- and 16th-century German painting are Hans Holbein's *Death of the Virgin* (around 1490), Albrecht Dürer's *Portrait of a Young Man*, as well as Lucas Cranach's *The Angel appears to St Joachim* (1518). Hans Baldung Grien and Albrecht Altdorfer are also represented. The artistic trends and associations of the Baroque epoch are introduced by way of a small, but representative selection of Austrian and German artists: Franz Anton Maulbertsch, Jan Kupetzky, Angelika Kaufmann and others.

Beyond the halls and several cabinet rooms for Italian painting there is the equally high-calibre Netherlands department. It is spread across two stories of the building. The early works are displayed on the first floor and the highlights of the Golden Age of Dutch art is shown on the second floor. An outstanding work of early Dutch painting is *John the Baptist's Sermon* (1566) by Pieter Brueghel the Elder, but Hans Memling, Petrus Christus and Gerard David and others are also represented. On the second floor the three Rembrandt paintings are indisputably the highlights of the art of the Golden Age, especially *The Old Rabbi* of 1642 and *The Angel Appears to St Joseph*, as well as portraits by Frans Hals. Dutch landscape painting is represented, among others, by Jan van Goyen, as well as by Salomon and Jacob van Ruisdael; but plenty of space is devoted to genre painting and still-lifes.

Flemish painting, spread across two rooms, includes paintings by Peter Paul Rubens, Anthony van Dyck and Jacob Jordaens alongside works of less well-known masters.

The department of **Spanish painting** is also of high quality. Spanish and Portuguese masters from the 15th and 16th century lead on to works by El Greco (*Repentant Mary Magdalene*, before 1580; *Annunciation*, c. 1595), the outstanding artist of Mannerism in Spain. Most of the famous names of Spanish Baroque are present, among others Francisco de Zurbarán, Jusepe de Ribera and Murillo. The museum possesses five works by Francisco di Goya, including *The Water Car-*

rier, The Grinder (both before 1812), and the *Portrait of Señora Bermúdez* (around 1785). One work by Diego Velázquez hangs in the exhibition: the stylistically early work, *Farmers' Meal.* English painting, with works by Gainsborough, Hogarth and Reynolds, and 17th- and 18th-century **French painting**, including canvases by Chardin, Lorrain and Poussin are represented as well.

The museum's sculpture collection encompasses predominantly Italian artists. The exhibits are spread among the relevant departments of painting. The highlight of the collection is the equestrian statue of French King François I by Leonardo da Vinci. Several Baroque sculptures are also remarkable, among others those by Georg Raphael Donner and Johann Christoph Mader.

El Greco's *Annunciation*

Nagytétény Palace

✦ **Excursion**

Location: XXII district
Railway station: Nagytétény

The main sight at Nagytétény is the Baroque palace, in which a department of the ▶Arts and Crafts Museum is now housed.

Nagytétény Palace (Nagytétényi Kastélymúzeum) is located in the Hungarian capital's rural southern district of the same name, on the Buda side of the Danube, where a Roman garrison existed from the 2nd to 5th centuries. Nagytétény is probably named after the Magyar leader Tétény, and had importance as a wine-growing area in the Middle Ages. It was granted a charter to hold markets in the 15th century. The settlement was for the most part destroyed during the Turkish wars, after which numerous families came to re-settle Nagytétény from south-western Germany. Their houses characterize the townscape to this day.

Immigrant town

Main sight at Nagytétény is the Baroque palace. This country residence was built in the 18th century, using building remains from the 15th century.

Baroque palace

MARCO ⊕ POLO TIP

! *Beware of sharks!* Insider Tip

In the Tropicarium (Nagytétényi út 37 – 45) the who is who of the ocean swims around: sharks, stingrays, alligators, iguanas, snakes as well as native fish. Opening hours: daily 10am–20pm: www.tropicarium.hu

The palace was badly damaged in the Second World War, but was painstakingly restored a few years ago and has now been made accessible as a museum. In addition to the superbly worked 15th–19th-century furniture, predominantly originating in Hungary and Germany, the collection is noteworthy for its oven tiles and its domestic ovens. There are valuable paintings, carpets, faïence and clocks from the 18th to 19th centuries in several rooms. Interesting exhibits from the Roman period are shown in the palace stables.

❶ Fri–Sun 10am–6pm;. www.nagytetenv.hu; admission: 600 HUF

✳ **National Museum**

✦ **D 7**

Location: VIII district, Múzeum körút 14–16
Metro: 3 (Kálvin tér)
Tram: 47, 49
Bus: 9

❶ Tue–Sun 10pm–6am
www.hnm.hu
Admission: 1100 HUF

With its eight conspicuous columns and huge outdoor steps, the National Museum is one of the city's most impressive buildings. The history of the country is comprehensively featured here, from the Stone Age to the present.

Classical-style building

In the 19th-century history of Budapest, the Széchényi family appears again and again; so too with the Hungarian National Museum (Magyar Nemzeti Múzeum), which owes its foundation to Count Ferenc Széchényi's commitment. Although the institution was already established in 1802, and Mihály Pollack was hired to design the building, the classical-style museum was not inaugurated until 1847. A memorial completed by Alajos Stróbl in 1893 for the famous Hungarian poet János Arany (1817–1882), stands in front of the museum. Further busts and memorials of famous people can be found in the park-like museum garden

Ground floor

The exhibition on the ground floor encompasses the pre-history of Hungary from the Stone Age, the Roman era and the early Middle Ages. The finds from Vértesszőlős and Sümeg are noteworthy in the department for pre-history. The highlight of the Bronze Age collection is the chariot from Pécel. From the migration era there is Hun-

Hungarian National Museum

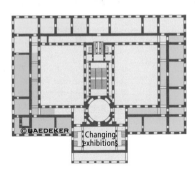

FIRST FLOOR

Hungarian history
1000-1990

▢ Hungarian history
1000-1700

▢ Hungarian History
1700-end of 19th Century

▢ Hungarian history
20th Century

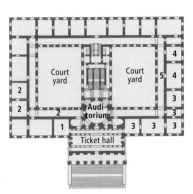

GROUND FLOOR

1 Coronation mantle
2 Changing exhibitions
3 Pre & Early History
4 Roman Era
5 Early Middle Ages

nish jewellery, a Carolingian sword, as well as utensils from Slavic tribes. Until 2000, the Hungarian monarchy's royal insignia could be viewed in a hall in the left wing, but it is now exhibited at ▶Parliament. Only the coronation mantel remains in the National Museum. It was given to the Székesfehérvár basilica by St Stephen in 1031 and only served as part of the ruling insignia from the end of the 12th century onwards. The coronation mantel is of gold-embroidered Byzantine silk with pearl decorations.

The first floor is reached via a magnificent stairway painted with a series of allegorical frescoes by Károly Lotz und Mór Than. The first room is a domed hall, which is dedicated to changing exhibitions, as is the large hall behind it. Hungarian history from the time its state

First floor

! *Old guidebooks please?* ^{Insider}
Tip

Opposite of the National Museum in the Múzeum körút antique bookstores are very well equipped with all kind of literature, not only in Hungarian. With some luck one could even find a small rarity: a Murray or Baedeker from the 19th century.

was founded – or rather from St Stephen I's coronation as Hungarian king in AD 1000 – to the expulsion of the Turks in the late 17th century, is highlighted in the rooms of the south wing. Hungarian history from Prince Ferenc Rákóczi's battles for independence at the beginning of the 18th century to the collapse of the socialist system in 1990 is vividly presented in the north wing. The individual independence battles of Hungarian history are accorded special prominence. The exhibits include Hungarian and Turkish weapons, memorabilia from the independence battles of Rákóczis, and Baroque art. Furthermore, documents and exhibits cover the 18th-century farmers' revolts, the Hungarian Jacobin movement and the revolution of 1848–49.

Lapidarium The Lapidarium with exhibits from the Middle Ages and early antiquity is housed on the lower ground floor and contains the museum's tombstone collection, as well as fragments of medieval architecture. The Roman rock and mineral collection on the lowest basement floor presents important Roman fragments from the Hungarian region, among them a floor mosaic from the 3rd century BC found in Baláca by Veszprém.

Népliget

✴ **F / G 8 / 9**

Location: X district
Metro: M 3 (Népliget)

At 112ha/27bac Népliget is the Hungarian capital's largest park. It was laid out to the south-east of the city centre in the 1860s. The planetarium is worth a visit in bad weather.

Largest park in the city The Népliget received a makeover according to the latest ideas in garden design on the occasion of the centenary jubilee celebrating the unification of Óbuda, Buda and Pest. Diverse monuments, water features, flowerbeds, meadows and mature trees make a stroll enjoyable, especially during the warmer times of year. The central bus station is also at the park, where coaches leave for and arrive from all over Europe. From time to time the park is also used for car and motorbike races. The park is also a meeting place for the local gay scene, especially after dark.

In the south-west part of the Népliget, the laser theatre of the planetarium transports visitors into a world of visual effects (every evening except Sun). Tickets can be had from the planetarium desk, from Music Mix Ticket Service (Váci utca 33), from the Central Ticket Office (Andrássy út 18), as well as at various hotel receptions. Programme information: www.lasertheater.hu (Hungarian only) or tel. 1 2 63 08 71.

Planetarium

Óbuda (»Old Oven«)

✦ A – C 1 – 3

Location: III district
Bus: 6, 34, 42, 86, 106
Suburban train HÉV: Batthyány tér – Szentendre
Tram: 1

Until its amalgamation with Buda and Pest in 1873, Óbuda was a sleepy little town and, in spite of large-scale urban renewal and modernization, it has managed to retain something of its former atmosphere.

According to tradition, the old settlement where evidence of settlement from prehistoric times has been discovered and where the Romans founded their garrison ►Aquincum shortly after the birth of Christ, was Attila the Hun's residence in the 5th century. The town experienced a significant upturn under the Árpáds and, during the Middle Ages, the Hungarian queens had a palace here. The town, which had been overshadowed by the developing royal city of Buda, was completely obliterated during the Turkish era,. In 1659 it came into the ownership of the Counts Zichy, who settled farmers from Austria and Moravia here to work their lands after the expulsion of the Turks, and in this way the town revived.

Prehistoric settlement

✱ FŐ TÉR AND ITS SURROUNDINGS

Fő tér is the old main square of Óbuda. Today it is surrounded by depressing high-rise residential blocks that provide an unattractive background for the pretty square lined by one- to three-storey houses. On the northern side of Fö tér stands the former neo-Baroque town hall of Óbuda. Opposite is the Sipos Halászkert fish restaurant. The **Imre Varga Museum** is not far from the figures with umbrellas. It is in one of the low single-storey dwellings (Laktanya utca no. 7), which leads off the square in a northerly direction. The museum contains numerous models of the master's great works, busts of famous

Main square

Sculptures by Imre Varga

people and copies of several other works. The small attractive garden of the house, with portrait sculptures of renowned Hungarian contemporaries, is also worth seeing.

Imre Varga Museum: Tue–Sun 10pm–6am

The oval building a few blocks north of Fő tér, at no. 44 on Harrer Pál utca, was built as a silk-weaving workshop by József Tallherr in 1785. Today it is a historic industrial monument and recalls the textile production in Óbuda that was promoted by Emperor Joseph II.

✳ ZICHY PALACE (ZICHY-KASTÉLY)

Three interesting museums

An unpretentious Baroque palace, built in the mid-18th century by Henrik János Jäger for Count Nikolaus Zichy, stands between Fő tér and Szentlelék tér adjoining to its south. It was restored after heavy damage during the Second World War and now serves as a cultural centre. Three interesting museums are ranged around the large courtyard of this building complex: the Lajos Kassák Museum and the Vasarély Museum. The Óbuda Museum for local history also has its departments and exhibition here.

The courtyard with the main palace building is reached via an entrance through the west wing of the palace, which faces towards Fő tér. A small **museum dedicated to Lajos Kassák** (1887 – 1967), the versatile proponent of Hungarian avant-garde, has been installed on the first floor of this beautifully renovated Baroque building. The life work of this writer, publicist and artist is shown in a three-room permanent exhibition that shows great attention to detail and commitment to the artist. Temporary exhibitions enrich an interesting show. Kassák, who lived in Óbuda from 1954, promoted the Hungarian avant-garde as publisher of the magazine »Ma« (Today), which appeared from 1916 to 1925 and combined the most diverse contemporary trends, from Dadaism and Constructivism to Expressionism and Futurism.

The entrance to the **Vasarély Museum** is located on Szentélek tér. Victor Vasarély (1908–1997), who originally came from Pécs in southern Hungary and made his home in France, is considered the most important representative of Op Art. The richly endowed exhibition gives a representative view of the artist's work.

Next door the **Óbuda Museum** for local history predominantly deals with Middle Age monasteries and rapid city development in the

19th and 20th century. Unfortunately explanations for many show-cases are only in Hungarian.

Laios Kassák Museum: Wed–Sun 10pm–5am

Vasarély Museum: Tue–Sun 10pm–5.30pm; www.vasarelv.hu

Óbuda Museum: Tue–Sun 10am–6pm

To the south of Zichy Palace, separated from it by the wide carriage-way, the Late Baroque parish church St Peter and Paul stands on Lajos utca, Buda's former main street. It was commissioned by the Zichys between 1744 and 1749 and designed by Johann Georg Paur.

St Peter and Paul

There was a synagogue for the resident Jewish community in Óbuda in the 18th century. When that community grew larger, András Landherr designed a larger house of worship, which was built at Lajos utca no. 161, to the south of the Óbuda parish church, between 1820 and 1825. The classical building is no longer used as a synagogue and nothing survives of its interior.

Former synagogue

ROMAN REMAINS

At Flórián tér, what is a major traffic axis today, a Roman militay camp stood in the 1st century AD. In its proximity a civilian town (▶Aquincum) emerged in time. Underneath the square a number of remains can still be seen, including the partly reconstructed ruins of a bath with underfloor heating, as well as hot and cold pools and surviving parts of a centurion's house. The bath was presumably in use from the 1st to the 4th century AD. The little Fürdő Museum provides a vivid description of Roman bathing culture. The medieval remains of the royal residence and Óbuda's 18th-century Reformed Church can be seen at the southern edge of the square, near Cálvin köz.

Roman bath

Fürdő Múzeum: May–Sep Tue–Sun 10am–6pm, second half of April– Oct Tue–Sun 10am–5pm

The remains of the Roman garrison were found during excavations in 1950, to the south of Flórián tér, on Pacsirtamezö utca. In addition to the surviving walls of the former south gate and other buildings dating from the 2nd to 4th centuries AD, tools, containers, burial gifts and sarcophagi came to light. A beautiful fresco from the 3rd century, which shows a hunting scene, was also revealed.

Roman garrison

Follow the broad Pacsirtamező utca even further south to the re-mains of an amphitheatre built in the 2nd century AD on the corner of Nagyszombat utca. The ruins were exposed in 1940. The elliptical arena, 131m/ long and 107mwide, once held around 12,000 specta-tors, who could follow Roman contests here.

Roman amphitheatre

*Hercules mansion   Even further north of Flórián tér, at Meggyfa utca nos. 19 – 21, the remains of a Roman villa, probably from the 3rd century, were exposed. The mosaics in the buildings show scenes from the legends of Hercules and Dionysus.

❶ only open for groups

The mural from the Hercules mansion

KISCELL

Kiscell, the quarter of Óbuda where the Counts of Zichy initially built a chapel, to which a monastery was added in the 1840s, is called Kleinzell or Kiscell. A copy of the pietà from the Austrian pilgrimage site Mariazell was brought to the chapel, which is how it got its name of Kleinzell (small chapel).

Kiscelli Múzeum   At the beginning of the 20th century the building, formerly part of the Trinitarian monastery (Kiscelli út 108) dissolved in 1783, came into the possession of an Austrian art and antiques lover, who also brought here the Baroque portal originally made in 1799 for the seat of the Jesuit order in Vienna. His art collection has been incorporated into the newly founded branch of Budapest's Historical Museum which has been installed in the rooms of the former Trinitarian monastery. An exhibition gives good insight into the economic and cultural life of the three Danube towns of Óbuda, Buda and Pest from the end of the Turkish occupation onwards.

❶ April–Oct Tue–Sun 10am–6pm, Nov–Mar Tue–Sun 10am–6 pm

* Palace of Arts

◆ D 9

Location: IX Komor Marcell sétanv
Tram: 1, 2, 24
www.mupa.hu

In 2005 the Palace of Arts (Művészetek Palotája) opened directly next to the National Theatre by the banks of the Danube. Instantly a new cultural centre was created, which has since established itself very well within the local art scene. The design by architects Gábor Zoboki and Nóra Demeter follows a functional nevertheless appealing concept.

The central element is the largest concert hall in Hungary. The national concert hall Béla Bartók holds 1700 people. During the spring festival famous concerts are held in the hall, which is renowned for its perfect acoustics. The largest concert organ is integrated in the concert hall. The small festival hall, which is also used by the National Theatre of Dance, is built next door.

*Concert Hall

Second major element of the palace is the Ludwig Museum for Modern Art. Its collection goes back to the German collector couple Irene and Peter Ludwig. It opened in the Royal Palace in 1991 as the first Ludwig Museum in Eastern Europe and moved to the Palace of Arts in 2005. It is the most important museum for modern art in Hungary. Hungarian as well as international artists of contemporary art are represented, the main focus is the 1960s and 1070s. Works on display include the Hungarian artists: Imre Bukta, Miklós Erdély, Sándor Molnár, Tibor Vilt, Valéria Sass und Tibor Csernus as well as international stars such as Andy Warhol, Pablo Picasso, Roy Lichtenstein, David Hockney, Jörg Immendorf, Gerhard Richter and Joseph Beuys. A chess game by Yoko Ono is on display as well (»Play it by trust«).

*Ludwig Museum for Modern Art

❶ Tue–Sun 10am–8pm; www.ludwig.muzeum.hu; admission: 1300 HUF

✱✱ Parliament

Location: V district, Kossuth Lajos tér   **Tram:** 2, 2A
Metro: M 2 (Kossuth tér)   **Trolley bus:** 7, 78

✦ B 5

The most imposing structure on the Pest side of the Danube bank is the giant neo-Gothic parliamentary complex. It is considered an outstanding achievement of Budapest architecture and is one of the landmarks of the Hungarian capital.

The building of a parliament in Budapest as a place where the legislative assembly, or rather the Hungarian estates, could meet was already agreed after the Compromise of 1867 with Austria, but was only realized with considerable delay. Until 1847 the legislative assembly had its permanent seat in Pressburg, today's Bratislava, and was then moved to Pest, where it met in various buildings until the new parliament was completed. After a 20-year period of construction, the huge complex was inaugurated in 1904. The neo-Gothic façade conceals a highly modern iron construction, which gives the complicated room designs the necessary stability.

Massive building complex (▶MARCO POLO Insight p. 216)

The focus of the building is the 96m/315ft-high dome over the central section. It is a synthesis of a neo-Gothic buttress system and a

Exterior

Parliament

It is the largest building in Hungary: with its 268m/884ft it is six meters (twenty feet) longer than British Parliament and approximately 100m high. The interior is equipped with almost 700 rooms, which were decorated and crafted by the best artist of the country's artists from the 19th century. By the way: the similarity with London Parliament is not a co- incidence – it was the ambition to dedicate oneself to the idea of English parliamentarianism.

Visits only possible with a guided tour
English language guided tours:
Mon–Sat 10am, 12am, 2pm. Sun
10am, 12am
Box office: Gate X. It is recommended
to wait in line between 1 and 2 hours.
Personal ID card must be presented.

❶ Assembly Hall
Galleries surround the assembly hall. It is 23m/76ft long and 25m/82ft wide.

❷ Congress hall
Center of the north wing is the con- gress hall

❸ Munkácsv Hall
The famous Hungarian artist Mihálv Munkácsv (1844 – 1900) created the painting »Hungarian Conquest«. It was disputed because it portrays the conquest of Prince Árpád as a peace- ful event.

Representative staircase

❹ Dome hall
In the centre of the building the pillar- supported dome hall has a total height of 27m/89ft. The pillars of the hall converge into a 16-pointed star.
The royal insignia with exception of the crowning cloak is displayed in the dome hall.

❺ Main Portal
Two stone lions guard the main portal.

❻ Statues
88 statues decorate the façade of the building. Various Hungarian sculptors crafted them.

Stephan's crown is displayed in Parliament

The dome finds its completion in a 16-pointed star.

❺

©BAEDEKER

In the marvellous assembly hall Parliament holds their meetings.

Renaissance dome. To left and right long symmetrical wings enclose no less than ten courtyards. The building is also remarkable for its total of 691 rooms. The south wing houses the parliamentary chamber for the House of Representatives, the northern one the congress hall. Both halls protrude from the roofline with their corner turrets and are therefore also recognizable from the outside. 88 statues from the workshops of a range of Hungarian sculptors decorate the façades of Parliament: on the Danube side are Hungarian tribal leaders and kings; on the eastern entrance side, facing Kossuth tér, eastern Hungarian army leaders and princes from the independence battles of the 17th and 18th century.

Parliament Building

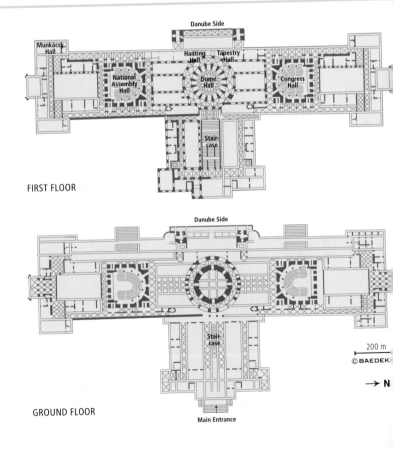

FIRST FLOOR

GROUND FLOOR

200 m

©BAEDEK

→ N

At Kossuth Lajos tér, steps lead to the tripartite main portal flanked by two bronze lions. The monumental nature of the exterior is also continued inside. The extensive entrance hall and stairwell is decorated with ceiling frescoes by Károly Lotz and sculptures by György Kiss. The bust of the architect Imre Steindl by Alajos Stróbl stands in a niche.

The magnificent 27m/89ft-high **domed hall**, sixteen-sided and borne by 16 pillars with portraits of outstanding Hungarian leaders, is on the first floor. Paintings by Aldar Körösfői-Kriesch hang in the hunting hall (Vadászterem), and behind that, in the tapestry hall (Gobelinterem), a truly colossal wall tapestry shows a gathering of the Magyar princes who founded the country. The large assembly chamber is especially impressive, with frescoes by the renowned artist Károly Lotz, and the large-format painting *Conquest*, with which the history painter Mihály Munkácsy made his name. The beautiful stained glass windows are by Miksa Róth, one of the leading glass painters of his time. The decorative grates over the heating vents cover up an ingenious system that also cools the building by means of huge blocks of ice in the summer.

The **Parliamentary Library** (Országgyülési Könyvtár), with its rich collection of legal, state and historic literature, can be reached via the southern gate on the Danube side of the parliament.

The coronation insignia, which were taken out of the country by Hungarian fascists in 1945, have been kept in Parliament since 1 January 2000, after an extensive political debate. American occupation troops found these valuable items in Austria and took them to the USA, where they were carefully held at Fort Knox until their repatriation to Hungary in 1978. St Stephen's crown, enameled with precious stones and pearls, is adorned by representations of saints and the characteristic crooked cross above the crossing point of the two headbands. Next to the crown lie the sceptre, orb and sword. The coronation mantel is exhibited at the ►National Museum. It remains undecided whether or not the coronation insignia will remain in Parliament long-term; a return to the National Museum or presentation in the ►Royal Palace are being considered.

Interior

*Coronation insignia

Rose Hill

──────────────── ✳ A 3 / 4

Location: II district, west of Margit híd
Bus: 91, 191, 291

Rose Hill (Rózsadomb) has long been part of the Hungarian capital's most favoured neighbourhoods. Exclusive villas, some with overgrown gardens, boulevards and pedestrian paths stretch all the way to the cool Hűvösvölgy valley.

*Tomb of Gül Baba

On the property of an old villa at (Mecset utca 14) stands the tomb (türbe) of Gül Baba (Turkish: »Father of Roses«), built from 1543 untill 1548 and surrounded by gardens. He lived in Buda as a Turkish dervish and died during a ceremony in 1541 at the Matthias Church when it was a mosque. The modest octagonal domed structure in which his sarcophagus is kept is today a museum commemorating Gül Baba.

❶ May–Sep Tue–Sun 10am–6pm, Oct Tue–Sun 10am–6pm

Béla Bartók Memorial

Before the great Hungarian composer Béla Bartók (▶Famous People) emigrated to the USA in protest against the emergence of fascism in Hungary, he lived in this villa on Rose Hill, at Csalán út 29, which has been open to the public for some time as a Béla Bartók Memorial (Bartók Béla Emlékház). Several items of his furniture and musical instruments have been left in their original places. Occasionally chamber concerts are also held here. The memorial in the garden was created by the Hungarian sculptor Imre Varga.

❶ Tue–Sun 10am–5pm

** **Royal Palace** (Budavári Palota)

─────────── ✣ **B 6/7** ●

Location: south tip of the castle hill
Chairlift: Clark Ádám tér – Szent György tér
Bus: 16, 16 A, 116

High above the Danube the Hungarian kings build their residency. Today the Royal Palace belongs to one of the highlights of the capital, already because of the marvellous view.

The construction of the first castle was closely linked to the Mongol invasions of the years 1241–42. King Béla IV had numerous fortifications built in the country in the 13th century as protection from further attacks and to control the Danube, and fortified Buda with a royal castle of which, however, nothing remains. A small palace was built in its place under King Charles Robert of Anjou in the 14th century, on top of which King Louis of Anjou built himself a magnificent palace after the royal residence had moved from Visegrád to Buda. A few fragments, for example the so-called Stephen's Tower, a Gothic residential tower, and the lower section of a palace chapel have survived from this period. His successor Sigismund had the residence massively extended to the north with the New Palace, which does not survive. The living quarters were equipped with heating systems and the fortifications were improved all around.

Royal Palace

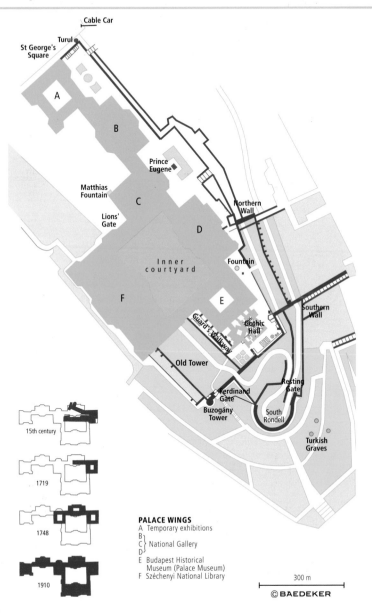

Cable Car

Turul

St George's Square

A

B

Prince Eugene

Matthias Fountain

C

Lions' Gate

D

Northern Wall

Inner courtyard

Fountain

F

E

Southern Wall

Guard's Walkway

Gothic Hall

Old Tower

Resting Gate

Ferdinand Gate

Buzogány Tower

South Rondell

Turkish Graves

15th century

1719

1748

1910

PALACE WINGS
A Temporary exhibitions
B
C } National Gallery
D
E Budapest Historical
    Museum (Palace Museum)
F Széchenyi National Library

300 m

© BAEDEKER

** *Royal Palace*

The former residence of the Hungarian Kings encompasses the entire south tip of Castle Hill. It dates back to the 13th century when King Béla decided to build a castle on this location. Ever since almost every dynasty left its stylistic mark. Parts were added to the castle, others renovated or expanded. During World War II quite a bit was destroyed. The later reconstructions put the castle back into the condition it had in the 19th century. A large amount of the former palace can be visited. Now it houses important museums.

❶ National Gallery
The National Gallery occupies three wings of the Royal Palace with its extensive collection of Hungarian art from the early Middle Ages until Modernity. The palace was destroyed completely by fire in 1945. The royal interior as well as numerous art treasures was burned. The reconstruction focused on the exterior shape. Therefore the interior is unostentatious and serves the presentation of the exhibitions. Pompous royal chambers are nonexistent.

❷ History Museum
Exhibition on the history of Budapest and the remains of the medieval Royal Palace.

❸ Széchenyi National Library
The Royal Palace is also the home of the largest and most important library of Hungary.

❹ Lions Gate
The Lions Gate leads to the backyard of the palace.

❺ Matthias fountain
The fountain was created by Alajos Strobl in 1904 and tells the story of King Matthias Corvinus and the girl Ilonka.

❻ Wall-walk
It comprises the oldest parts of the palace.

❼ Dome
It was constructed in a classicist style after the original Baroque dome was destroyed in the Second World War. The view on the city is marvellous from here.

The bird Turul stands on the north side of the palace front. It is the symbol of the Hungarian people.

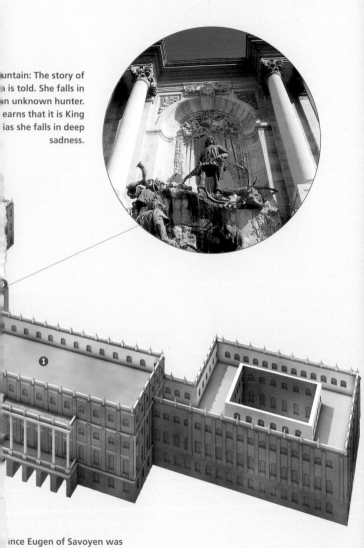

untain: The story of
a is told. She falls in
n unknown hunter.
earns that it is King
ias she falls in deep
sadness.

❶

ince Eugen of Savoyen was
ctorious against the Turks
nd established the Habsburgs
osition as a great power.

©BAEDEKER

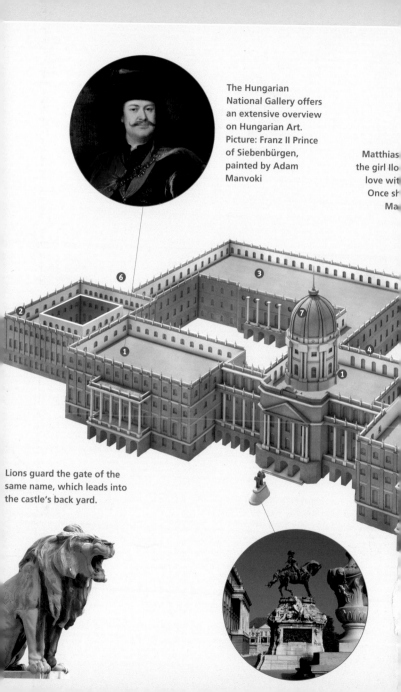

The Hungarian
National Gallery offers
an extensive overview
on Hungarian Art.
Picture: Franz II Prince
of Siebenbürgen,
painted by Adam
Manvoki

Matthias
the girl Ilo
love wit
Once sh
Ma

Lions guard the gate of the
same name, which leads into
the castle's back yard.

Under King Matthias Corvinus, who is remembered as a promoter of the Renaissance and humanism, the royal palace was extended magnificently in the style of the early Renaissance. The Turks did not destroy the royal palace during their 150-year rule, nor did they do anything towards its maintenance. Sigismund's so-called New Palace served as an armoury and was totally destroyed by an explosion in 1578, while the other royal buildings fell victim to the sieges and battles of 1686. After victory over the Turks by the Holy Alliance, the damaged fortifications were initially restored and renewed, but it was only in the 18th century that the Habsburg kings undertook the building of a new palace. A new residence was built north of Stephen's Tower under Charles III in 1719, to plans by the Italian architect Fortunato Prati. Maria Theresa finally ordered the further extension of the rather humble palace, which was completed in 1770. From then on, the palace was a symmetrical three-part building, comprised of a south wing (the original palace and today's E wing), a higher central wing (today's D wing), and a northern wing (today's C wing). The planning was placed in the hands of Jean Nicolas Jadot, who was active as an architect at the court of Vienna. The Baroque architect Franz Anton Hillebrandt supervised the construction.

For almost a hundred years no further building works were undertaken on the palace, in which the representatives of the Habsburg emperors (palatines) had lived since 1790. Only in 1867, after the Austro-Hungarian Compromise, were renewed plans made for an extension, which was this time entrusted to the Hungarian architect Alajos Hauszmann. Ybl built a massive wing (F) on the western side of Castle Hill, which was completed in 1891. Hauszmann completed the imposing construction with a central-domed building (62m/204ft) facing the Danube, as well as the adjoining two wings (A and B), which were matched stylistically to the existing sections. Reconstruction of the palace, as well as the excavation and preservation of the medieval remains was begun in 1950.

WHAT TO SEE IN THE ROYAL PALACE

Szent György tér

Insider Tip

From the Castle District or coming up by funicular (Sikló) from the first place reached is the Szent György tér, the northern forecourt of the Royal Palace, which becomes Disz tér to the north. The forecourt of the Royal Palace facing the Danube, which is also where the main entrance to the Hungarian National Gallery is located, can be reached via a neo-Baroque double staircase »guarded« by the eagle named Turul, the emblem of the Arpáds.

Equestrian statue

The bronze memorial for the conqueror of the Turks, Prince Eugene of Savoy, was built in the tradition of Baroque equestrian statues by

József Róna in 1900, and was placed in front of the domed building of the Royal Palace.

Near the equestrian statue an opening leads to the western forecourt of the Royal Palace, on whose south side (the northern wall of C wing) a monumental fountain encased by Corinthian columns, designed by Alajos Stróbl in the style of a Roman Baroque fountain (1904), catches the eye. The wall behind it is like a stage set for the raised bronze figure of the youthful King Matthias, who is styled as a hunter. Below the king, to the left, is the mournful seated figure of a girl, which originates in a folk legend that grew up around the ruler and is intended to express his popularity among the people. According to this legend, the farm girl Ilonka fell in love with Matthias when the king went hunting incognito. When the girl later realized that the unknown youth was her king, she fell into deep sorrow for the rest of her life.

*Matthias Fountain

The centre of the forecourt is decorated with a sculpture called the *Horse Guardian*, created by Gyögy Vastagh in 1898, and originally intended for a different place in the palace grounds.

»Horse Guardian«

The inner prestige courtyard of the palace grounds is reached through the Lion's Gate, a work of the Hungarian sculptor János Fadrusz (1904). Here the entrances to the Széchenyi National Library (see below) and the Budapest History Museum (see below) can be found, as well as an entrance to the National Gallery, whose main entrance is on the Danube side. The two aggressive-looking stone lions at the gate guard access to the inner courtyard, where two further roaring stone sentinels await.

Lion's Gate

** THE HUNGARIAN NATIONAL GALLERY (MAGYAR NEMZETI GALÉRIA)

❶ Tue–Sun 10am–6pm; www.mng.hu; admission: 1200 HUF

The Hungarian National Gallery, which was founded in 1957 from various municipal and private collections, along with stored departments from the Museum of Fine Arts, is housed in the three main wings of the palace over four floors. Until its move to the rooms of the Royal Palace in 1975 the works used to be viewed in the former Palace of Justice on Kossuth tér, which today exhibits the treasures of the Ethnographic Museum. The National Gallery's holdings encompass Hungarian art from the early Middle Ages to the present, as well as a collection of medals. The development and characteristics of Hungarian painting, sculpture and graphics are extremely well documented by the works gathered here. The rooms with medieval pic-

Collection

Hungarian National Gallery

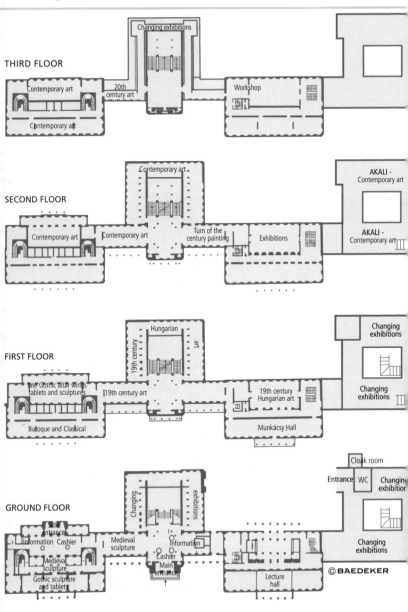

THIRD FLOOR

Changing exhibitions

Contemporary art

20th century art

Contemporary art

Workshop

SECOND FLOOR

Contemporary art

Contemporary art

Contemporary art

Turn of the century painting

Exhibitions

AKALI - Contemporary art

AKALI - Contemporary art

FIRST FLOOR

Hungarian

19th century

art

late Gothic altar wings tablets and sculptures

19th century art

Baroque and Classical

19th century Hungarian art

Munkácsy Hall

Changing exhibitions

Changing exhibitions

GROUND FLOOR

Changing

exhibitions

Slide entrance

Information Cashier

Medieval sculpture

Gothic sculpture and tablets

Medieval sculpture

Information

Cashier

Main entrance

Cloak room

Entrance WC Changing exhibition

Changing exhibitions

Lecture hall

©BAEDEKER

tures and 19th-century paintings and sculpture on the first floor are especially interesting (B wing). In the former quarters of the Ludwig Museum (A wing) the museum now holds special exhibitions. The passage to the main building can be found in the first floor.

In the hallway of D wing, on the ground floor, medieval stone carvings are displayed, especially architectural fragments from the country's most notable Romanesque and Gothic churches, as well as wooden sculptures and paintings from the 14th and 15th centuries. The so-called »soft style«, which was common throughout Europe around 1400, is impressively illustrated by the wooden sculpture of St Dorothea from Barka, and by the Toporc Madonna; the altarpieces from Jánosrét, which were made in the final third of the 15th century, are also worth seeing.

Ground floor

The first floor houses three sections: late medieval altarpieces and sculptures from the 15th and 16th centuries, painting and sculpture of the late Renaissance and Baroque, and painting and sculpture from the 19th century.

First floor

The staircase leads first to a long room with 19th-century paintings and sculptures. These works mostly illustrate significant events in Hungarian history. Late Gothic altar wings from the 15th and 16th centuries are gathered in the **Great Throne Room** and several smaller rooms around it.

The *Visitation of the Virgin* is of particular interest. It was part of an altar in Selmecbánya and was signed by a master M.S. and dated 1506. The work stands at the transitional point between late Gothic and the modern age: while the rendering of the folds in the clothes of the two women, ornamental and without depth, is still faithful to medieval concepts, the representation of the landscape already heralds the arrival of a new era that looks beyond medieval conceptions of form.

A relatively high standard is also maintained in the section for **Baroque painting and sculpture** from the 17th and 18th century, which can be found in the room facing the Danube. If, next to the few Hungarian artists such as Jakáb Bogdány or Ádám Mányoki, the names in the collection are almost exclusively German, Austrian and Bohemian – among others, Joseph Heintz the Elder, Johann Kupetzky, August Querfurt, Franz Anton Maulbertsch and Franz Sigrist – then the exhibition is simply a reflection of the fact that artistic life in 17th- and 18th-century Hungary was dominated by foreign painters, who were brought into the country by their noble patrons. The works exhibited represent almost all genres: still life, as well as landscapes, royal portraits, allegories and biblical themes.

The **art of the 19th century** housed in B wing is entirely Hungarian once more. A stroll through the many rooms amply illustrates that this

Historical paintings let Hungarian history come to life

era of Hungarian painting has been unjustly neglected abroad. The first room after the staircase is, just as in D Wing on the opposite side, dedicated to historical painting, mostly in large format. Important representatives of this genre are Bertalan Székely, Gyula Benczur and Viktor Madarász. The most significant and popular representative of his era, Mihály Munkácsy, belongs to the few internationally renowned artists and therefore is given an entire room, where the painter's famous village and tavern scenes (among others, including *The Condemned Man's Last Day*, 1870) can be found. In the second half of the century, László Paál, whose landscape pictures are scattered around the Munkácsy exhibition, pioneered Hungarian open-air painting, along with Pál Szinyei Merse.

The small sculptures in the Munkácsy room are by György Zala. The most significant sculptors at the turn of the 20th century were György Zala, Alajos Stróbl and János Fadrusz, whose works in Budapest are not only encountered at the National Gallery.

Tivadar Csontváry, one of the few internationally famous painters from Hungary, was an outsider in his own land, who never found recognition during his lifetime. Csontváry (1853–1919), famous for his expressive naïve pictures, is represented through several paintings in the exhibition. One of his major works hangs in the National Gallery's main stairwell: *The Ruins of Taormina Theatre* (1905).

The development of Hungarian art is presented in the second floor. Works of the members of the artist colony Nagvabánvai are on display. One of them is Károly Ferenczy (1862-1917) who was an influential representative of non-academic styles such as Pleinair, impressionism and art nouveau. One of the greats is definitly József Rippl-Rónai (1861-1927) who incorporated his experiences of France within his artworks.

2nd and 3rd floor

In the second and third floor the collection of Hungarian paintings and sculptures from the post 1945 era is on display. Different stylistic directions from abstract Expressionism to Pop Art are represented.

Exhibits from the numismatic collection and collection of small sculptures are spread throughout the exhibition rooms of the different epochs. The National Gallery also owns an extensive graphics collection, part of which is shown in the museum.

Numismatic collection, graphics

SZÉCHÉNYI NATIONAL LIBRARY

Széchenyi National Library (Nemzeti Széchenyi Könyvtár) is housed in F wing of the Royal Palace since 1985. This institution, founded by Count Ferenc Széchenyi in 1802, is Hungary's largest and most important library. Around six million books, manuscripts and a whole range of writings are stored here, including more than 625,000 manuscripts and around 183,000 maps. Prize pieces of the collection are the »Budapest Notes«, which are among the oldest medieval song scores, as well as some of the codices from King Matthias Corvinus' library. This manuscript collection of originally around 2000 volumes was already famous far beyond Hungary's borders during the Renaissance ruler's lifetime.

F wing

✳ BUDAPEST HISTORICAL MUSEUM (BUDAPESTI TÖRTÉNETI MÚZEUM)

❶ Mar–Oct Thu–Sun 10am–6pm Nov–Feb Thu–Sun 10am–4pm; www.bhm.hu; admission: 1500 HUF

The Budapest Historical Museum in the E wing of the Royal Palace introduces the history of the Hungarian capital from pre-history to modern times. Visitors can see not only remains of the medieval

E wing

royal palace, but also precious works of art and other items found during excavations. The exhibition on the upper floors of the museum provides vivid information on the development of Budapest, or rather its municipal districts of Óbuda, Buda and Pest, which were independent until 1873. The historical survey ranges from the Stone Age and the Roman era, when a garrison and civilian settlement was built in Óbuda, right up to the end of the Second World War and the post-war years. Archaeological finds, tools and craftwork, as well as artistic metal and ceramic items, textiles, photos, domestic goods and other objects convey a lively and all-encompassing picture of life in the Hungarian metropolis.

Medieval remains of the royal castle

The medieval remains of the royal castle are especially worth seeing. A model of the medieval royal residence in the entrance hall of the lower ground floor helps to give an idea of the overall design of the former castle. In the partly reconstructed rooms of the medieval castle that follow, woodcarvings, painted oven tiles, kitchen utensils and weapons from the 14th and 15th century royal palace are shown. In

Medieval castle chapel

the **Renaissance Hall**, which was not part of the medieval castle, there is, among other paintings, a portrait of King Matthias Corvinus and Beatrice of Aragon – his second wife – under whose reign Italian Renaissance artists came to the royal court at Buda. The so-called **Gothic Hall**, with its two aisles and low-reaching cross-rib vaulting, is very beautiful. The cool dim passages and vaults of the southern part of the medieval castle section, as well as the dark chapel and the royal cellar in the northern section are also very interesting to explore.

Medieval fortifications

To the south, below wings E and F of the Royal Palace, several sections of the medieval fortifications of the castle, mostly built in the first half of the 15th century, have been reconstructed and can be seen from the terrace of the Historical Museum. The square tower (Buzogány torony) next to Ferdinand's Gate is especially imposing. In front of it is the southern rondel, above which is the wall-walk which completes the fortification above, along with the tower gate with portcullis and drawbridge, which was named **»Gate of Rest«**. Outside of the castle walls there are still several tombs from the time of the Turks.

✱ St Stephen's Basilica

✦ **C 6**

Location: V district, Szent István tér
Metro: M 1 (Arany János utca)

The Basilica of St. Stephen, built in the neo-Renaissance style, is one of the most impressive religious buildings in the Hungarian capital. Marble and stucco adorn the interior and one of Europe's largest bells hangs in the tower. A visit to the basilica treasury is also worthwhile.

The monumental size of the basilica is underlined by its 96m/316ft-tall central dome and two west towers in height 80m/264ft. In 1845 the design of the church was entrusted to József Hild, who had already made a name for himself as the architect. He was still largely a devotee of the classical style, and the ground plan of the building in the shape of a Greek cross and the central dome survive from his plan. After Hild's death in 1867, Miklós Ybl brought new ideas that eventually gave the church its monumental neo-Renaissance style. St Stephen's was completed by József Kauser after the death of Ybl in 1905.

Impressive basilica

One of the special features of the Basilica is Leó Feszler's sculptural decoration on the façade. The twelve apostles embellish the choir apse, while the four evangelists stand in niches on the drum of the

Sculptural decoration

St Stephen's Basilica

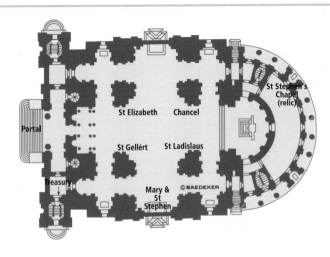

Portal

Treasury

St Elizabeth

Chancel

St Gellért

St Ladislaus

Mary & St Stephen

St Stephen's Chapel (relic)

©BAEDEKER

St Stephen's Basilica: opulent view at the end of the street

dome. Portraits of the church fathers are set into the two tower façades and Patrona Hungariae surrounded by saints occupies the tympanum above the narthex. A new nine-ton bell, one of the largest in
Europe, has rung from the basilica since 1989. It was donated as an
expression of thanks to the Hungarian people for their participation
in the political events that led up to the reunification of Germany.

Interior   The marble and gold-leaf stuccoed interior is predominantly the
work of Ybl, who recruited Hungary's leading contemporary artists
for the various tasks. A sculpture on the first right-hand pier of the
dome representing Bishop Gellért and St Emmerich was made by
Alajos Stróbl; on the second right-hand pier is the holy King Ladislaus, a work by János Fadrusz. St Elizabeth by Károly Senyei stands
on the second pier on the left. The dome mosaics representing biblical scenes were produced in the Salviati workshop in Venice to designs by Károly Lotz. A sculpture of St Stephen by Alajos Stróbl in
Carrara marble under the magnificent semi-circular canopy over the
high altar is a further reference to the patron saint of the basilica. The
bronze reliefs by E. Mayer on the apse wall show scenes from the

saint's life. Of the paintings in the side altars, special mention should be made of the second altar to the right of the main entrance, which originates from the workshop of Gyula Benczúr: it shows St Stephen offering the crown to the Virgin, the Patrona Hungariae – a popular subject in the country's Catholic iconography.

St Stephen's »Holy Right«, supposedly his right hand, is kept in a shrine in St. Stephen's Chapel. Every year on 20 August, the national holiday in honour of the canonized king, the relic is carried through the city in procession.

St Stephen's »Holy Right«

The treasury of St Stephen's Basilica holds magnificent vestments and extremely valuable liturgical objects from various Hungarian, Austrian and German workshops.

Treasury

❶ April–Sept daily 9am–5pm, Oct–Mar daily 10am–6pm

There is a wonderful view across the city from the platform around the basilica dome. Even the ascent of the dome is interesting. Visitors who are daunted by the steps can complete two thirds of the stretch by elevator, after which iron steps lead to the space between the inner and outer part of the dome. Here it is hard to escape the question of why such dome constructions don't regularly collapse – as this one actually did in 1868.

Platform

❶ April–May daily 10am–6.30pm, June–Aug. 9.30am–6pm, Sept–Oct 10am–5.30pm

In the summer sometimes Szent István tér and its surroundings are used as a concert stage. Many of cafés set their tables out in the open. Due to the transformation of the Zrínvi utca into a pedestrian zone the basilica is now very well connected to the Széchenvi István tér and the Chain Bridge.

Concerts and cafés

State Opera House

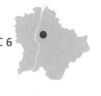

✦ C 6

Location: VI district, Andrássy út 22	**Ticket sales:**
Metro: M 1 (Opera)	Mon–Fri starts:
Trolley bus: 70, 78	11am, Sat, Sun
Bus: 4	11am–11am ???
Guided tours: daily 3pm, 6pm	**www.opera.hu**

The State Opera House is one of the most beautiful opera houses in the world. A tour provides an impression of its splendour, but it is even better to experience a performance here.

The State Opera House is a glamorous surrounding for special music experiences

Huge and magnificent building

The State Opera House was built in neo-Renaissance style between 1875 and 1884 to designs by Miklós Ybl on the newly created ▶Andrássy út, which was also laid out on the basis of plans supplied by Ybl. As one end of the opera house borders the magnificent boulevard, it is necessary to step into the adjoining side streets in order to get an idea of the vast dimensions of the building. The entrances lie behind a covered driveway for vehicles, which is constructed along the first floor as a balustraded loggia. In the niches on both sides of the vehicle access, sculptures by Alajos Stróbl commemorate the composer Franz (Ferenc) Liszt, as well as Ferenc Erkel, the first director of the opera house. The balustrade above is crowned by sculptures of famous composers by Gyula Donáth, György Kiss and again Alajos Stróbl.

*Interior

The heart of the opera house is the magnificent foyer with its double marble staircase at the centre. Ybl engaged the most renowned Hungarian artists of his day for the painting and sculptural decoration. The ceiling frescoes, which partly create the illusion of a coffered ceiling, are by Bertalan Székely, the wall paintings with scenes from Greek mythology by Mór Than. Stróbl completed the bust of the architect Ybl. The three-storey auditorium, designed as a loggia theatre, has exceptionally good acoustics. The ceiling and wall frescoes there were painted by Károly Lotz und Mór Than.

Szabadság tér

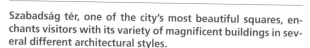

✦ C 5/6

Location: V. district
Metro: M 2 (Kossuth tér)
Bus: 15

Szabadság tér, one of the city's most beautiful squares, enchants visitors with its variety of magnificent buildings in several different architectural styles.

Freedom Square was laid out in the late 19th century after the decommissioning of a military barracks there. The commanding building on the square is the former stock exchange on the west side, built between 1902 and 1905, a magnificent edifice at the transition between historicism and art nouveau which is now home to the Hungarian State Television (MTV). Opposite stands the National Bank (Magyar Nemzeti Bank), designed by the Ignác Alpár which by now takes up an entire block with its offices including the former ▶ Post Savings Bank building behind it to the east. A few steps left of the National Bank the corner building housing the American Consulate is also worth a glance.

Various styles of architecture

To the north, a semi-circle of office blocks designed in a unified style at the end of the 19th century and the beginning of the 20th century closes off the square. The obelisk with a relief by the artist Károly Antal at the centre of the semi-circle has a special status, as it is apparently the only Soviet memorial that was allowed to remain in the city after Hungary's political turnaround. Some of those memorials are today on view at the ▶Memento Park.

In the back of the National Bank the formal Post Savings Bank stands on Hold ut-ca 2. Including the ▶Museum for Fine Arts it is one of Hungary's major examples of the national style.

Post Savings Bank

This architecture style developed around 1900 as a Hungarian variation of the European art nouveau. The pioneer and most important proponent of the national style was Ödön Lechner, who also produced the designs for the Post Savings Bank building, which opened in 1901. Characteristic of art nouveau as a whole are the broad spatial treatment of the façade and the continuous flowing form details, such as can be seen on the small gable ornamentation and the divisions of the windows. The Hungarian element is particularly apparent in the roof zone, with its colourful glazed tiles – from the Zsolnay

Art nouveau Post Savings Bank

factory in Pécs, of course – and the folk art flower motifs on the bat-
tlement-style gables.

House of
Hungarian
Secession

Next to the Post Savings Bank the House of Hungarian Secession
(Honvéd utca 3) opened thanks to a private initiative. Here Tivadar
Vad displays his private collection of art nouveau. The collection is
adjoined by the attractive Art Nouveau Café. The house used to belong to Béla Bedő who was a lover of the arts. The house is a felicitous
example of private culture commitment in Budapest.

❶ Mon–Sat 10am–5pm

Széchenyi István tér

B 6

Location: V district
Tram: 2, 2 A
Bus: 16, 105

The Palais Gresham is the largest eye catcher on the dual
square of the Pest side of the ▶Chain Bridge. It surpasses even
the neighbouring Academy of Science, especially when im-
pressively illuminated at night.

Square of the
»Reform
Count«

The square was named after former US President F.D. Roosevelt until 2011 when the name was changed and the square renamed after
the great Hungarian count István Széchenyi who was a driving force
in the modernisation process of Hungary. The building of the Chain
Bridge was undertaken due to his initiative. At the beginning of the
19th century the square was used as a place for markets and landing
station for cargo ships that went up and down the Danube from here,
until the Chain Bridge was build.

Colossal monuments on the square represent Széchenyi and another
distinguished statesman, who also had a massive influence on Hungary's political and economical development in the 19th century. On
the northern side of the square József I. Engel created an impressive
statue of the »count of reform« while Ferenc Deák is eternalized on
the south side. He played a major part in the negotiations that led to
the compromise between Austria and Hungary in 1866/67.

Hungarian
Academy of
Sciences

The north side of the square is dominated by the Hungarian Academy of Sciences whose foundation goes back to an initiative by István
Széchenyi in 1825. This centre of Hungary's highest-ranking scientific establishment was completed on construction plans of the Berlin
architect Friedrich August Stüler. The design for the building took as
its model the palace architecture of the Italian High Renaissance, the

era when scientific research was born. The statues of famous scientists that decorate the façade also indicate the building's purpose. A bronze relief from 1893 showing the foundation of the academy by Count Széchenyi in 1825 is especially noteworthy. Frescoes by Károly Lotz adorn the hall of the academy. Today numerous research institutes are affiliated with the academy. Its internationally renowned scientific library possesses an important collection of oriental literature.

Gresham Palace is one of the defining examples of architecture in the Secessionist style in Budapest. It was build in 1907 according to the design of Zsigmond Quittner and the brothers Lázló and József Vágó for the English insurance company Gresham. Until a buyer with the necessary financial resources was found, the impressive building was left to go to ruin but, after many years of meticulous renovation, the elegant Four Seasons Hotel opened its doors in Gresham Palace in 2003.

Gresham Palace

Details of Gresham Palace

The small **Eötvös tér** adjoins Széchenyi István tér to the south, with a memorial by Adolf Huszár created in honour of the author József Eötvös. The two five-star hotels Sofitel Atrium and Intercontinental occupy the southern side of the square; both were built in the early 1980s. Though built by Hungarian architects, their international architectural style does not really fit Budapest's historic building framework. Nevertheless, the roofed courtyard of the Sofitel Atrium is worth seeing for a model of Hungary's first airplane suspended high up.

Szentendre

✳ **Excursion**

Location: 20km north of Budapest
Access: HÉV Budapest – Szentendre; during the summer boats depart from Budapest's Vigadó tér

The charming Danube town of Szentendre, with its crooked lanes and bumpy cobblestones, has attracted artists since the beginning of the 20th century. Today visitors come from all over the world to visit the little galleries and museums, marzipan and souvenir shops.

Popular
excursion
venue

The small town on the hilly right-hand bank of the Danube is one of the most popular destinations for a short excursion from the capital – especially during the warmer times of year, when it is possible to arrive by boat. Consequently this »Hungarian Montmartre« gets very crowded during the high season. The origins of this settlement go back to the 4th century BC, when Celts settled here. The Romans built a garrison on the shores of the Bükkös stream in the first century AD, and called it Ulcisia Castra (Wolf Castle). It was first mentioned in documents in the 12th century, and Serbs came to Szentendre in several waves from the 14th century onwards, bringing their culture, Orthodox religion, customs and building traditions to Hungary. Szentendre experienced an economic upturn in the 18th century, when the town became the religious and cultural centre of the Hungarian Serbs and seat of the Greek Orthodox church. The tourist development of the town began in the early 20th century.

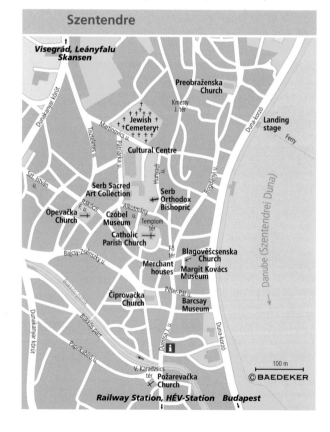

WHAT TO SEE IN SZENTENDRE

The main square of Szentendre, which has long been protected by a ***Fő tér**
preservation order, is the triangular Fő tér, surrounded by pretty
merchant houses of the Baroque and Rococo style. A merchant's
cross donated after a catastrophic plague epidemic has stood in the
middle of the square since 1763: a richly embellished cast-iron cross
on a pediment decorated with icons. The beautiful Serbian Orthodox
Blagoveštanska church, stands on
the east side of the square, which was
built to designs by Andreas Mayerhoffer in the middle of the 18th century. The iconostasis created in 1790
for the church interior is the work of
a Serbian artist.

The neighbouring former Serbian
school (Fö tér 6) build in late Rococo
style dates back to 1797 and was giv-
en back to the Serbian Orthodox
community. After the Károly Fernc-
zy museum has moved out it is
planned to move a part of the Serbi-
an Orthodox collection here, at the moment it is still completely held
in the Belgrade church. It remains unclear whether a new building
will and can be found for the Károly Fereczy Museum.

> **MARCO POLO TIP**
>
> ! *Sweet seduction* **Insider Tip**
>
> The name Szamos stands for up-
> scale pastry products in Budapest
> and its surroundings, chocolates
> and marzipan. In Szentendre the
> pastry dynasty has opened its own
> Marzipan Museum (Dumtsa lenő
> utca 16) with exquisite creations.
> In the neighbouring house a nice
> café invites for a sweet break.
> Tel: 0626 31 05 45

The work of Hungary's most famous female sculptor and ceramic art-   **Margit Ko-**
ist Margit Kovács (1902–1977), who combined folk art motifs with   **vács museum**
modern elements, can be viewed in the Baroque building on Vastagh
György utca 1.

❶ Apr–Oct daily 9am–6pm, Nov–Mar Tue–Sun 10am–4pm; www.pmmi.hu

The walled Templom tér on the top of castle hill was the centre of the   **Templom tér**
medieval settlement. Today it makes for a wonderful viewpoint, with
many market stalls selling folklore souvenirs. The foundations of the
Catholic parish church go back to the 13th century. The present
church is predominantly 18th-century, but the tower window and the
sundial still survive from the 14th and 15th century.

In a small house opposite the church, the artistic inheritance of the   **Béla Czóbel**
painter Béla Czóbel (1883 – 1976) is presented in a museum. The art-   **Museum**
ist left for Paris with only 22 years where he joined the Fauves and
exhibited together with Matisse. After his return to Hungary he made
the Hungarian art scene hum. He was a cofounder of the Group of
the Eight (Nyolcak), which however only was active together for a
short period of time. Czóbel, however, continued to be one of the

One should visit Szentendre not only for the Marzipan Museum but also because of its picturesque town centre

most creative and expressive Hungarian painters. After some years in the Netherlands and in Berlin Czóbel frequently stayed in Szentendre in the summer. One can be convinced that Czóbel was a painter of European format in the museum. Works from almost his entire artistic scope such as the paintings »*Boy holding a Ball*« (1916) as well as the *Venus of Szentendre* (1968) which he painted at 85, can be seen.
❶ Wed–Sun 10am–6pm

Belgrade Church The most elegant of Szentendre's total of seven Baroque churches is the Serbian Orthodox cathedral on Alkotmány utca, which was consecrated in 1764 and is known as the Belgrade Church. Inside the church the painted and gold-leaf iconostasis carved out of lime wood is worth seeing. Diagonally across, the collection of Serbian sacred art housed in the former bishop's palace displays art and religious objects.

*Skanzen An excursion to the Hungarian open-air museum approx. 3km/2mi north-west of Szentendre is highly recommended. A visit to this exhibition of Hungarian folk architecture and domestic culture and lifestyle, also called Skanzen after the famous open-air museum in Stockholm, is a journey into Hungary's rural past, introducing the lives of different social groups and classes of country people between the late 18th century and the early 20th century.

On view are characteristic settlement groups with buildings typical of regions from western Transdanubia, from the Upper Tisza area, the Small Plain and the Great Plain, as well as from the Balaton Uplands. In addition to the domestic homes furnished in historically precise detail, a whole range of different agricultural and craft installations, mills, animal sheds, barns, a smithy, a weaving workshop, as well as village churches and cemeteries give insight into the daily life of the rural population. On the hill above this settlement group stands the Greek Orthodox church built in log-house style from the small village of Mándok, which represents the basic type of an Orthodox church in the northern and eastern Carpathian mountains. Since 2009 a historical train huffs and puffs along the broad area.

● Mar–Oct Tue–Sun 10am–4pm; www.skanzen.hu

Tabán

✳ B 7

Location: I district
Tram: 18, 19, 41
Bus: 5, 7, 78, 86, 173

Green areas and arterial roads characterize Tabán today and visitors go to the Semmelweis Museum or take the steps up towards the castle.

The Tabán district lies between Castle Hill and ►Gellért Hill. In the 18th century, Serb refugees settled here in Tabán and the old district was one of the most appealing quarters of Budapest until the historic houses were demolished in the 1930s. Relics of the former district have survived on Szarvas tér, where the Golden Stag tavern and the parish church can be found.

Modernized district

The Golden Stag tavern (Aranyszarvas; Szarvas tér 1) at the bottom of the steps leading to the magnificent Royal Palace specializes in game dishes. It was built in Rococo style in the 19th century and has a golden stag (Arany Szarvas) above the entrance.

Golden Stag tavern

The Tabán parish church (Tabáni plébánia-templom) dedicated to St Catherine of Alexandria was built between 1728 and 1740. The treasures of the Baroque church include a copy of the carved Tabán Christ underneath the gallery. The 12th-century original can be seen in the Budapest Historical Museum (►Royal Palace).

Tabán parish church

The birthplace of the famous Hungarian doctor Ignác Semmelweis (►Famous People) stands at Apród utca 1–3, at the south-eastern

Semmelweis Museum

base of Castle Hill. Today the Baroque building with Rococo façade houses a museum of the history of medicine.

Semmelweis Orvostörténeti Múzeum: mid-March–Oct Tue–Sun 10.30am–6pm; Nov–mid-March until 4pm; www.semmelweismuseum.hu

Miklós Ybl tér

The elongated square on the banks of the Danube underneath the Royal Palace carries the name of the famous architect Miklós Ybl (1814–91), who significantly contributed to the appearance of Budapest with his buildings in the second half of the 19th century, including the great ▶St Stephen's Basilica. The memorial to him on the square dates from 1896 and is the work of sculptor E. Mayer. Several buildings designed by Ybl are ranged around the square.

The broad and magnificent flight of stairs that lead up from the banks of the Danube to the Royal Palace, built between 1875 and 1882, are one of the most impressive legacies of this architect, who carried out many commissions.

Town Hall (Városháza)

✳ C 6 / 7

Location: V district, Városház utca 9 – 11
Metro: M 1, M 2, M 3 (Deák tér)
Tram: 47, 49

The mighty 190m/210yd-long Baroque building in the heart of Pest, which has been used since 1894, was originally built as a hospital for invalids returning from the Turkish wars.

Hospital for veterans

The Viennese architect Anton Erhard Martinelli supplied the designs for the building complex, which takes up an entire block. It was commissioned by Emperor Charles VI and built between 1716 and 1728, and accommodated up to 2000 people. At the time of its construction the building stood at the north-eastern edge of Pest. Above the gates of the main body of the building there are two beautiful reliefs: one commemorates Charles VI as its patron, representing him as King Charles III of Hungary, the other shows Prince Eugene of Savoy, who emerged as a hero of the Turkish Wars.

District council of Pest

A building complex (Városház utca 7) with three courtyards erected in the 19th century, which now houses the district authority for Pest, adjoins the town hall.

Szervita tér

To the west of the town hall lies Szervita tér.**Two remarkable art nouveau houses** stand on the west side of the square: on the former bank building Török at no. 3, built in 1906 by Ármin Hegedüs and

Henrik Böhm, the sweeping gable with its shining gold mosaic stands out. The female figure in the centre of the picture embodies Patrona Hungariae. By contrast, the façade with its large areas of glass on the department store at no. 5 is considerably more sober. It was built by the design of Béla Lajta in 1912.

University Church

Location: V district, Papnövelde utca 5 – 7
Bus: 15

⟡ C 7

A Turkish mosque once stood on the site of today's University Church, which is considered the most beautiful Baroque church in the city.

The University Church would hardly be discovered on a casual stroll, as it lies in southern Pest on Egyetem tér, facing a narrow side street that barely allows its imposing exterior to make an impression. It was built for the Pauline order on top of a Turkish mosque between 1725 and 1742. The architect was an Austrian, Andreas Mayerhoffer. The two massive towers were only completed in 1771. The main façade of the church is topped by a pediment with representations of the hermits Paul and Anthony, as well as with the emblem of the Pauline order: a palm between two lions and a raven. A Madonna on a globe can be seen under the pediment.
Budapest's most beautiful baroque church

The interior is aisle-less with pilasters and enclosed side chapels. The vaulted ceiling was embellished with a fresco containing scenes from the life of the Virgin by Johann Bergl in 1776; here the architecture of the church is continued in the painting after the example of Italian Baroque art. The choir stalls and the sculptures on the main altar – the hermit saints Paul and Anthony – were carved by József Hebenstreit in 1746. At the centre of the altar there is a copy of the Black Madonna from Czestochowa in Poland, which was probably made in 1720. The pulpit, stalls and doors, as well as the sacristy cupboards with inlaid decoration, which contain valuable monstrances, cups and vestments, all originate from different workshops of the Pauline order of monks.

The 18th-century former Pauline monastery adjoins the church and was designed by Matthias Drenker. There is a ceiling fresco, painted by Pietro Rivetti in 1803, in the library, which also holds some medieval manuscripts. Since 1805 it has been used by the theological faculty of Hungary's first university, as the Pauline order was dissolved by Joseph II in 1786.
Former Pauline monastery

University Library The library building of the University (Ferenciek tere 10) stands a little further towards the city centre. Where it was completed in 1775. The collection possesses numerous medieval codices amongst other treasures. Its interior has wonderfully decorated bookcases with a continuous gallery and two spiral staircases. The ceiling fresco was painted by Pietro Rivetti in 1803.

Váci utca

✳ C 6/7

Location: V district
Metro: M 1 (Vörösmarty tér), M 2, 3
(Deák tér), M 3 (Ferenciek tere)

Bus: 5,7,8,112,173

The Hungarian publicist György Dalos once aptly described Váci utca as »a mixture of flea market and respectable shopping street«. This description fits very well in so far as György Dalos truly is a very popular street for strolling and shopping.

Pedestrain zone of Pest Here, in the busy pedestrian zone of Pest city centre, the capital's most elegant shops can be found, as well as the chic boutiques of international fashion houses, shoe and leatherware shops, new and antiquarian bookshops – among others Libri for foreign-language books – antique shops, jewellery and craft shops, espresso bars, wine bars and the offices of leading airline companies, but also cheap book stalls and street artists, all of which combines to give the street its characteristic flavour. The much less frequented section of Váci utca to the south of Szabadsajtó út is comparatively humble, quiet and much less hectic – more charming, in fact, than the overdone, highly commercialized northern part. The underground walkway that connects

Váci utca

the northern section of Váci utca with the southern one is decorated with interesting historic **photographs** by the Hungarian artist György Klösz of Budapest street scenes from around 1900.

A former hotel where the eleven-year-old Franz Liszt gave his first concert in Pest in 1823, is now home to the Pest Theatre (no. 9). The foyer with its beautifully crafted dark mosaics is very elegant. The **New Town Hall** (no. 62–64) was built in the neo-Renaissance style by Imre Steindl, the architect of Parliament, between 1869 and 1875.

Pest Theatre

Shortly before Váci utca meets ►Fövám tér, turn left onto Szerb utca to see the Serbian Church on the corner of Veres Pálné utca. Numerous Serbs were resident in the city at the beginning of the 19th century, and their church is said to have been designed by the famous architect Andreas Mayerhoffer in the 18th century. The nave is divided into three parts; the raised women's section is separated from the men's section by a wooden balustrade.

Serbian Church

Vízivaros

A / B 5 – 6

Location: I district
Suburban train HÉV: Batthyány tér
Metro: M 2 (Batthyány tér)
Tram: 19, 41
Bus: 86

Vízivaros, »Watertown«, extends along the narrow terrace between Castle Hill and the western side of the Danube.

Right up to the era of Turkish rule, this quarter was fortified. The Ottomans installed baths in the area predominantly populated by fishermen, artisans and merchants, and turned the existing churches into mosques. The name Watertown is explained by the repeated floods to which Vízivaros was once exposed. There was a lot of building here during the Baroque era, when craftsmen and merchants settled on Castle Hill as a result of the construction of the Royal Palace. This is when, among other buildings, St Anne's Church (►Batthyány tér) was erected. The character of the quarter has been permanently changed by the building of multi-storey apartment blocks from the end of the 19th century onwards.

Freequent flooding

The house at Fő utca 20, whose origins reach back to the 15th century, was rebuilt in the 18th century and given its attractive Rococo façade in 1811. The corner bay crowned by a turret is particularly

Historic building

pretty, as are the reliefs under the windows. The Biedermeier interior dates from the mid-19th century.

St Elizabeth Church A Baroque church was built in 1757 on the foundations of a Turkish structure which originally belonged to the Franciscans. It was transferred to the Elizabethan nuns in 1785, who set up a hospital, which today serves as an old people's home (Fő utca 41 – 43). Details worth seeing are the sculptures on the church façade and the pulpit made by the Franciscan monks.

Király bath ▶MARCO POLO Insight p.174

St Florian's Chapel The little St Florian's Chapel (Fő utca 90) dates from 1759–60 and is the work of the architect Matthäus Nepauer. Today it is used as a parish church by members of the Greek Orthodox community. Beautiful statues of the saints Nicolas, Florian and Blasius adorn the façade of the chapel. The paintings and sculptures that used to be inside the chapel can now be seen in the Historical Museum on Castle Hill (▶Royal Palace).

Corvin tér South of ▶Batthyány tér, about halfway to Clark Adam tér, lies Corvin tér. It is lined by several noteworthy buildings from the 18th century (nos. 2, 3, 4, and 5). The former Capuchin monastery stands on the southern side of the square and still shows evidence of Turkish construction and ornamentation.

Foundry Museum The Foundry Museum (Bem József utca 20), an old foundry established by Abraham Ganz in the middle of the 19th century, was the foundation of the Ganz industrial concern. This company, which became famous far beyond Hungary, built locomotives, wagons and cranes etc. The museum illustrates the history of the Hungarian iron industry.
❶ April–Nov Tue–Sun 9am–5pm, Dec–Mar Tue–Sun 9am–4pm

Vörösmarty tér

✦ C 6

Location: V district
Metro: M 1 (Vörösmarty tér)

Named after the poet Mihály Vörösmarty, this traffic-free square is the lively heart of Pest city centre, where it is a great pleasure to watch the world go by from one of the street cafés.

Lively city centre Immaculately renovated former office buildings around the square now house all manner of shops. The steel-glass building that was built

2008 on the west side of the square houses offices, stores and luxurious appartments. On the other side of the square the building of the former Luxus department store is discreet, but nevertheless architecturally interesting for its skeleton construction. Today smaller boutiques and shops are housed here.

At the centre of the square, surrounded by trees, the memorial to Mihály Vörösmarty (1800–1855) shows the poet enthroned in an armchair. The figures at his feet – children, adults, old and young – represent the Hungarian people that Vörösmarty's prophetic poem *Szózar* eulogizes. The first line of this work is etched into the marble base of the monument: »Hazádnak rendületlenül légy híve, óh magyar« (»Hungarians, always retain love and loyalty to your homeland«). To the right, underneath the first stanza's line, a black mark is noticeable, supposedly a »lucky forint« donated by a beggar when the memorial was built. The construction of Carrara marble is the work of the artists Kallós and Telcs from the year 1908.

Vörösmarty Monument

The famous Café Gerbeaud, which was founded by Henrik Kugler in 1858 and later became the property of the Swiss patissier Emil Gerbeaud, is at the northern side of the square. Gerbeaud's original interior survives to this day. The café was temporarily called Café Vörösmarty and was an extremely popular society rendezvous in the early 20th century. In the summer months it is pleasant to spend time here, watching the colourful life on the square from the terrace while savouring a cup of excellent coffee. Nevertheless, even in good weather a look at the beautiful 19th-century interior should not be missed.

** Pastry shop Gerbeaud

In order to get to the Vigado tér from Vörösmartv tér one merely has to follow Vigado tér. Pest's Vigado ballroom and concert hall are among the most impressive creations of the Romantic era in Hungary. The designs for Pest's Vigadó ballroom and concert hall on the banks of the Danube were supplied by the architect Frigyes Feszl (1821– 84), a commission he received in 1859, ten years after the old concert hall had been destroyed during the 1848–49 revolution. The new ballroom and concert hall was inaugurated with pomp and circumstance in 1864. The richly embellished main façade facing the Danube, with its high rounded arches opening from the large concert hall on the first floor, is decorated by female figures symbolizing music and dance. A frieze above the window arches contains the Hungarian coat of arms as well as representing Hungarian rulers and politicians. The building was used for all kinds of festive occasions and musical presentations; Liszt and Bartók, among others, conducted here. It has been under renovation for years now and still awaits its reopening.

*Pesti Vigadó

PRACTICAL
INFORMATION

Where can one get informed? Which Hungarian books are recommendable? How do you say »Thank you« in Hungarian? Look it up – best before your trip!

Arrival · Before the Journey

HOW TO ARRIVE IN BUDAPEST

By air There are direct flights from destinations around the world, including the USA, to Budapest. The Hungarian national carrier Malev serves a large number of routes, sometimes via Amsterdam, Madrid or Prague. Direct connections within Europe are operated by low-cost airlines such as Easyjet (e.g. from London Gatwick, flight time 2.5 hrs, www.easyjet.com), Ryanair (from Liverpool and Dublin, flight time 3 hrs, www.ryanair.com) and Wizzair (from London Luton, www.wizzair.com). Budapest's Ferenc Liszt International airport lies at the south-east end of the city and has two totally separate terminals: The older Terminal 1 is closer to the town and is the destination for cheaper airlines; Terminal 2 A and Terminal 2 B are the newer additions to the airport and therefore further away. The Sky Court connects them with each other. Terminal 2 A serves as station for flights that are uncontrolled according to the Schengen agreement. The international flights arrive and depart from Terminal 2 B.

The official **airport taxi** is Zónaltaxi. The prices depend and are bound to according zones. A taxi ride into town takes round about half an hour, depending on the traffic.

The **airport minibuses** take the air passengers to any address in Budapest. Each person pays the same amount. A group of several people pays less when they take a taxi. Tickets can be bought at the booths in the arrival hall. A trip back to the airport must be reserved 24 hours in advance (Tel. 061 2 96 85 55).

A transfer by train is no problem as well since a station is included in Terminal 1. The train's destination is the West Train Station (Nyugati pu.). Tickets are available at the tourist information in Terminal 1.

A further possibility to get into town is via bus or metro. First take the fast bus 200 E from terminal 1 or 2 to the Kőbánya-Kispest Metro station, where there is a fast metro no. 3 link to the city centre. Desks of the car hire firms can be found in the airport terminals.

By rail The most direct rail journey from London to Budapest goes via Paris and Munich. Other routes from western and central Europe are via Nuremberg, Passau, Linz and Vienna; or via Berlin, Dresden, Prague and Bratislava. Connections from the east (Moscow) and south (Rome) are also often routed through Bratislava. Most international trains arrive at Budapest's East Railway Station (Keleti pu.).

Train travel can be very convenient and cheap if tickets are booked early in advance. The Savings Tickets of the rail companies offer large reductions.

AIRLINES
Malév
www.malev.hu

easyjet
www.easyjet.com

Ryanair
www.ryanair.com

Wizzair
www.wizzair.com

FERENC LISZT AIRPORT
Information
Arrival: Tel. 1 2 96 80 00
Departure: Tel. 1 2 96 70 00

TRAIN INFORMATION
Tel. 1 4 44 44 99

RAILWAY STATIONS
East Railway Station
(Keleti pályaudavar)
VIII, Baross tér
Trains to Austria and Switzerland as well as Germany, the Czech Republic and Slovakia depart from here.

West Railway Station
(Nyugaati pályaudavar)
VI, Nyugati tér
Trains depart to the northeast Danube region (Vác. Nagymaros ect.) and to Terminal 1 of the airport.

South Railway Station
(Déli pályaudavar)
I, Alkotás út
Many trains run to Austria and Slovenia as well as Croatia, Serbia and Bosnia. It is also the starting point for the regional transportation to Lake Balaton, Pécs, Tapolca, Szombathely and Győr.

BUSES
Volánbusz Eurolines
Reservation in Budapest:
IX, ÜllŐ ut 131
Tel. 1 2 19 80 00
www.volanbusz.hu

BOATS
Mahart
V, Belgrád rakpart
Tel. 1 4 84 40 13
www.mahart.hu

By bus
Volánbusz AG in cooperation with Eurolines has an all-year-round service to Budapest at regularly scheduled times from many European cities, though the number of direct connections is limited. Journey time from London to Budapest is around 24 hrs.

By car
The easiest way to reach Budapest from Western Europe is via Austria. From Vienna, the Austrian motorway leads to the Nickelsdorf/Hegyeshalom border crossing, and from there it's the Hungarian M 1 motorway, for which you need a vignette. From the north, the best route is via the Czech motorway D 1 (Prague to Brno) and then the Slovak motorway D 2 (Brno to Bratislava), crossing the Hungarian border for Budapest at Rajka.

By ship
From the beginning of May to September, there are hydrofoils between Vienna (landing stage: Reichsbrücke/Mexikoplatz) and Buda-

pest (landing stage: Belgrád rakpart) that run 3 times a week. Journey time from Vienna to Budapest is about five hours heading downstream and around six hours heading upstream. Several very comfortable cruise ships travel from Germany and Vienna to the Hungarian capital. Information available from any travel agent

TRAVEL REQUIREMENTS

Documents

Hungary is participant in the Schengen Agreement between the countries of the European Union. This allows travel between EU countries without identity check.

Citizens of the European Union, USA, Canada, Australia and New Zealand need a valid passport or identity card for visits to Hungary. South African citizens need a visa. Children now require their own passport. Car drivers must carry their driving license and vehicle registration documents, and insurance is recommended. Damaged cars can enter or leave Hungary only with the relevant documentation issued at the border or at the accident site in Hungary.

Animals

The importation of animals to Hungary is only permitted with an official veterinary certificate that may not be more than eight days old at the time of entry. A rabies vaccination certificate must be produced and, in addition, dogs require a vaccination for canine distemper. Dog owners must bring a lead and muzzle; the import of so-called dangerous fighting dogs is prohibited.

Custom regulations

Since 2004 Hungary has been a member of the European Union. Movement of goods for private purposes is largely duty free within the area of the European Union. Certain restrictions on quantities apply (e. g. for visitors, 800 cigarettes, 400 cigarillos, 200 cigars, 10 liters of spirits, and 90 litres of wine and 110 litres of beer).

All personal items may be taken out duty free for travellers by air or sea, as well as presents and souvenirs to a maximum total value of €430. For train and car travellers the maximum amount is €300. For children under 15 the limit is at €175, irrespective of the transportation method. The export of artefacts, precious metals and precious metal products, as well as of stamps, is only possible with special permission. Precise information is available from the customs authorities.

Electricity

The Hungarian alternate voltage runs at 220 Volt. Adapters are not required.

Emergencies

General emergency number: Tel. 112	*Tourist police* Tel. 1 4 38 80 80 (English)
Police Tel. 107	*Accidents/emergency doctors* Tel. 104
	Fire department Tel. 105

Etiquette and Customs

Hussars galloping across the Puszta plains to the sound of passionate gypsy music; later »goulash communism« or »the happiest hut in the camp«: these are the clichés that come to mind when speaking of Hungary. Beyond that, the impossible, unintelligible language with its unbelievably long words might come to mind – or the famously beautiful Hungarian women. It is true that Hungary's communist state was a lot more relaxed and colourful than its fellows behind the grim Iron Curtain. However, privately, Hungarians reject the other clichés without wanting to constantly deny them either. After all, it is these – predominantly positive – clichés that year on year draw many millions of visitors to their state on the Danube. For a country without significant reserves in raw materials, tourism is an essential economic factor. It is therefore not beyond the realms of possibility that when a western tourist sees a genuine-looking rider with a whip in his hand on the legendary plains of the Hungarian Puszta Hortobágy, he is actually watching a philosophy student from the University of Debrecen earning money in the summer holidays to finance a trip to Majorca.

Hungary from the outside

Loneliness and tragic pathos – always spiced with a positively insistent hope that good will triumph –are the sentiments that make the Hungarian soul come alive. This small nation feels alone, surrounded by great and important nationalities, and its thousand-year history seems a tragic chain of disasters. Of course, no one, much less a nation, can endure only sadness, and therefore the positive milestones are noted with great pride: 1456, when Marshal János Hunyadi expelled the Turks from Belgrade; 1848–49 when the country flew the flag of the European revolution to the last; or October 1956, when the uprising temporarily toppled the communist dictatorship. Despite

Hungarian self-image

the ultimately tragic outcome of all these events, despair and hope lie very close together in Hungary. Apart from this, Hungarians in the 21st century appreciate the same values as in the rest of Europe: independence, a united family, education, security, property and holidays abroad.

Drinking
It is said that »the Magyar amuses himself by crying«. Crying, but never without wine. Hungarian drinking was and is a defiant expression of a love of life. In hardly any other literature is there so much and such passionate boozing, and so it is at parties and festivals in real life as well. Hungarians are friendly hosts and like to spoil their guests with their national dishes. Small presents for the host, such as flowers, chocolates or wine are always welcome.

Greetings
As a rule, people introduce themselves by their surname, occasionally followed by their first name (Kovács Sándor). Adults normally greet each other with a firm handshake, good friends embrace each other and offer a kiss on the cheek, to the left and right. It counts as especially polite to address people by their title (Doctor, Profesor …), followed by their surname. Colloquial greetings include, among others, Szervusz oder Szia. And when you say good-bye, you say Viszontlátásrá or simply Viszlát.

Health

First aid
First aid is always provided free of charge. Since 2005 the European Health insurance card (EHIC) is in effect. However mostly a part of the doctors or the pharmaceutical bill has to be paid. The cost of repatriation is generally not carried by medical insurance, and it is therefore usually best to arrange private travel insurance.

Pharmacies
In each municipal district at least one pharmacy (Patika, Gyógyszertár) each day has 24-hour service, usually on a rotating basis. Every pharmacy has a notice displaying the address of the nearest pharmacy offering a night service; several are always open around the clock.

Ambulance
Tel. 1 04

Medical on-call service
Falck SOS Hungary
II. Kapv utca 49 B, tel. 1 2 00 01 00

Dental emergencies
SOS Dental Service
VI. Király utca 14
Tel. 2 67 96 02

Information

IN UK
Hungarian National Tourist Office
46 Eaton Place
London SW1X 8AL
Tel. 0080036000000
(free of charge)
www.gotohungary.co.uk

IN USA
Hungarian National Tourist Office
350 Fifth Avenue, Suite 7107
New York, NY 10118
Tel. (212) 6951221
www.gotohungary.com

IN BUDAPEST
Hungarian Tourism Office
Magyar Turizmus Rt., PO Box 215
1364 Budapest
fax 266–7477
info@budapestinfo.hu
www.hungarytourism.hu
www.budapestinfo.hu
(only for written queries)

Tourinform main office
V, Sütö utca2 (Pest)
tel. 438–8080, fax 317–9656
www.tourinform.hu

Tourinform branch offices
Liszt Ferenc Square 11
(Pest, near Oktogon)
Tel. 322-4098, fax 342-9390

Castle Hill
Szentháromság Square (Buda)
Tel. 488-0475, fax 488-0474

Tourinform Call Centre
Tel. 438–8080 (24 h)

Fax 356–1964
hungary@tourinform.hu

Touchscreen information
Electronic information pillars can be
found all over the city. They provide information, for example, on sights, museums, opening hours, local transport and
accommodation options

INTERNET
www.budapestinfo.hu
Website for the Budapest Tourist Office
with information on sights, the Budapest Card, shopping, excursions and
much more

http://hotels.hu
Hotels, restaurants, holiday rental
properties

http://english.budapest.hu
The Budapest portal, internet presentation of the city in English

www.visitorsguide.hu
Online information from the Budapest
Sun

EMBASSIES IN BUDAPEST
Australia
XII, Királyhágó tér 8–9
Tel. 457–9777
www.hungary.embassy.gov.au

Canada
II, Ganz utca 12–14
Tel. 392–3360
http://geo.international.gc.ca/
canada-europa/hungary/

Ireland
Bank Center, Granite Tower
V Szabadság tér 7
Tel. 301–4960

United Kingdom
V, Harmincad utca 6
Tel. 266–2888
www.britishembassy.gov.uk/hungary

USA
V Szabadság tér 12
Tel. 475–4164
http://hungary.usembassy.gov/

HUNGARIAN EMBASSIES
AND CONSULATES
Australia
Suite 405, Edgecliff Centre, 203-233
New South Head Road
Edgecliff, Sydney, NSW 2027

Tel. 02/ 93287859
Fax 93271829

Canada
299 Waverley Street
Ottawa, Ontario K2P OV9
Tel. 613/230 2717, fax 230 7560

Ireland
2 Fitzwilliam Place, Dublin 2
Tel. 01/661290200, fax 6612880

UK
35 Eaton Place
London SW1X 8BY
Tel. 0207/2355218, fax 8231348

USA
223 East 52nd Street
New York, N.Y.10022
Tel. 212/7520669, fax 755 5986

Language

It is rarely difficult to communicate in Budapest, as most young people speak English.

Hungarian language guide

Pronunciation Vowels

a	as in »pot«
á	as in »father«
e	as in »pet«
é	as in »air«
i	as in »pit«
í	as in »peat«
o	as in »saw«, but short
ó	as in »shawl«
ö	as in »curt«, but short with no »r« sounded
u	as in »hull«

| ú | as in »rule« |
| ü | as in French »tu« |

Consonants

c	as »ts«in »pits«
cs	as »ch« in »chips«
dz	as in »adze«
dzs	as »j«in »jump«
gy	as »du« in »duel« (British)
j/ly	as in »yes«
ny	as in »canyon«
r	rolled
s	as in »shut«
sz	as in »sit«
ty	as »tu« in »tune« (British)
zs	as »s« in »leisure«

At a glance

Yes/No	Igen/Nem.
Maybe	Talán.
Please	Kérem.
Thank you	Köszönöm.
It's a pleasure	Szívesen.
Sorry!	Bocsánat!
What did you say?	Tessék?
I don't understand you	Nem értem.
I only speak a little ...	Csak egy kicsit beszélek ...
Do you speak ...	Beszél ...
... English?	... angolul?
Please write it down for me	Kérem írja fel!
Can you please help me?	Tudna nekem segíteni kérem?
I want	Szeretnék
I (don't) like that	Ez (nem) tetszik.
Do you have ...?	Van ...?
How much is it?	Mennyibe kerül?
What time is it?	Hány óra (van)?

Greetings

Good morning!	Jó reggelt!
Good day!	Jó napot!
Good evening!	Jó estét!
Hello!/Hello!	Szia!/Sziasztok!
How are you?	Hogy van/vagy?
Thank you. And you?	Köszönöm. És Ön/te?

Good bye!	Viszontlátásra!
Bye!	Szia/Sziasztok!
See you soon!/See you later!	Viszlát!

Out and About

left/right	balra /jobbra
straight ahead	egyenes(en)
near/far	közel /messze
Excuse me, where is... ?	Hol van kérem a(z) ... ?
How far is it?	Milyen messze van?
You can take...	Mehet ...
... the bus ...	... busszal.
... the tram ...	... villamossal.
... the metro ...	... metróval.

Breakdowns

My car has broken down	Defektem van.
Could you please send me a towing vehicle?	Tudna nekem egy vontatókocsit küldeni?
Where is there a garage near here?	Hol van itt a közelben egy muhely?

Petrol station

Where is the next petrol station please?	Hol (van) a legközelebbi benzinkút?
I want ... litres ...	... liter ... kérek.
... leaded petrol.	... normálbenzint
... super.	... szupert.
... diesel.	... dízelt.
... unleaded.	... ólommenteset
Fill it up please.	Tele kérem.

Accident

Help!	Segítség!
Careful!	Figyelem!
Watch out!	Vigyázat!
Please quickly call ...	Hívjon gyorsan ...
... an ambulance.	... mentot.
... the police.	...a rendorséget.
... the fire brigade.	... a tuzoltókat.
It was my fault.	Ön vagyok a hibás.
It was your fault.	Ön a hibás.
Please give me your name and address.	Adja meg kérem a nevét és a címét!

Eating

Where can I find ...	Hol van itt ...
... a good restaurant?	... egy jó étterem?
... a not too expensive restaurant?	... egy nem túl drága étterem?
Is there a cosy tavern here?	Van itt valahol egy nyugodt, ... hangulatos kocsma?
Please reserve a table for us for this evening.	Foglaljon kérem nekünk ma ... estére egy asztalt.
The meal was excellent.	Az étel kituno volt.

Numbers

0	nulla	1	egy
2	ketto két	3	három
4	négy	5	öt
6	hat	7	hét
8	nyolc	9	kilenc
10	tíz	11	tizenegy
12	tizenketto/ tizenkét	13	tizenhárom
14	tizennégy	15	tizenöt
16	tizenhat	17	tizenhét
18	tizennyolc	19	tizenkilenc
20	húsz	21	huszonegy
22	huszonketto/.. huszonkét	30	harminc
40	negyven	50	ötven
60	hatvan	70	hetven
80	nyolcvan	90	kilencven
100	száz	101	százegy
200	kétszáz	300	háromszáz
1000	ezer	2000	kétezer
10,000	tízezer	1/2	fél
1/3	harmad	1/4	egy negyed
3/4	háromnegyed		

Accommodation

Can you recommend ...	Tudna ajánlani egy ...
... a good hotel ...	... jó szállodát?
... a pension ...	... panziót?
Do you have a room available?	Van még szabad szobájuk?
a single	egy egyágyas szobát
a double	egy kétágyas szobát
with bathroom	fürdoszobával
for one night	egy éjszakára
for one week	egy hétre

What does the room with … cost?	Mennyibe kerül a szoba …?
… breakfast	… reggelivel
… half-board	… félpanzióval

Doctor

| Can you recommend a good doctor? | Tud nekem egy jó orvost ajánlani? |
| It hurts here. | Itt fáj. |

Bank

| Where is there a bank here? | Hol van itt kérem egy bank? |
| I want to change … euros (pounds/dollars) into forint. | Szeretnék … Euro (svájci frankot) forintra átváltani. |

Post

What does it cost to send …?	Mibe kerül …?
… a letter …	… egy levél …
… a post card …	… egy levelezolap …
stamp	bélyeg

Étlap (menu)

Reggeli	Breakfast
feketekávé	black coffee
tejeskávé	white coffee
tea tejjel	tea with milk
tea citrommal	tea with lemon
lágytojás	soft egg
rántotta	scrambled egg
szalonnás rántotta	egg and bacon
kenyér/zsemle/pirítós	bread/rolls/toast
kifli	croissant
vaj	butter
sajt	cheese
kolbász	sausage
sonka	ham
méz	honey
lekvár	jam
müzli	muesli
joghurt	yogurt
gyümölcs	fruit
Eloöételek ès Levesek	Starters and soups
bableves	bean soup
burgonyaleves	potato soup
eroleves	bouillon
hortobágyi palacsinta	pancake with meat filling

libamájpástétom	goose liver paté
májgombócleves	liver dumpling soup
töltött paradicsom	stuffed tomatoes
zöldségleves	vegetable soup
Húsételek és Szárnyas	**Meat and poultry**
báránypaprikás	paprika lamb with sour cream
bécsi szelet	Viennese Schnitzel
bélszínjava	steak
birkapörkölt	mutton goulash
borjúpaprikás	veal goulash with cream
csirke	chicken
fott marhahús	stewed beef
hagymás rostélyos	onion roast meat
(vad)kacsa	(wild) duck
(vad)liba	(wild) goose
naturszelet	schnitzel without breadcrumbs
pirított máj	chopped liver
pulyka	turkey
sertéskaraj	pork cutlet
sült kolbász	bratwurst
vagdalt	minced meat
Nemzeti Ételek	**National dishes**
bográcsgulyás	goulash
csirkepaprikás	paprika chicken with sour cream
gulyásleves	goulash soup
Gundel palacsinta	pancake with nut filling and chocolate sauce
halászlé	spicy fish soup
hideg meggyleves	cold sour cherry soup
káposztás kocka	cabbage
kapros-túrós rétes	quark strudel with dill
lecsó	cooked whole paprika, tomatoes and onions
máglyarakás	bread pudding with apples
somlói galuska	Schomlau dumplings
töltött káposzta	meat-filled cabbage
töltött paprika	stuffed paprika
túrós csusza pirított szalonnával	noodles with sour cream and lard
Halak	**Fish**
angolna	eel
csuka	pike
fogas/süllo	pikeperch
lazac	salmon
pisztráng	trout
ponty	carp

tonhal	tuna
Zöldség és Köretek	**Vegetables and side dishes**
bab	beans
borsó	peas
fejes saláta	lettuce
fokhagyma	garlic
fott burgonya	boiled potatoes
galuska	dumplings
gomba	mushrooms
(zsemle)gombóc	(bread dumplings
hagyma	onion
hasábburgonya	French fries
karfiol	red cabbage
kelbimbó	cabbage
kelkáposzta	curled lettuce
lencse	lentils
paradicsom	tomatoes
paprika	paprika
póréhagyma	mashed potatoes
rizs	rice
sárgarépa	carrots
spagetti	spaghetti
sparga	asparagus
sült burgonya	sautéed potatoes
vegyes saláta	mixed salad
szpresszó	**Café**
dobostorta	Dobos gateau (six layers of pastry with chocolate cream and caramel icing)
fagyaltkehely	ice cream
kávé	coffee
sütemény	cake
teasütemény	biscuits
tejszínhab	cream

Itallap (drinks menu)

Borok	Wine
asztali bor	table wine
különleges minöségü bor	premium-quality wine
evjarat	vintage
édes	sweet
fröccs	mixed with mineral water
könnyu	light
fehér	white
vörös	red
száraz/fanyar	dry

fèlédes	semi-sweet
fèlszáras	semi-dry
pezsgo	champagne, sparkling wine
Szeszes Italok	**Alcoholic Drinks**
sör	beer
pohár	glass
korsó	small jar
üveg	bottle
gyomorkeseru	schnaps (digestif)
pálinka	schnaps
Alkoholmentes Italok	**Soft Drinks**
almalé	apple juice
(ásvány)víz	(mineral) water
gyümölclé	fruit juice
narancslé	orange juice
szódavíz	soda water

Literature

Attila Jószef, *Selected Poems*, iUniverse.com 2005. Moving collection of poems. Jószef (1905–37) grew up in the poor working-class district of Ferencváros.

Imre Kertész, *Fateless,* Vintage Books 2006. The Nobel prize-winner for literature in 2002 (►Famous People) attempts the demystification of Auschwitz in this great book; it is the semi-autobiographical tale of a young man's journey to the concentration camp.

Insider Tip

Imre Kertész, *Liquidation,* Vintage Books 2007. Set in Budapest after the end of communism, this book explores the attempts of a man to come to terms with the suicide of a friend.

Arthur Phillips, *Prague,* Duckworth 2006. No, the title is not a mistake. In this novel about life in Budapest during the post-communist years, many of the characters find the Czech capital more attractive than their own.

Giorgio and Nicola Pressburger, *Homage to the Eighth District: Tales from Budapest,* Readers International 1990. Tales of life and survival in the Jewish quarter during the Nazi era and Stalinism.

Betty Schimmel/Joyce Gabriel, *To See You Again: the Betty Schimmel Story,* Simon & Schuster 1999. The tragic love story between

Betty and Richie during the Second World War is shattering, and not just for its authenticity.

Bryan Cartledge, *The Will to Survive: A History of Hungary*, Timewell Press 2006. Detailed history, well written and researched, by a former British ambassador to Hungary.

John Lukacs, *Budapest 1900: A Historical Portrait of a City and its Culture*, Grove Press 1988. This classic description of Budapest portrays the city in its golden age.

Sándor Márai, *Memoir of Hungary: 1944–48*, Central European University Press 1996. The playwright Márai was forced to flee Hungary in 1948. Here he tells of the destruction of Budapest in the war and the post-war establishment of communism.

Kriztián Ungváry, *The Siege of Budapest: 100 Days in World War II*, Yale University Press 2006. Details of the battle that resulted in the loss of 25,000 civilian lives and the destruction of or severe damage to most of the city's historic buildings.

Lost and Found

In Budapest all transportation companies as well as train stations and the airport have their own lost and found (Talált tárgvak oztálva). Things that are found in public areas or in regular and department stores are usually redirected to the lost and found of the appropriate city district.

Ferihegy Airport
Terminal 2A
Tel. 296–8108 or 296–7217
Terminal 2B
Tel. 295–3480 or 296–7690

Metropolitan Transport BKV
VII, Akácfa u.18
Tel. 267–5299
(lost on the same day)

Media

International Press

International newspapers and magazines can be bought at newsstands in the inner city, the airport, in the three large train stations and the newsstands of the large hotels.

Two English-language newspapers are published weekly: the tabloid *Budapest Sun* (www.budapestsun.com) on Thursdays, with a useful arts and events section, and the *Budapest Times* (www.budapest-times.hu) on Mondays with reviews of what's on in the city. *Budapest Week* (www.budapestweek.hu). For serious reading on Hungary, its culture and current issues, read the high-brow *Hungarian Quarterly* (www.hungarianquarterly.com)

Hungarian Press

Apart from the above papers and the information available frree of charge from the tourist offices and hotels in *Budapest Panorama* and *Budapest City Magazine*, it is worth consulting the English-language brochures *Budapest In Your Pocket* (www.inyourpocket.com) and *Budapest Pocket Guide* (www.budpocketguide.com), which are updated four or five times a year and contain relevant information for tourists, including addresses, opening times and an events calendar.

Brochures, listings magazines

Money

The Hungarian currency is the Forint (HUF). Coins as much as 5, 10, 20, 50, 100 and 200 Forint as well as notes with the value of 500, 1000, 2000, 5000, 10.000 and 20.000 Forint are in circulation.

Currency

Foreign currency as well as native currency above 1 million Forint must be declared. Other restrictions on imported currency do not exist.

Restrictions

EXCHANGE RATES
100 HUF = £ 0.24
1 £ = 414 HUF
100 HUF = 0.37 US$
1 US$ = 269 HUF
100 HUF = € 0.32
1 € = 305 HUF

LOST OR STOLEN CARDS
The following numbers can be used to report and stop lost or stolen bank and credit cards:

American Express
tel. +44 1273 696 933

MasterCard
tel. +44 20 7557 5000

Visa
tel. +1 410 581 9994

Diners Club
tel. +44 1252 513 500

HSBC
tel. +44 1442 422 929

Barclaycard
tel. +44 1604 230 230

NatWest
tel. +44 142 370 0545

Lloyds TSB
tel. +44 1702 278 270

Currency exchange   Currency exchange outside of hotels, official currency exchanges and banks is highly unadvisable. It is illegal and dangerous. As a tourist it is recommendable to buy Hungarian Forint when one has arrived in the country. The exchange rate is substantially better. When trading Forint back to other currency it is recommendable to do so in Hungary again. It is advisable as well to check the very different exchange rates of the banks and the currency exchanges. The conditions are much better in the city centre than in the outskirts. The receipts must be kept and presented to custom officials when asked for.

Credit cards   Banks, larger hotels, restaurants of better category, car rentals as well as the department stores and regular stores frequented by tourists accept the standard credit cards.

ATM machines   ATM machines are installed in the whole city. Cash can be withdrawn with all standard bank and credit cards. The machines have explanations in various languages.

Banks   Hungarian banks are usually open from Monday till Friday 8am – 3pm. Some banks close on Fridays already at 1pm. There are currency exchanges open Sundays on Castle Hill.

Personal Safety

Average crime rate   Crime against tourists in Hungary does not exceed the average of other European holiday destinations. The number of car thefts has declined drastically, although valuable new cars continue to be objects of desire among professional car thieves. Budapest visitors are well advised to park their cars at supervised car parks and not to leave any items in the car that are even slightly valuable. The places in Budapest with a strong tourist presence are naturally an Eldorado for pickpockets. Their activities can be noted everywhere, especially in the Castle District, on Váci utca, Heroes' Square and in the large market hall by the Freedom Bridge. Take care at ticket booths for metro and tram tickets too.

Taxis   A few brazen taxi drivers have specialized in tricking uncertain and inexperienced visitors. Inattentive tourists can already fall into the hands of such drivers during arrival at the airport or at one of the Budapest train stations. It is therefore highly recommended to establish clearly at the outset of a journey that the taximeter is not only switched on, but also clearly shows the price per kilometer. It is therefore highly recommendable to use a taxicab of one of the larger companies: e.g. Fő Taxi, City Taxi or Zóna Taxi.

During the tourist high season, from 1 June to 1 September, special-   **Tourist police**
ly trained tourist police accompanied by translators are present on all
streets and squares heavily frequented by tourists. These law-enforc-
ers are entitled to see your passport on request, but they are not allowed to ask for money or credit cards. The tourist police have established a phone number for tourist victims of crime: the Budapest
number is 1 4 38-80-80 (area code if calling from outside Budapest is
06-1). Victims of crime can get help and information in English,
French, German or Spanish. The hotline is operational around the
clock. In the event of any damage or harm do seek the local police
(rendőrség). Dial 1 07 for the police emergency number or go to the
next Budapest police station. The central Budapest police station can
be found in XIII Teve utca 6).

Post · Telecommunications

POST

Budapest post offices open: Mon–Fri, 8am–6pm, Sat 8am–1pm; post   **Post offices**
office at the West Railway Station (Nyugati pályaudvar): Mon–Fri   **and rates**
7am–8pm, Sat 8am–6pm. Postcards to EU countries and Switzerland
cost 240 Ft. For letters below 20g the EU standard fare is required.
Stamps are available from post offices and almost everywhere that
sells post cards. Hungarian post boxes are red, decorated with a post
horn

TELEPHONE

For telephone booths can be used with 10-, 20-, or 100-Forint coins   **Public call**
or telephone cards. These may be acquired in post offices, at newspa-   **boxes**
per stands, gasoline stations or in tobacco stores.

PREFIXES AND
SERVICE NUMBERS
Within Hungary to Budapest
Tel. 06-1

From other countries
Tel. 00 36-1

From Budapest
First 00, then country code, e.g. to
UK 00 44, to USA 00 1

National Service:
Tel. 1 98

International Service:
Tel. 1 99

Telephoning Within cities and communities it is only necessary to dial the personal number of the recipient. When making a phone call within Hungary first dial 06, wait for the signal sound and then dial the regional prefix as well as the number of the recipient. In case of making a phone call beyond Hungary the 00 has to be dialed first, wait for the signal sound again, then dial the number of your choice. Do not forget to add the country prefix and leave out the 0 when dialing the regional prefix within the chosen country. Telephone booths for international calls are marked as such.

Mobile phone Hungarian mobile phone numbers have 11 digits. Depending on the telephone company they start with either 06 20, 06 30, 06 60 and 06 70. When calling from conventional network or a non-Hungarian proprietor all 11 digits have to be used. If one should call a number that is with the same telephone company the first four digits may be left out. It the number you are calling is a different Hungarian telecommunications proprietor the 06 can be dropped.

Prices · Discounts

Prices are rising in Budapest. In the top restaurants and hotel chains they are on a par with those in western Europe, and naturally shops and restaurants in the tourist districts adapt their prices to the financial resources of their international customers. Nevertheless, it is possible to eat and drink well for little money in most cafés and restaurants. Souvenirs, CDs and local specialties remain good value even today, and high-quality Hungarian wine and spirits are available at low prices.

? MARCO ❖ POLO INSIGHT

What does it cost?

A cup of coffee: 300 HUF
A liter petrol: 320 HUF
A beer: 400 HUF

Prices for restaurants
►p. 92
prices for hotels:
►p. 58

Hungarian Tourist Card For exploring the environs of Budapest, it is worth taking advantage of the reductions offered by the Hungarian Tourist Card. It is valid for 13 months and provides discounts on rail and boat tickets, in many taxis, and in hotels and restaurants.

Budapest Card The discount card of the Budapest tourist authorities can be aquired fot 24, 48 and 72 hours. It offers free public transport in the metropolitan area (except on the cable car up Castle Hill), and reduced entry to many museums and sights; in a few small museums the entry is free. Many shops, restaurants, spas and car rental firms also grant significant discounts to cardholders. Special treats are the free English guided city tours through the Buda castle and downtown Pest. The Budapest Walking Card is designed especially for seniors, who may use public transportation for free anyway. The Junior Cards discounts activities and needs of children and youths. The Budapest Card can be purchased at the airport, hotel receptions or at the larger metro stations.

EU citizens who are age 65 or above can use all of Budapest's public transportation for free (do not for get your ID for confirmation). From the age of 70 and onward entry is also free in many museums. With an international students ID many museums offer a 50% discount.

Seniors and students

Transport

Urban public transport in Budapest is run by BKV. This includes suburban trains HÉV, the metro, trams, trolley buses and ordinary buses which, as a rule, operate between 5am and 11.30pm, with a 24-hour service on some routes.

Public transport

The four routes of the suburban rail service HÉV provide rapid transport between the city centre and suburbs, as well as to the neighbouring towns of Gödöllő, Csepel, Ráckeve and Szentendre.

HÉV

The metro (▶map in the back folder) consists of three lines. Line 1 was inaugurated in 1896 and is therefore the oldest on the European mainland; it was incorporated in the UNESCO World Heritage list in 2002. An east-west connection was opened in 1973, and a north-south route in 1979. The metro network is still being expanded.

Metro

The narrow-gauge railway on Szabadság-hegy (hill), the chairlift up János-hegy (hill), the cable car onto Castle Hill are part of the BKV.

Other city transport

The Danube boats run between Boráros tér and Fünkosd fürdő from May till August on a daily basis from 8am – 8pm. The local boats are also included in the BKV. Numerous excursion boats vitalize traffic on the Danube between Esztergom and Budapest during the high season.

Boats

Tickets for all public transport can be bought at ticket booths at all metro stations, at all tram and suburban train (HÉV) terminals, as well as at bus terminals, and at many newspaper kiosks and hotel re-

Tickets

PUBLIC TRANSPORTS
Tel. 1 2 58 - 46 36
www.bkv.hu

TAXI COMPANIES
Pest Taxi
Tel. 4 33 33 33

City- Taxi
Tel. 2 11 11 11

Fő Taxi
Tel. 2 22 22 22

Rádió Taxi
Tel. 7 77 77 77

Tele 5 Taxi
5 55 55 55

Zóna Taxi
Tel. 3 65 55 55

6 x 6 Taxi
Tel. 4 66 66 66

TRAIN
Magyar Államvasutak (MAV)
Tel. 06 40 49 49 49
www.mav.hu

ceptions. Tickets must be validated on entering the relevant transport. Travelling without a valid ticket is punished by heavy fines. Single tickets are not valid for changing to another vehicle. Holders of the Budapest Card (▶Prices and Discounts p.268) can use the entire urban public transport network for free.

For all EU citizens age 65 or above the public transportation are free as well. The ID has to be presented if verification is required.

Single tickets can be bought in stacks of 10 or 20 tickets and multiline tickets may be purchased also. The 24- until 72-hour tickets as well as the 7-day ticket are especially interesting for tourists.

Regional transport
The rail and bus network plays an important role in regional transport. In the Budapest/Danube Bend area, passenger boats and car ferries run by the Mahart Pass Nave Shipping Company are also in service.

Taxis
Taxis have yellow number plates in Budapest. They are best ordered by phone. They normally arrive at the requested location within ten minutes. Many taxi drivers have at least basic knowledge of English. Every taxi has to have a taxi meter installed, and visitors should make sure it is switched on.

Railway
Budapest is an important national and international transport hub. The state operated Hungarian railway company is Magyar Államvasutka (MAV). Its express trains provide comfortable and reliable connections between Budapest and all other important Hungarian cities.

When to Go

The best time to travel is between the months April to October. Spring and autumn are especially attractive. It can get very dry and hot, sometimes also humid and stormy in the summer. That is why many locals retreat to Lake Balaton, not a lot goes on in Budapest in August. Hungary is one of Europe's sunniest countries. It gets quieter in Budapest during the cold time of year, roughly from mid-October, and the tourist trade only revives again during the Christmas holidays and around New Year. Hungarian winters have a tendency of being comparatively dry and cold.

Index

List of Maps and Illustrations

Photo Credits

Publisher's Information

1st Edition 2015
Worldwide Distribution: Marco Polo
Travel Publishing Ltd
Pinewood, Chineham Business Park
Crockford Lane, Chineham
Basingstoke, Hampshire RG24 8AL,
United Kingdom.

Photos, illlustrations, maps:
103 photos, 32 maps and and
illustrations, one large map
Text:
Stefanie Bisping, György Dalós, Matthias
Eickhoff, Carmen Galenschovski, Odin
Hug, Helmut Linde, Silwen Randebrock,
Peter Renyi, Monika Wucher, Andrea
Wurth
Editing:
John Sykes, Rainer Eisenschmid
Translation: Barbara Schmidt-Runkel,
Natascha Scott-Stokes, Sabine Welter
Cartography:
Klaus-Peter Lawall, Unterensingen
MAIRDUMONT Ostfildern (city map)
3D illustrations:
jangled nerves, Stuttgart
Infographics:
Golden Section Graphics GmbH, Berlin
Design:
independent Medien-Design, Munich

Editor-in-chief:
Rainer Eisenschmid, Mairdumont
Ostfildern

Printed in China

Despite all of our authors' thorough
research, errors can creep in. The pub-
lishers do not accept any liability for thi
Whether you want to praise, alert us to
errors or give us a personal tip Please
contact us by email or post:

MARCO POLO Travel Publishing Ltd
Pinewood, Chineham Business Park
Crockford Lane, Chineham
Basingstoke, Hampshire RG24 8AL
United Kingdom
Email: sales@marcopolouk.com

FSC
www.fsc.org
MIX
Paper from
responsible sources
FSC® C011918

MARCO POLO

HANDBOOKS

www.marco-polo.com

Budapest Curiosities

Be it communist sculptures, an unusual means of transport, toll for noble pedestrians – Budapest has some unusual things on offer.

►**Name Change**
The streets of Budapest have experienced many name changes. Andrássy út was hit especially hard: From Radial Street to Stalin Street, Street of Hungarian Youth to Street of the People's Republic it went. Since 1989 Count Gyula Andrássy has graced the street signs.

►**Cave City**
Budapest down under: The city is known for the wonderful caves in the Buda Hills.

►**Budapest Spa**
120 hot springs bubble within the city limits – they have officially turned the Danube metropolis into Budapest Spa.

►**Unusual Means of Transport**

Had enough Metro or bus? The city on the Danube can also offer a funicular, a cog railway, a children's railway and a chairlift for your explorations.

►**First Bridge over the Danube**
The Chain Bridge was inaugurated in 1849 as Hungary's first Danube crossover. A revolutionary idea: Even the nobility had to pay a toll.

►**Communist Relics**
In other places they were destroyed, in Budapest the communist monuments are kept in the outdoor museum Memento Park.

►**Danube Skaters**
Hydrofoils regularly run in the summer between Vienna and Budapest – and that since communist times already.

►**Castle Without a King**
The impressive Buda Castle dominates the skyline on Castle Hill – but not a single member of the Hapsburg dynasty ever lived in it because they preferred Vienna.